INSIGHT GUIDE

Bangkok

Part of the Langenscheidt Publishing Group

W9-AAV-106

ABOUT THIS BOOK

Editorial

Editor
Clare Griffiths
Editorial Director
Brian Bell

Distribution

UK & Ireland
GeoCenter International Ltd
The Viables Centre , Harrow Way
Basingstoke, Hants RG22 4BJ
Fax: (44) 1256-817988

United States
Langenscheidt Publishers, Inc.
46–35 54th Road, Maspeth, NY 11378
Fax: (718) 784-0640

Canada
Prologue Inc.
1650 Lionel Bertrand Blvd., Boishriand
Québec, Canada J7H 1N7
Tel: (450) 434-0306. Fax: (450) 434-2627

Australia & New Zealand
Hema Maps Pty. Ltd.
24 Allgas Street, Slacks Creek 4127
Brisbane, Australia
Tel: (61) 7 3290 0322. Fax: (61) 7 3290 0478

Worldwide
**Apa Publications GmbH & Co.
Verlag KG (Singapore branch)**
38 Joo Koon Road, Singapore 628990
Tel: (65) 865-1600. Fax: (65) 861-6438

Printing

Insight Print Services (Pte) Ltd
38 Joo Koon Road, Singapore 628990
Tel: (65) 865-1600. Fax: (65) 861-6438

©1999 Apa Publications GmbH & Co.
Verlag KG (Singapore branch)
All Rights Reserved
First Edition 1988
Third Edition 1999

CONTACTING THE EDITORS
Although every effort is made to
provide accurate information, we
live in a fast-changing world and
would appreciate it if readers
would call our attention to any
errors or outdated information
that may occur by writing to:
**Insight Guides, P.O. Box 7910,
London SE1 1WE, England.
Fax: (44 171) 403-0290.**
e-mail:
insight@apaguide.demon.co.uk

This guidebook combines the
interests and enthusiasms of
two of the world's best known
information providers: Insight
Guides, whose titles have set the
standard for visual travel guides
since 1970, and the Discovery
Channel, the world's premier
source of nonfiction television
programming.

Insight Guides' editors provide practical advice and general understanding about a
place's history, culture, and
people. Discovery Channel
and its extensive web site,
www.discovery.com, help millions of viewers explore their
world from the comfort of their
home and also encourage them to
explore it firsthand.

How to use this book

The book is carefully structured
to convey an understanding of
Bangkok and its culture and to
guide readers through its
sights and attractions:

◆ The Features section,
with a yellow colour bar,
covers the city's history
and culture in lively
authoritative features
written by specialists.

◆ The Places section,
with a blue bar, provides

EXPLORE YOUR WORLD

Discovery
CHANNEL

– and the experience and sensations and opportunities – into a guidebook can be a daunting and perplexing experience.

This new edition, which builds on the first edition edited by **Steve Van Beek**, was managed and edited by **Clare Griffiths**, who lived and worked in Bangkok in the early 1990s.

Contributing to this new edition with updated material and new essays on architecture, sports, the National Museum, Jim Thompson's House, Thai script and the tuk-tuk, was a team of writers and updaters lead by journalist and editor **Kanokchan Patanapichai**.

Chapters on the southeast and northeast of Bangkok, Sukhothai, people and society and culture were updated by long-term Bangkok resident **Joe Feinstein** and colleagues, while the essay on Food and Drink was brought up-to-date by the original author, **Robert Halliday**. Thanks also goes to **Marcel Barang** in Bangkok for his help and guidance on the project. **Marcus Wilson-Smith, Gerald Cubitt** and **David Henley** provided much of the new photographs for this edition.

Previous contributors whose work remains include **Aporanee Buatong, Robert Burrows, Jerry Dillon, Nancy Grace, Frank Green, Neil Kelly, Sara Lai, Gayle Miller, Siripimporn Phoosomporn, M. R. Priyanandana Rangsit, Savika Srisawat, John Stirling, Tony Wheeler** and **Kultida Wongsawatdichart**. The book was proofread by **Cathy Muscat** and indexed by **Elizabeth Cook**.

full details of all the sights and areas worth seeing. The chief places of interest are coordinated by number with specially drawn maps.
◆ The Travel Tips listings section, with an orange bar, at the back of the book offers all the information you'll need on the practical aspects of the city. Information can be located quickly using the index printed on the back cover flap, which also serves as a handy bookmark.

The contributors

Bangkok simply overwhelms and attempts to condense the place

Map Legend

── ··	International Boundary
⊖	Border Crossing
─ · ─	National Park/Reserve
─ ─ ─ ─	Ferry Route
✈ ✈	Airport: International/ Regional
🚍	Bus Station
🅿	Parking
❶	Tourist Information
✉	Post Office
✝ ✝ ✝	Church/Ruins
✝	Monastery
☾	Mosque
✡	Synagogue
🏰	Castle/Ruins
∴	Archaeological Site
∩	Cave
⚡	Statue/Monument
★	Place of Interest

The main places of interest in the Places section are coordinated by number with a full-colour map (e.g. ❶), and a symbol at the top of every right-hand page tells you where to find the map.

Main picture: shophouses in Bangkok, where display and presentation of goods is an artform

INSIGHT GUIDE
BANGKOK

CONTENTS

Maps

Inside front cover:
Bangkok
Inside back cover:
Thailand

Intense
sensations
of color,
taste and
smell in
Bangkok's
Chinatown

Insight on ...

Information panels

Travel Tips

Places

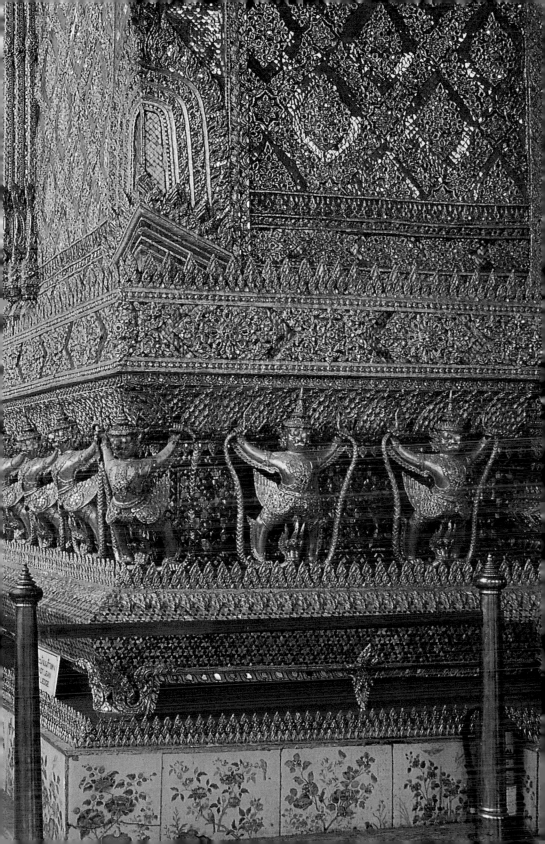

THE CITY OF ANGELS

Stopover visitors will be dazed by the traffic fumes and noise.

Those staying a little longer will discover Bangkok's allure

A t first glance, Bangkok appears to be a place desperately in need of a competent city planner. It certainly seems a place where no one has sat down and thought things through to an orderly outcome. In fact, Bangkok, whose full name translated as City of Angels, Abode of the Emerald Buddha, never has had much order imposed on it, save for Rattanakosin, the royal core of the city where the kings built their palaces and temples. The rest of the city simply happened, and as one moves outward from the royal island, which is defined by canals and the Chao Phraya River, the city increasingly looks like a challenge to cartographers.

Yet it is undeniably one of the world's most fascinating cities, and travelers inevitably leave Bangkok with a wealth of impressions, opinions and stories to tell. Yes, it is polluted and it is noisy and it is traffic-clogged. Yes, it can take hours to travel a few kilometers by car. And, yes, the situation never seems to improve.

Bangkok began as a city of canals and elephant paths. When motor vehicles redefined urban transportation, the old thoroughfares were simply filled in or paved over for the new wheels. Little attempt was made to accommodate the different needs of a motorized society. Construction begat chaos, and a large part of what assaults the eye today started in the late 1950s. The population of the city has grown nearly tenfold since World War II. Today, about one out of every eight Thais live in Bangkok – from 8 to 11 million people, depending upon the statistical source. The city is Thailand's only metropolitan area, and its only true cultural, economic and political center.

Metropolitan Bangkok was once two separate urban entities: Thonburi on the west side of the Chao Phraya, and Krung Thep (Bangkok) on the eastern side. In the early 1970s, the two were united into a single metropolitan government, and the expanded city was then merged with the two surrounding provinces into one densely-populated province: Bangkok Metropolis. This metropolitan area is slightly over 1,500 sq. km (600 sq. miles) in size.

About 50 km (30 miles) from the Gulf of Thailand, Bangkok is atop the gulf delta of the Chao Phraya River, which flows from the north. Since it is on an alluvial plain, Bangkok is quite flat and without geographical boundaries, save for the river itself.

Bangkok's challenge is simple: to sort out the mess of its infrastructure. Telecommunications have noticeably improved. The transportation network is, well, continuing to pose problems. In any case, whether the city planners manage to unknot the traffic or not, and whether the city eventually stabilizes its growth, or else implodes, or explodes, Bangkok will never fail to elicit a response. ❏

PRECEDING PAGES: early morning trading at Damnoen Saduak floating market; girl guides; monk at Wat Phra Kaeo (Temple of the Emerald Buddha); lighting of incense at a temple. **LEFT:** samlor driver takes a break.

Decisive Dates

PRE-THAI CIVILIZATION

3600–250 BC Ban Chiang culture flourishes in northeastern Thailand.
Circa **250 BC** Suvannabhumi trading with India.
4th–8th centuries AD Influence of Mon and Khmer empires spreads into Thailand.
9th–13th centuries Khmer Empire founded at Angkor. Thai peoples migrate south from Yunnan Province of China into northern Thailand, Burma, and Laos. Lopburi becomes an important provincial capital in Khmer Empire.

THE SUKHOTHAI ERA

1238 Khmer power wanes. Kingdom of Sukhothai founded under Intaradit.
1277–1318 Reign of Ramkamhaeng in Sukhothai. Often called Thailand's "Golden Age," the period saw the first attempts to unify the Thai people, the first use of Thai script, and flourishing of the arts.
1281 Chiang Rai kingdom founded in north.
1296 Lanna kingdom founded at Chiang Mai. Mengrai controls much of northern Thailand and Laos.
1318–47 Lo Thai reigns at Sukhothai. The slow decline of the Sukhothai kingdom begins.
1438 Sukhothai is now virtually deserted; power shifts to the Kingdom of Ayutthaya, to the south and along the Chao Phraya River.

THE KINGDOM OF AYUTTHAYA

14th century Area around Ayutthaya settled by representatives of the Chiang Rai kingdom.
1350 City of Ayutthaya founded by Phya U-Thong, who proclaims himself Ramathibodi I. Within a few years he controls the areas encompassed by the kingdoms of Sukhothai and the Khmer empire.
1369 Ramesuen, son of Ramathibodi, becomes king.
1390 Ramesuen captures Chiang Mai.
1393 Ramesuen captures Angkor in Cambodia.
1448–88 Reign of King Trailok, who finally unites the Lanna (Chiang Mai) and Ayutthaya kingdoms.
1491–1529 Reign of King Ramathibodi II.
1569 Burmese capture and destroy Ayutthaya.
1584 Naresuen declares independence of Siam.
1590 Naresuen becomes king, throws off Burmese suzerainty. Under Naresuen, Ayutthaya expands rapidly at the expense of Burmese and Khmer empires and flourishes as a major city.
1605–10 Ekatotsarot reigns, begins significant economic ties with Europeans.
1610–28 Reign of King Songtham. The British arrive and obtain land for a trading factory.
1628–55 Reign of Prasat Thong. Trading concessions expand and regular trade with China and Europe is established.
1656–88 Reign of King Narai. British influence expands. Reputation of Ayutthaya as a magnificent city and a remarkable royal court spreads in Europe.
1678 Constantine Phaulkon arrives at Narai's court and gains great influence; French presence expands.
1688 Narai dies, Phaulkon executed.
1733–58 Reign of King Boromakot. Ayutthaya enters a period of peace, and of arts and literature.
1767 Burmese King Alaungpaya captures and sacks Ayutthaya, destroying four centuries of Thai civilization. Seven months later General Phya Tak Sin returns and expels the Burmese. He moves the capital from Ayutthaya to Thonburi, near Bangkok.

BEGINNING OF THE CHAKRI DYNASTY

1767 Phya Tak Sin crowned as King Taksin.
1779 Generals Chao Phya Chakri and his brother Chao Phya Sarasih conquer Chiang Mai, expel the Burmese from what is now Thailand and add most of the Khmer and Lao kingdoms to the Thai kingdom. The Emerald Buddha brought from Vientiane, Laos, to Thonburi.
1782 Taksin deposed and executed, and Chao Phya Chakri is offered the throne, founding the Chakri dynasty and assuming the name Ramathibodi and later Rama I. Capital is moved across the river to the city that becomes known to the West as

Bangkok. Under Rama I, the Siamese Kingdom consolidates and expands its strength. Rama I revives Thai art, religion, and culture and starts to build the Grand Palace and Wat Phra Kaeo in Bangkok.

1809–24 Reign of Rama II; best known for construction of Wat Arun and many other temples and monasteries. Rama II reopens relations with the West, suspended since the time of Narai.

1824–51 Reign of Rama III, who left as his trademark the technique of embedding Chinese porcelain fragments as decorations on temples.

1851 King Mongkut (Rama IV) ascends the throne. He is the first Thai king to understand Western culture and technology. Builds Bangkok's first paved road, Charoen Krung.

1868 Chulalongkorn (Rama V) ascends the throne, reigning for the next four decades, the second-longest reign of any Thai king. Chulalongkorn ends the custom of prostration in royal presence, abolishes slavery, and replaces corvée labor with direct taxation. Schools, infrastructure, military, and government modernized.

1910–25 Reign of Vajiravudh (Rama VI), Oxford-educated and thoroughly Westernized.

1925–35 Reign of Prajadhipok (Rama VII). Economic pressures from the Great Depression encourage discontent.

END OF THE ABSOLUTE MONARCHY

1932 A coup d'état ends the absolute monarchy and ushers in a constitutional monarchy.

1935–46 Reign of Ananda (Rama VIII).

1939 The name of the country is officially changed from Siam to Thailand, "Land of the Free."

1941 Japan invades Thailand with the acquiescence of the military government, but a spirited if small resistance movement thrives.

1946 King Ananda is killed by a mysterious gunshot, and Bhumibol Adulyadej (Rama IX) ascends the throne. The royal family becomes symbol of national spirit and unity.

1973–91 Bloody clashes between the army and demonstrating students bring down the military government; political and economic blunders bring down the resulting civilian government just three years later. Various military-backed and civilian governments come and go for almost 20 years.

1992 Another clash between military forces and civilian demonstrators results in the military leaving government to civilian politicians. Thailand begins five years of unprecedented economic growth. Growth reaches 9 percent annually.

1996 King Bhumibol Adulyadej celebrates his golden jubilee of 50 years on the throne, becoming the world's longest-reigning monarch.

1997 A few months later, Thailand's banking system and economy begins a free-fall as the baht loses half of its value. Other regional economies also falter.

1998 While other Asian economies continue to wallow in crisis, Thailand follows guidelines established by the International Monetary Fund to resuscitate its financial systems and economy.

1999 The economy shows signs of recovery. ❑

CHAKRI MONARCHY		
Since 1782, a single royal dynasty – known as Chakri – has ruled over Thailand.		
Rama I (Chakri)		1782–1809
Rama II (Phutthalaetia)		1809–1824
Rama III (Nangklao)		1824–1851
Rama IV (Mongkut)		1851–1868
Rama V (Chulalongkorn)		1868–1910
Rama VI (Vajiravudh)		1910–1925
Rama VII (Prajadhipok)		1925–1935
Rama VIII (Ananda)		1935–1946
Rama IX (Bhumibol)		1946–present

PRECEDING PAGES: 19th-century mural in Wat Ratchasilaram. **LEFT:** Thai manuscript showing royal parade, 1600s. **RIGHT:** Chulalongkorn (Rama V), 1893.

THE DAWN OF BANGKOK

It wasn't until 1782 that Bangkok became the power center of Thailand, the last in a line of capitals established over many centuries

Although an important town for hundreds of years, Bangkok sat on the sidelines, located beside the Chao Phraya River between the ancient capital of Ayutthaya to the north and the sea to the south. It was only following a sequence of kingdoms and invasions in the regions to the north that Bangkok evolved into what it is today.

The story of Bangkok begins in the far north of Thailand. The soil from which tall buildings now sprout once provided sustenance for rice. At that time, as little as 1,500 years ago, the site of the future capital city lay beneath the ocean's waters. Each monsoon season, the powerful currents of the Chao Phraya River swept southwards, carrying the soil from eroded farmland into the sea, gradually nudging the shoreline a little further into what is known today as the Gulf of Thailand.

Eventually, the mudbanks rose above the waterline, the mangrove trees took root, and the lungfish moved in. Soon, houses started to rise up on stilts above the tidal mudflats. Their inhabitants used their self-made islands as bases for fishing expeditions into the nearby sea. Each year, the river deposited more soil and silt until the delta became high enough that farmers could start to till and plant rice in it. Around those fields grew villages, then towns, and finally a city. Because it originated on top of an alluvial plain, Bangkok has remained a flat city, with no natural point more than a few meters above any other. Floods have always swamped the city during the October monsoon season, when the Chao Phraya River breaks its banks and spills into the streets. Every year, the city sinks by about 10 cm (4 inches).

Bangkok's origins

Bangkok's history as a town began in the 16th century, when a small-time king commanded that a 2-km (just over a mile) long canal be dug across the neck of a 17-km (11-mile) loop of

LEFT: terracotta figure from the Sukhothai period.
RIGHT: illustration of two early indigenous Thai men.

the Chao Phraya to cut the distance between the sea and Ayutthaya. The annual monsoon floods scoured the banks of the canal like sandpaper until the canal widened to become the main course of the river. On its banks rose two towns – trading posts along the river route up to Ayutthaya, 75 km (47 miles) upriver – Thon-

buri on the west and, on the east, Krung Thep, later to become Bangkok. At the time, Bangkok was little more than a village (*bang*) in an orchard of what were thought to be wild plum trees (*kok*). Hence, the town's name, Bangkok, which translates as "village of the wild plum."

During the 17th century, the town was inhabited by a few Chinese merchants and farmers who tended their *kok* trees on low ground. As the area was subject to flooding, it had little commercial value and there was no logical reason for it to grow. But grow it did, becoming one of Asia's grandest cities. To understand why the city developed as it did, one must look to the development of Thailand as a whole.

Ban Chiang culture

A sophisticated ancient civilization is known to have inhabited the Chao Phraya valley several thousand years ago, long before the ethnic Thai people are thought to have arrived. The first discovery of prehistoric relics was made during World War II, by a Dutch prisoner of war forced to work on the "Death Railway" to Burma.

By mistake he uncovered Stone Age implements at Ban Kao, in the western province of Kanchanaburi, which led to

BURIAL POTS

Each of the pots unearthed in the village of Ban Chiang has a unique design. Red-painted jars, decorated with fingerprint whorl patterns, were buried in funeral mounds as offerings.

from about 3600 BC. Settlement seems to have lasted until 250 BC, after which the people mysteriously faded from history. While they thrived, they farmed rice and domesticated animals, in addition to making their highly original pottery. The Ban Chiang culture illustrates the high level of technology achieved by prehistoric people in Southeast Asia.

Indian influence

Ancient texts discuss the presence of people from India in the region from around the 3rd

the discovery of paleolithic and neolithic caves, and cemeteries that contained a wealth of tools and other artifacts.

The most archaeological important site, however, is the tiny village of Ban Chiang, near the province of Udon Thani, in the northeast of the country. Systematic excavation here revealed both practical and decorative items including painted pottery, jewelry, and examples of bronze and iron tools.

The identity of the Ban Chiang people is a mystery. According to archaeological timetables, the existence of pottery normally suggests a culture already 2,000 years along the road to civilization; Ban Chiang's pottery dates

century BC, though archaeological evidence has yet to be unearthed to support this. In later centuries, Buddhism and Hinduism – along with Indian ceremonial rites, iconography, law codes, and cosmological and architectural treatises – were adopted *en bloc* by the Southeast Asian ruling elite and modified to suit local requirements and tastes. Sanskrit became the court language, while Pali was the language of the Buddhist canons.

Native chiefs wanting to consolidate power and increase their prestige may have been responsible for this diffusion of culture, calling in *Brahmans* (Indians of the priestly caste) to validate their rule.

The arrival of the Thais

The origin of the ethnic Thai has been hotly debated for decades. Popular tradition claims that the first people fled to Siam (as Thailand was known until 1939) from China to escape the depredations of Kublai Khan's hordes sweeping southward out of Mongolia. Another theory suggests they originated in Thailand a millennium or two ago and those Thais found in today's China are said to have emigrated north from Thailand about 1,000 years ago. One of the most persuasive theories says that from perhaps as early as the 10th century, a people living in China's Yunnan province

Whichever conjecture is correct, it is accepted that the Thais' first home in Thailand was in the northern hills. They formed themselves into principalities, some of which became independent kingdoms. The first was in 1238, at Sukhothai, at the southernmost edge of Thai penetration. Then came Chiang Rai, in 1281, and Chiang Mai, in 1296. Long after the main group of Thais moved farther down the peninsula to establish more powerful states, Chiang Mai continued to rule more or less autonomously over the northern region, maintaining a distinctive culture. As the centuries passed, they shared the country with ethnic

migrated down rivers and streams into the upper valleys of the Southeast Asian river system. There, they branched off. The Shans, also known as *Thai Yai* (Great Thais), went to Upper Burma; the Ahom Thais established themselves in Assam; another group settled in Laos; yet another occupied the island of Hainan, off the Vietnamese coast. The greatest number of *Thai Noi* (Little Thais) first settled in the north of modern Thailand, around Chiang Saen and valleys to the south.

Left: terracotta figures found in central Thailand, thought to be southern Indian in origin.
Above: Sukhothai stone engraving.

Laotians, who populated the northeastern area, bringing a similar language and culture. The southern isthmus linking Thailand (from Bangkok south) with the Malay Peninsula became the home of Muslims.

Kingdom of Sukhothai

The name *Sukhothai* translates into "the dawn of happiness," and if early inscriptions are to be believed, its people enjoyed considerable freedom to pursue their livelihoods. This first independent Thai kingdom was a land of plenty, governed by just and paternal kings who ruled over peaceful, contented citizens. Sukhothai represented early Thai tribal society in its purest form. The most famous king of Sukhothai was Ramkamhaeng. He was the first Thai ruler to leave epigraphical accounts of the Thai state, beginning with his own early life. At 19 he earned his title on a campaign with his father against a neighboring state, in which he defeated the enemy leader in hand-to-hand combat on elephant-back.

A GOLDEN ERA

The Sukhothai era is often looked back upon with great nostalgia and the kingdom thought of as the ideal Thai state.

Reign of Ramkamhaeng

At the time of Ramkamhaeng's accession in about 1279, the Sukhothai kingdom was quite

the idyllic conditions of his kingdom: fertile land and plentiful food, free trade, prohibition of slavery and guaranteed inheritance. However, some experts now doubt its authenticity and believe the inscription to be a much later work.

The king was a devout and conscientious Buddhist, following the Theravada school practiced in Sukhothai. During this period, Buddhism flourished and became more deeply rooted in the Thai way of life. In 1287, with the continuing progress of the Kublai Khan's powerful armies,

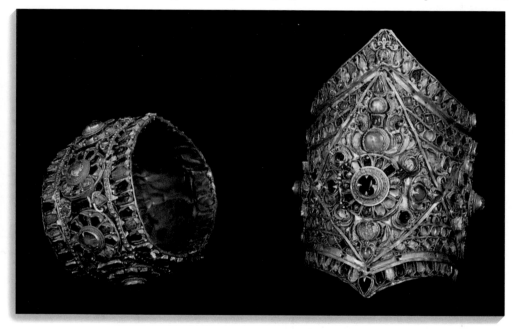

small, consisting only of the city of Sukhothai and surrounding areas. By the end of his reign, he had increased its size tenfold – from Luang Prabang in the east, through the Central Plains to the southern peninsula. The Mon state in Lower Burma also accepted his control. Ramkamhaeng was noted as an administrator, legislator and statesman – and sometimes as an amorous king.

He is credited with the invention of Thai script, which he achieved by systematizing the Khmer alphabet with Thai words. A stone inscription bearing the date 1292 and employing the new script has been attributed to Ramkamhaeng. In the inscription, he depicted

Ramkamhaeng formed a pact with two northern Thai princes, Mengrai of Chiang Rai and Ngam Muang of Phayo. They agreed not to transgress, but to protect each others' borders against common enemies. The alliance was maintained during their lifetimes.

Founding of Chiang Mai

Mengrai completed Thai political ascendancy in the north by annexing the last Mon kingdom of Haripunjaya, in about 1292. He first sent an *agent provocateur* to sow discord, and when the time was right, his army "plucked the town like a ripe fruit." Wishing to found a new capital, Mengrai invited his two allies to help him select a site. The location they agreed upon as truly auspicious was one where two white sambars, two white barking deer, and a family of five white mice were seen together. On that spot by the river Ping, Mengrai laid the foundation of Chiang Mai (New Town) in 1296, supplanting his former capital at Chiang Rai and giving him a more centralized location from which to administer the southern portion of his newly expanded kingdom.

Decline of Sukhothai

Tradition says Ramkamhaeng drowned in the rapids of the Yom River at Sawankhalok. His son, Lo Thai (who ruled from 1318 to 1347), preferring religion to war, lost the feudatory states as fast as he had gained them. He was called Dharmaraja, "the Pious King," an epithet his successors also bore. The relationship between Sukhothai and Sri Lanka, the center of orthodox Buddhism, intensified during his rule; Lo Thai recorded that he built many monuments to house sacred relics of the Buddha newly obtained from Sri Lanka.

Lo Thai's son, Li Thai, was as pious as his father. As heir to the throne, he composed a famous treatise on Buddhist cosmology, the *Traibhumikatha* (Tales of the Three Worlds). When he became king in 1347, he laid down laws in accordance with the Ten Royal Precepts of the Buddha. He pardoned criminals, for example, as he desired to become a Buddha, "to lead all creatures beyond the oceans of sorrow and transmigration." The prioritizing of religion over military affairs might have permitted the meteoric rise of one of Sukhothai's former vassal states, Ayutthaya.

The southern kingdom expanded rapidly, extending its control over the Chao Phraya River valley, until Li Thai was forced to acknowledge its hegemony. Deprived of his independence, the pious king took deeper refuge in religion, eventually assuming the yellow robe of the monk. His family ruled for three more generations, but in 1378 power shifted south to Phitsanulok, and Sukhothai's population followed. By 1438, Sukhothai was nearly deserted. The Sukhothai period saw the Thai people, for the first time, develop a dis-

tinctive civilization with their own administrative institutions, art and architecture. Sukhothai Buddha images, characterized by refined facial features, linear fluidity, and harmony of form, are perhaps the most beautiful and most original of Thai artistic expressions. Many say that the Sukhothai aesthetic is the high point of Thai civilization.

Rise of Ayutthaya

Historically, U-Thong was an independent principality in today's Suphan Buri. Its rulers were members of the prestigious line of Chiang Saen kings. During the reign of Phya U-Thong, a

cholera outbreak forced the ruler to evacuate his people to the site of Ayodhya (Ayutthaya), an ancient Indianized settlement named after Rama's legendary kingdom in India.

The location of Phya U-Thong's new capital was blessed with several advantages. Situated on an island at the confluence of the Chao Phraya, Lop Buri and Pasak rivers, not far from the sea and surrounded by fertile rice plains, it was an ideal center of administration and communications. Phya U-Thong officially established the city in 1350, after three years of preparation. Within a few years, the king united the whole of central Siam – including Sukhothai – under his rule, and extended

---

LEFT: Ayutthayan royal jewelry found at Wat Ratchaburana.
RIGHT: 12th–13th-century bronze seated Ganesh.

control to the Malay Peninsula and Lower Burma. He and his successors pursued expansionist campaigns against Chiang Mai and the Khmer civilization in Cambodia.

Ironically, although the Thais were responsible for the decline and eventual collapse of Angkor, the old Khmer capital, the Ayutthaya kings adopted Khmer cultural influences from the start. No longer the paternal and accessible rulers that the kings of Sukhothai had been, Ayutthaya's sovereigns were absolute monarchs, Lords of Life, enhanced by royal trappings reflective of a Khmer *devaraja* (god-king). The king's son, Ramesuen, captured Chiang

shaped the administrative and social structures of Siam up until the 19th century. He brought Ayutthaya's loosely controlled provinces under centralized rule, and regulated *sakdi na*, an ancient system of land ownership that had stratified society, dictated responsibilities of both overlord and tenants, and determined salary levels of the official hierarchy.

Trailok also defined a system of corvée labor, under which all able-bodied men were required to contribute labor during part of each working year to the state. This system indirectly increased the status of women, who became responsible for the welfare of their families.

Mai in 1390, reportedly using cannon, the first recorded use of this weapon in Siam. Ramesuen's army sacked Angkor three years later, and according to the *Pongsawadan*, the Annals of Ayutthaya, some 90,000 prisoners of war were taken. Given the economics of the time, acquisition of people for labor was more precious than any amount of gold.

Reign of King Trailok

Two centuries of wars between Chiang Mai and Ayutthaya reached a climax during the reign of King Boroma Trailokanath, more popularly known as Trailok (ruled 1448–1488). He is important for having introduced reforms that

Trailok's Palace Law of 1450 spelled out the relative ranks of members of the royal family, prescribed functions of officials, and regulated ceremonies. It also fixed punishments, which included death for "introducing amatory poems" into the palace, or for whispering during a royal audience, and amputation of the foot of anyone kicking a palace door. While these sentences may not often have been carried out, they certainly exalted the aura of the king and deterred malefactors. Royalty was not spared punishment, although the Palace Law stipulated that no menial hands could touch royal flesh. The executioner would beat the condemned royalty at the nape of the neck with a club.

Burmese aggression

The 16th century was marked by the first arrival of Europeans, and by continual conflict with the Burmese. Alfonso de Albuquerque, of Portugal, conquered Malacca in 1511, and soon thereafter his ships sailed to Siam. King Ramathibodi II (ruled 1491–1529) granted the Portuguese permission to reside and trade within the kingdom, in return for arms and ammunition. Portuguese mercenaries fought alongside the king in campaigns against

A FLUID SOCIETY

Many of King Trailok's rules persist today. Ranks of nobility were, and are, earned rather than inherited. Titles of royal descendants degenerate, reaching a common status within five generations.

Naresuen, was taken to Burma as a guarantee for Maha Thammaraja's good conduct. The boy was repatriated to Siam at the age of 15.

Together with his younger brother, Ekatotsarot, Naresuen began to gather followers. Naresuen had gained an insight into Burmese armed strength and strategies during his formative years. He trained his armed troops in the art of guerrilla warfare; their effective hit-and-run tactics earned them the nicknames Wild Tigers and Peeping Cats.

Chiang Mai and taught the Thais the arts of cannon foundry and musketry. But this did nothing to stem the rising tide of Burmese aggression. The Burmese invasion of 1549 was doomed to failure. But 20 years later, Ayutthaya fell to Burmese forces. The invading Burmese thoroughly ransacked and plundered the city, and forcibly removed much of Ayutthaya's population to Burma.

Maha Thammaraja, the defeated king's leading deputy, was appointed by the Burmese to rule Siam as a vassal state. His eldest son,

LEFT: 15th-century *Yaksa* (guardian) ceramic bust.
ABOVE: King Narai and Constantine Phaulkon.

Naresuen's opportunity to restore Siamese independence came following a period of internal chaos in Burma. Naresuen declared Ayutthaya's freedom in 1584. During the following nine years, the Burmese made several attempts to resubjugate Siam, but Naresuen had taken thorough defensive measures and repulsed all invasions.

Naresuen reconsolidated the Siamese kingdom, then turned the tables on Burma with repeated attacks that contributed to the disintegration of the Burmese empire. The Khmers, who had been whittling away at Siam's eastern boundary during Ayutthaya's period of weakness, were also subdued. Under Naresuen,

Ayutthaya prospered and became the thriving metropolis that was vividly described by 17th-century European visitors.

Door to the East

The reign of Naresuen's brother, Ekatotsarot, between 1605 and 1610, coincided with the arrival of the Dutch in Siam. Ekatotsarot was not interested in pursuing Naresuen's militaristic policies; instead, he sought to develop Ayutthaya's economy. The Dutch opened their first trading station at Ayutthaya in 1608.

The time of peace initiated by Naresuen had given rise to a surplus of wealth, which created

The Greek favorite

It was the French who gained greatest favor in Narai's court. Their story is interwoven with that of a Greek adventurer, opportunist and interloper named Constantine Phaulkon.

Phaulkon arrived in Siam in 1678. A talented linguist, he learned the Thai language in just two years, and with the help of his English benefactors, he was hired as interpreter within the court. Within five years, Phaulkon had risen through Thai society to the rank of *Phya Vijayendra*. In this powerful position, he had continual access to the king, whose confidence he slowly and surely cultivated.

a demand in Thai society for imported luxury items such as porcelain and silk. The Dutch effectively established maritime dominance in the Far East when they drove the Portuguese out of Malacca, in 1641.

Later, they persuaded the Thais to agree to various trade concessions, giving them virtual economic control in Siam. King Narai (ruled 1656–88) despised the Dutch and welcomed the English as an ally in order to counter Holland's growing influence in the region. But another Dutch blockade, in 1664, this time at the mouth of the Chao Phraya River, won them a monopoly on the hide trade and, for the first time in Thai history, extraterritorial privileges.

As Phaulkon moved firmly into the French camp, so did King Narai. He sent two ambassadors to Louis XIV's court, and the French reciprocated with a visit to Ayutthaya in 1685. Following another exchange of embassies between the courts of Louis and Narai, a French squadron accompanied French and Thai delegations aboard warships to Siam. Following Phaulkon's advice the small but disciplined and well-equipped French force of 500 soldiers was given landing rights by King Narai.

Then the tables began to turn against Phaulkon's influence and his extravagant lifestyle. His unpopularity was fueled not only by the ominous French military presence, but also by a rumor that Phaulkon had converted King Narai's adopted son to Christianity, intending to secure succession to the throne.

When Narai fell ill in 1688, a nationalistic, anti-French faction took action. The ailing king was confined to his palace. Phaulkon was arrested for treason, and in June was executed outside Lop Buri. Narai died a month later. The French eventually removed their soldiers from Thailand.

The presence of Europeans throughout

HUMBLE BEGINNINGS

The adventurer Constantine Phaulkon, the son of a Greek innkeeper, worked his way from cabin boy with the East India Company to a high ranking position at King Narai's court.

"the most beautiful city in the East." The kings who succeeded Narai ended his open-door policy. A modest amount of trade was maintained and missionaries were allowed to stay, but the Kingdom of Ayutthaya embarked on a period of isolation that would last for 150 years.

Golden Age

Although the reign of King Boromakot (1733–58) began with a particularly violent struggle for power, Boromakot's 25-year term was an unusually peaceful one and

Narai's reign gave the West most of its early knowledge of Siam. Voluminous literature was generated by Western visitors to Narai's court. Their attempts at cartography left a record of Ayutthaya's appearance, though few maps remain. Royal palaces and hundreds of temples were crowded within the walls encircling the island on which the capital stood. There were also accounts of extravagant royal barges decorated with gold lacquer and rowed by numerous oarsmen. Some Western visitors called it

LEFT: 19th-century mural at Wat Suwannaram.
ABOVE: religious mural at Wat Ratchasitaram from the 19th century.

became known as Ayutthaya's Golden Age. Poets and artists abounded at his court, enabling literature and the arts to flourish.

These tranquil years proved to be the calm before the storm. Boromakot's son, Ekatat, ascended the throne in 1758, after a bitter succession struggle with his brother, and surrounded himself with female company to ensure his pleasure.

Meanwhile, the Burmese once again set their sights on Ayutthaya, and, in 1767, successfully captured Ayutthaya after a siege lasting 14 months. The Burmese then killed, looted and set fire to the whole city, thereby expunging four centuries of Thai civilization. Burmese forces plundered Ayutthaya's many rich temples, melting down all the available gold from images of the Buddha. Members of the royal family, along with 90,000 captives and the accumulated booty, were removed to Burma.

Despite their overwhelming victory, the Burmese didn't retain control of Siam for long. A young general named Phya Tak Sin, popularly known as Taksin, gathered a small band of followers around him during the final Burmese siege of the Thai capital. He recognized the hopelessness of the Siamese

---
TAKSIN'S DREAM

Taksin revealed to his troops that the old kings had appeared to him in a dream and told him to move his capital away from Ayutthaya.

---

withdrawal easier. During the 17th century, the small fishing village of Bangkok located downstream had become an important trade and defense outpost for Ayutthaya, containing fortifications built by the French during their military presence. The settlement straddled both banks of the Chao Phraya, at a place where a short-cut canal had widened into the main stream. On the west bank, at Thonburi, Taksin officially established his new capital, and here he was proclaimed king.

Taksin ruled until 1782. In the last seven years of his reign, he relied heavily on two trusted generals, the brothers Chao Phya Chakri and Chao Phya Sarasih, who were given absolute command in military campaigns. They liberated Chiang Mai and the rest of northern Thailand from Burmese rule, and brought Cambodia and most of present-day Laos under Thai suzerainty.

The Emerald Buddha

It was from the victorious Laotian campaign that Thailand obtained the famed Emerald Buddha (Phra Kaeo). Chao Phya Chakri carried the Buddha from Vientiane to Thonburi in 1779. Carved of solid jadeite, the image was allegedly discovered at Chiang Rai, in 1436, inside a pagoda struck asunder by lightning. The stucco originally surrounding the image gradually flaked away, revealing the jadeite form inside. The Emerald Buddha is regarded by Thais as the most sacred of all Buddha images, and is believed to guarantee the independence and prosperity of the nation.

At Thonburi, Taksin's personality underwent a slow metamorphosis from strong and just to cruel and unpredictable. When a revolt broke out in 1782, Taksin abdicated and entered a monastery.

A minor official who had engineered the revolt offered the throne to Chao Phya Chakri upon his return from a Cambodian campaign. General Chakri assumed the kingship on April 6 – a date still commemorated as Chakri Day – thereby establishing the still-reigning Chakri dynasty. Taksin, unstable in mind and regarded by a council of generals as a threat to stability in the country, was executed in a royal manner. ❏

situation. He and his comrades broke through the Burmese encirclement and escaped to the southeast coast. There, Phya Tak Sin assembled an army and a navy. Only seven months after the fall of Ayutthaya, General Taksin and his forces returned to the capital and expelled the Burmese occupiers.

Move to Bangkok

Taksin had barely spent a night at Ayutthaya when he decided to transfer the site of his capital. A location nearer to the sea would be better strategically, both facilitating foreign trade and ensuring the relatively easy procurement of arms. It would also make defense and

---

LEFT: 18th-century Ayutthaya-style lacquer door.
RIGHT: jewelry collection from the Ayutthaya period.

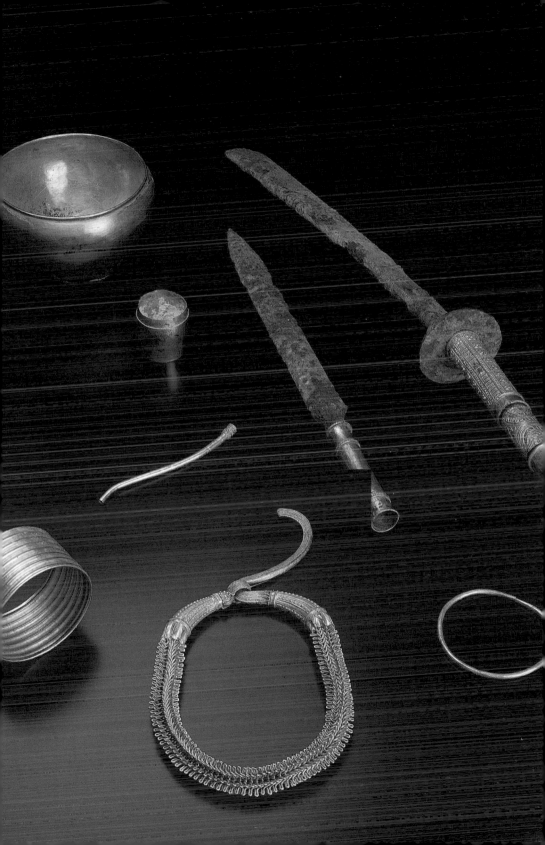

THE ABSOLUTE MONARCHY

The Chakri dynasty modernized and consolidated Thailand, turning Bangkok

into one of Asia's most modern cities by the early 20th century

U pon assuming the throne, General Chakri took the name of Ramathibodi. Later known as Rama I, he ruled from 1782 until 1809. His first action as king was to transfer his administrative headquarters from the marshy confines of Thonburi to the more spacious Bangkok, across the river.

The Chakri dynasty

Rama I was an ambitious man eager to re-establish the Thai kingdom as a dominant civilization. He ordered the digging of a canal across a neck of land on the Bangkok side, creating an island and an inner city. This canal, Khlong Lawd, runs north from today's Pak Klong Talat market, and served as a boundary, a moat, and an artery of communication and commerce.

Rama I envisioned this artificial island as the core of his new capital. Within its rim, he would concentrate the principal components of the Thai nation: religion, monarchy, and administration. To underscore his recognition of the power of the country's principal Buddha image, he called this island *Rattanakosin*, or the "Resting Place of the Emerald Buddha."

To dedicate the area solely to statecraft and religion, he formally requested that the Chinese living there move to an area to the southeast. This new district, Sampeng, soon sprouted thriving shops and busy streets, becoming the commercial heart of the city in what is now known as Chinatown.

On April 6, 1782, at a time and place chosen by geomancers and astrologers, the new monarch proclaimed both the establishment of a new City of Angels and the Chakri dynasty, which continues today.

Rama I modeled Bangkok's defensive system on that of Ayutthaya. Recognizing that Bangkok would need room to expand, he ordered 10,000 Cambodian captives to dig a second canal in a concentric arc some 800 meters (2,600 ft) east of Khlong Lawd.

LEFT: the Golden Mount.
RIGHT: early map of Bangkok showing waterways.

To gird and guard the city, 5,000 Laotian captives built a high, stout wall along the inner banks of the second canal and the river, lining it with 14 octagonal watchtowers, only two of which remain today. He next sent his workers north to Ayutthaya to dismantle the ruined city's buildings. Transported downriver to Bangkok,

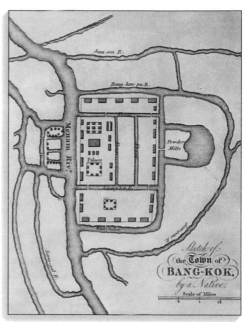

the bricks were cemented together to form the wall. Rama I thus ensured that Bangkok would be imbued with the spirit of ancient Ayutthaya.

As the city grew, a third canal was dug a further 800 meters (2,600 ft) to the east, again in a concentric arc. A network of canals was then dug to connect them. In the early days, the city had only three dirt roadways, tracks really: Bamrungmuang, an elephant path running east from the city wall; a road circling the outside of the city wall; and a third one inside the wall.

It would be another 80 years before Bangkok would have its first paved road. By the middle of the 20th century, most of the canal network had been filled in to make way for roads.

Building for the future

Rama I then turned his attention to constructing the royal island's principal buildings. First was a home for the Emerald Buddha, the most sacred image in the realm, which, until then, had been resting in a temple in Thonburi. Two years later, in 1784, Wat Phra Kaeo was completed.

In commemoration of the event, a new word was added to the lengthy official title of the capital city (the longest city name in the world): Krung Thep Phra Maha Nakorn Amorn

NEW FINERY

Because the royal regalia had been destroyed with everything else during the siege of Ayutthaya, Rama I had a new crown and robes made for his coronation.

National Theater, and various government offices.

Modern Thailand is indebted to Rama I for his assiduous cultural revival program. He appointed experts to review and assemble fragments of historical and religious treatises, few of which had survived Ayutthaya's destruction in 1767.

Rama I perpetuated another Ayutthaya tradition by appointing his brother as *maha uparaja,* a "second" or deputy king, with powers almost equal to his own. His home, the *Wang Na* or "palace at the back," is now part of

Rattanakosin... et cetera. The new word altered the title to mean "City of Angels, Abode of the Emerald Buddha..." It was shortened to Krung Thep, but Bangkok became the accepted name.

Rama I then turned his attention to building a palace. The Grand Palace was more than a home; it contained buildings for receiving royal visitors and debating matters of state. The last building to be constructed, the Chakri Maha Prasad with its triple crowns, was not erected until late in the 19th century. Until 1946, the Grand Palace was home to Thailand's kings.

The palace grounds also contain Wat Po, the National Museum, one of the nation's two most prestigious universities (Thammasat), the

the National Museum and once extended across the northern half of Sanam Luang.

In his old age, he commissioned a golden urn to be prepared for his body, in accordance with ancient court protocol prescribing that the bodies of high-ranking royalty be placed in urns between death and later cremation.

The king was so pleased with the golden urn created by his craftsmen that he placed it in his bedroom so he could admire it fully. Upon seeing the urn, one of his wives burst into floods of tears. It was a bad omen, she said. "Nonsense," replied the king, laughing. "If I don't see it from the outside while I'm alive, how do you think I can ever see it?"

Rama II and Rama III

Rama I's successors, Rama II and Rama III, completed both the consolidation of the Siamese kingdom and the revival of Ayutthaya's arts and culture.

If Rama I laid the foundations of Bangkok, it was Rama II who instilled it with the spirit of the past. Best remembered as an artist, Rama II (ruled 1809–24), the second ruler of the Chakri dynasty, was responsible for building and repairing numerous Bangkok monasteries. His most famous construction was Wat Arun, the Temple of Dawn, which was later enlarged to its present height by Rama IV. He is said to

have carved the great doors of Wat Suthat, throwing away the chisels so his work could never be replicated.

During his father's reign, Rama II had gained renown as a great poet. His *magnum opus* was the *Inao*, an epic poem adopted from a Javanese legend. His classic version of the *Ramakien*, the Thai interpretation of the Indian classical saga, *Ramayana*, was completed during his reign, with large sections composed by the king himself, as well as by other poets. At his court,

LEFT: Bangkok *khlong*, late 19th century.
ABOVE: Mongkut (Rama IV) and his queen.
ABOVE RIGHT: Chulalongkorn (Rama V) and entourage.

Rama II employed *khon* and *lakhon* dance-drama troupes to enact his compositions, just as in the courts of Ayutthaya.

Rama II reopened relations with the West, which had been suspended since the time of Narai, and allowed the Portuguese to open the first Western embassy in Bangkok. Rama III (ruled 1824–51) continued to open Siam's doors to foreigners.

The ready availability of Chinese porcelain led him to decorate many temples, including Wat Arun, with ceramic fragments. This vogue did not survive his lifetime, so that today, when visiting any temple with porcelain-decorated

gables, travelers can immediately ascribe it to the reign of Rama III. A pious Buddhist, Rama III was considered to be "austere and reactionary" by some Europeans. But he encouraged American missionaries to introduce Western medicine, such as smallpox vaccinations, to Siam.

Mongkut (Rama IV)

With the help of Hollywood, Rama IV (ruled 1851–68) became the most famous king of Siam. More commonly known as King Mongkut, he was portrayed by Yul Brynner in *The King and I* as a frivolous, bald-headed despot – but nothing could have been further from the truth. He was

Thai Script

The Thai script is believed to have been created in 1283 during the landmark reign of King Ramkamhaeng. In fact, the inscribed stone bearing the first example of written Thai (dated 1292) is attributed to the Sukhothai king, and the monarch himself is credited with having invented the script.

In the days before the Thai language had a script, records were maintained using characters from Khmer and ancient Indian languages, such as Sanskrit and Pali. However, these languages did

not always have characters that could adequately represent the nuances of spoken Thai. The Thai script was, therefore, born of necessity rather than simply at the whim of an ambitious ruler.

Ramkamhaeng's characters were mainly adapted from Khmer and Devanagri (the script in which Sanskrit and Pali were written). In the beginning, consonants and vowel signs, as well as tone markers, were all written continuously in a line, without breaks. The script on the first stone inscription, now displayed at the National Museum in Bangkok, thus looks quite different from the Thai script used now. The outline of the characters is rough and they are not easy to read. There are also only two signs to denote tone.

Over the course of the next 100 years, the Thai script evolved into something more user-friendly. It became simpler and plainer, and the characters acquired smoother, more flowing outlines. More tonal marks were also added to represent all the tones – unlike many Western languages, the Thai language relies heavily on tone to give similar sounding words different meanings. So if you don't get the tone right, the chances are you are saying the wrong thing.

Although the Thai script is now much simpler than it was in Sukhothai days, it can still easily confuse foreigners, and sometimes even Thais. There are 44 characters in the Thai alphabet, but they represent only 21 sounds, which means that quite a few characters share the same sound. One of the reasons for this is that many Thai words that come from Pali or Sanskrit were pronounced differently to begin with, but have now come to sound the same in speech, though they have retained their different spellings.

There is also the difficulty that many Thai letters look very similar to others, and a short straight line added to a character or a little circle placed in the wrong position can produce a different character with a completely different sound. Moreover, there are 21 vowel signs signifying 32 sounds, and four tonal marks representing five tones.

Like most Western scripts, Thai writing proceeds from left to right. But what makes it radically different is the order in which characters and vowel and tonal signs have to be written to make any sense. Vowel signs have to be written before, after, above, below, and in between characters depending on what is being said. Tonal marks, too, have to be inserted above characters and vowel signs in the right position to produce meaningful words and sentences. Though this may sound quite complex and arbitrary, there are clear rules governing what goes where. Learning to write Thai, therefore, requires a lot of patience, a good memory and an eye for detail.

Reading Thai also presents difficulties because words derived from other languages are spelt in complex ways but contain characters that are not usually pronounced. An example of this can be seen when Thai words are transliterated into English. A road in downtown Bangkok is called Surawong Road, but it is often written as "Surawongse" even though the "se" at the end is silent. ❑

LEFT: stone inscription attributed to King Ramkamhaeng, inventor of the Thai writing system.

the first Thai – and in many instances, the first Asian – king to understand Western culture and technology, and his reign has been described as the bridge spanning the new and the old.

The younger brother of Rama III, Mongkut spent 27 years as a Buddhist monk prior to his accession to the throne. This gave him a unique opportunity to roam as a commoner among the populace. He learned to read Buddhist scriptures in the Pali language; missionaries taught him Latin and English, thus enabling him to read European texts. As a monk, Mongkut delved into many subjects: history, geography and the sciences – he had a particular passion for astronomy.

Even as an abbot, he established himself as a reformer, ridding the Buddhist scriptures of their superstitious elements and founding a sect, the Dhammakaiya, which stressed strict adherence to Buddhist tenets. Today, these monks can be recognized by their brown robes.

Opening doors

Mongkut instituted a policy of modernization, and England was the first European country to benefit from this, when an 1855 treaty – gained after some coercion by the British – granted extraterritorial privileges: a duty of only 3 percent on imports, and permission to import Indian opium duty-free. Other Western nations followed suit with similar treaties. When Mongkut lifted the state monopoly on rice, it rapidly became Siam's leading export.

In 1863, Mongkut built Bangkok's first paved road – Charoen Krung (prosperous city) or, as it was known to foreigners, New Road. This 6-km (4-mile) long street, running from the palace southeast along the river, was lined with shops and houses. He paved other dirt roads, and introduced new technology to encourage commerce.

The foreign community quickly moved into the areas opened by the construction of New Road. They built their homes in the area where the Oriental Hotel now stands, and along Silom and Sathorn roads, both rural retreats at that time. Numerous letters to the editor of the *Bangkok Times* in 1900 complain of the writers'

RIGHT: a son of Chulalongkorn (Rama V).

> ### MODERNIZATION
>
> Mongkut believed that traditional Thai values would not save Siam from Western encroachment, but that modernization would bring Siam into line with the West, reducing hostilities with foreigners.

inability to take the evening air or ride in their carriages along Windmill Road (Silom) due to the prevalence of "foul odors" from the gardens that the Chinese farmers nourished with fertilizer.

Mongkut wanted his children to gain the same benefits from the English language as himself. For this purpose, he engaged Anna Leonowens as an English teacher. The self-elevated governess greatly exaggerated her role in the Thai court in her autobiographical writings, misrepresenting the king as a cruel

autocrat permanently involved in harem intrigues. In fact, her five years in Siam are hardly mentioned in Thai chronicles.

Mongkut's beloved hobby, astronomy, was to be the indirect cause of his death. From observatories at his favorite palaces, the Summer Palace at Bang Pa-in and the Palace on the Hill at Petchburi, he successfully calculated and predicted a total eclipse of the sun in 1868. European and Asian skeptics joined him on the southeastern coast of the Gulf of Thailand to await the event. As the moon blocked the sun's light, both the Europeans and the scoffers among the royal astrologers raised an exclamation of great admiration, elevating the king's esteem among both parties. But his triumph was short-lived. The king contracted malaria during the trip, and died from it two weeks later.

Chulalongkorn

Mongkut's son, Chulalongkorn, or Rama V, was only 15 when he ascended the throne. The far-sighted Chulalongkorn immediately revolutionized his court by ending the ancient custom of prostration, and by allowing officials to sit on chairs during royal audiences. He abolished serfdom in stages, giving owners

LONG REIGN

Chulalongkorn reigned over Siam as Rama V for 42 years – longer than any Thai king until the present King Bhumibol, who surpassed that record in 1988.

lighting. He hired Danish engineers to build an electric tram system 10 years before the one in Copenhagen was completed. He encouraged the importation of automobiles about the same time they began appearing on the streets of America.

Chulalongkorn changed the face of Bangkok. By 1900, the city was growing rapidly eastward. In the Dusit area, on the northeastern outskirts of the city, he built a palace and constructed roads to link it with his palace. Other noble families followed, building elegant man-

and serfs time to readjust to the new order, and replaced corvée labor with direct taxation.

His reign was truly a revolution from the throne. When Chulalongkorn assumed power, Siam had no schools, and few roads, railways, hospitals, or well-equipped military forces. To achieve the enormous task of modernization, he brought in foreign advisors and sent his sons and other young men to be educated abroad. He also founded a palace school for children of the aristocracy, following this with other schools and vocational centers. Previously the only schools in Siam had been monasteries.

During his reign, he abolished the last vestiges of slavery and, in 1884, introduced electric

sions. In the same area, he arranged the construction of Wat Benjamabophit, the last major Buddhist temple built in Bangkok.

A watershed year was 1892, when the four government ministries were expanded to 12, a post-and-telegraph office was established, and construction of the first railway was begun. Chulalongkorn's brothers were leading figures in his government, especially Prince Devawongse, the foreign minister, and Prince Damrong, the first interior minister and a historian who has come to be known as the father of Thai history. Chulalongkorn's elder children returned from their European schools in the 1890s, helping to modernize both the army and navy.

The first hospital, Siriraj, was opened in 1886 after years of unrelenting opposition – most of the common people preferred herbal remedies to *farang* medicine. Besides, there was a serious shortage of doctors. Eventually, though, the obstacles were overcome.

Defining borders

In the area of foreign relations, however, Chulalongkorn had to compromise and give up parts of his kingdom in order to protect Siam from foreign colonization. When France conquered Annam in 1883 and Britain annexed

> ### A NEW TITLE
>
> Chulalongkorn was posthumously named *Piya Maharaj*, meaning the Beloved Great King.

up 120,000 sq. km (46,300 sq. miles) of fringe territory. But that seemed a small price to pay for maintaining the country's peace and independence.

Chulalongkorn made two European tours during his reign, in 1897 and 1907. These led him to seek more spacious surroundings than those of the Grand Palace, so he built the on the site of a fruit orchard to the north, in Dusit. It was directly connected to the Grand Palace by the wide Ratchadamnern Avenue. At the Dusit palace, he held intimate parties and sometimes

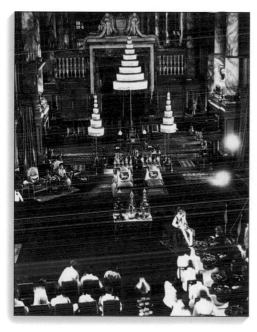

Upper Burma in 1886, Siam found itself sandwiched uncomfortably between two rival expansionist powers.

Border conflicts and gunboat diplomacy forced Siam to surrender to France its claims to Laos and western Cambodia. Similarly, certain Malay Peninsula territories were ceded to Britain in exchange for renunciation of British extraterritorial rights in Siam. By the end of Chulalongkorn's reign, Siam had given

LEFT: Chulalongkorn's (Rama V's) family; Vajiravudh and Prajadhipok are at center top and lower right. ABOVE: Prajadhipok (Rama VII) delivering a new constitution. ABOVE RGHT: Plowing Day, 1930.

even fancy-dress balls, often cooking the food outside himself.

Chulalongkorn's many and wide-ranging reforms bore fruit within his lifetime. The economy of the country flourished, and the Thai peasantry – by comparison with their counterparts in French Indochina and British Burma – were very well-off. It is no wonder that Chulalongkorn was posthumously named *Piya Maharaj*, the Beloved Great King. As Rama V, Chulalongkorn was conscious of worldwide democratic trends, but judged his country to be unprepared for such a change. It is said that he managed to bring progress to Siam through the judicious exercise of his absolute power.

Vajiravudh (Rama VI)

King Chulalongkorn's successor, Vajiravudh, started his reign (1910–25) with a lavish coronation. He was educated at Oxford and thoroughly anglicized, and his Western-inspired reforms aimed at modernizing Siam had a profound effect on modern Thai society.

One of the first changes was a 1913 edict which commanded his subjects to adopt surnames. In the absence of a clan or caste system, genealogy was virtually unheard of in Siam at that

NATIONAL PRIDE

An accomplished author, Vijiravudh (Rama VI), fostered nationalism by glorifying Thai legends and historical heroes in plays. Under a pseudonym, he also wrote essays extolling the virtues of the nation.

time. Previously, Thais had used first names, a practice that the king considered uncivilized. The law generated much initial bewilderment, especially in rural areas, and Vajiravudh personally coined patronymics for hundreds of families. To simplify his forebears' lengthy titles for foreigners, he invented the Chakri dynasty name, Rama, to be followed by the proper reign number. He started with himself, as Rama VI.

As Thai standards of beauty did not conform to Western ideals of femininity, women were encouraged to keep their hair long instead of having it close-cropped, and to replace their *dhoti,* or wide-legged Thai trousers, with the *panung,* a Thai-style sarong. Primary education was made compulsory throughout the kingdom; Chulalongkorn University, the first in Siam, was founded, and schools for both sexes flourished during Vajiravudh's reign.

At the outbreak of World War I, Siam remained neutral, but late in the war, in 1917, Vajiravudh effectively joined the Allies by sending a small expeditionary force to fight in France, thereby securing Siam's admittance to the League of Nations. The then-Thai flag, a white elephant against a red background, was flown with others at Versailles, but the pachyderm was unfortunately mistaken for a small domestic animal. The incident greatly discomfited the king, who then decided to change the flag to red, white and blue stripes to represent the nation, the religion and the monarchy, elements now recognized as essential to the structure of modern Thailand.

Vajiravudh preferred individual ministerial consultations to summoning his appointed cabinet. His regime was therefore criticized as autocratic and lacking in coordination. Members of his family were dissatisfied because he rarely saw them, enjoying more the company of his courtiers. His extravagance soon emptied the reserve funds built up by Chulalongkorn; towards the end of his reign, the national treasury had to meet deficits caused by the ruler's personal expenses.

The king married late. His only daughter was born one day before he died in 1925. He was succeeded by his youngest brother, Prajadhipok, who reaped the consequences of his brother's brilliant but controversial reign.

Prajadhipok (Rama VII)

The early death of his elder brother propelled Prajadhipok to royal succession, although being an old Etonian, he would have preferred a soldier's career to that of a ruler. Once king, however, he stressed economy and efficiency within the government.

Unlike his brother, he tried to cut public expenditure by drastically reducing the civil service and royal household expenses. Prajadhipok's economic policies, combined with the increased revenue from foreign trade, amply paid off for the kingdom.

In the early years of his reign, communications were improved by the advent of a wireless service, and the Don Muang Airport began to operate as an international air center. It was also during the course of Prajadhipok's reign that Siam saw the establishment of the Fine Arts Department, the National Library and the National Museum, institutions that continue today as important preservers of Thai culture.

Hard-working and conscientious, Prajadhipok was personally concerned with improving the welfare of his subjects. He was aware of the rising demand for greater participation in government by a small foreign-educated fac-

resorting to a retrenchment of the armed services. Discontent brewed among army officials and bureaucrats, who felt promotions were due.

Coup d'état

Rumors and speculation were rampant during the 150th anniversary celebrations of the Chakri dynasty in 1932. Prajadhipok was the last regal representative of traditional Thai kingship to preside over grand pageantry, which featured a royal barge procession.

Two months later, a coup d'état ended the absolute rule by Thai monarchs. The coup was staged by the People's Party, a military and

tion, but felt that the Thais were, on the whole, not ready to accept democracy. In 1927, he publicly commented that the people must first be taught political consciousness before democracy could effectively be introduced.

The worldwide economic crisis of 1931 affected Siam's rice export. By the time Prajadhipok dropped the gold standard, linking the Thai baht to the pound sterling, it was too late to stem the financial crisis. The government was forced to implement further economies by cutting the salary of junior personnel, and by

LEFT: Chulalongkorn (Rama V).
ABOVE: Prajadhipok's (Rama VII) 1925 coronation.

civilian group masterminded by foreign-educated Thais. The chief ideologist was Pridi Panomyong, a young lawyer trained in France. On the military side, Capt. Luang Pibulsongram (Pibul) was responsible for gaining the support of important army colonels.

With a few tanks, the 70 conspirators sparked off their "revolution" by occupying strategic areas and holding the senior princes hostage. Other army officers stood by as the public watched. At the time, the king was in Hua Hin, a royal retreat to the south. Perceiving he had little choice and to avoid bloodshed, he agreed to accept a provisional constitution by which he "ceased to rule but continued to reign." ❏

MODERN TIMES

Thailand has seen phenomenal economic growth and building on a huge scale in Bangkok. But the price has been unstable government and financial crisis

Originally motivated by idealism, the People's Party, who took power following the 1932 coup d'état, soon succumbed to internal conflicts and competitions. A National Assembly was appointed, but universal suffrage was postponed while the public was to be tutored in the rudiments of representative democracy. The Thai people didn't show much interest, however. They wouldn't voluntarily attend the party's educational rallies, and other parties were initially outlawed.

The party's military factions quickly outmaneuvered the civilian contingents. They had greater cohesion, and more extensive connections with traditional elite power brokers. The officers exercised their influence when Pridi Panomyong presented a vague and utopian economic plan in 1933. It called for the nationalization of land, and for the creation of peasant cooperatives. When his opponents attacked the plan as communistic, Pridi slipped into his first overseas exile. The power of Pibul and the army was further strengthened in October of 1933 by the decisive defeat of a rebellion led by Prince Boworadct, who had been the war minister under King Prajadhipok.

The king had no part in the rebellion, but had become increasingly dismayed by quarrels within the new government. He moved to England in 1934 and abdicated in 1935. In a farewell message, he said that he had wished to turn over power to the entire people and not to "any individual or any group to use in an autocratic manner." Sadly, the subsequent history of coups, aborted coups, and bloodbaths has caused the king's words to be often quoted. Ananda Mahidol (Rama VIII), a 10-year-old half-nephew, agreed to take the throne, but remained in Switzerland to complete his schooling.

The governments of the 1930s had some achievements. Most notably, public primary education, totaling four years, was extended to many rural areas. Indirect and, later, direct elections to the lower house meant that for the first time representatives from provincial areas had a voice at the national level.

After a series of crises and an election in 1938, Pibul became prime minister. His rule grew more authoritarian. While some Thai officers favored the model of the Japanese military

regime, Pibul admired – and sought to emulate – Hitler and Mussolini. Borrowing many ideas from European fascism, he attempted to instill a sense of mass nationalism in the Thai people.

With tight control over the media and a creative propaganda department, Pibul whipped up sentiment against the Chinese residents. Chinese immigration was restricted, Chinese workers were barred from certain occupations, and state enterprises were set up to compete in Chinese-dominated industries. By changing the country's name from Siam to Thailand in 1939, Pibul intended to emphasize that it belonged to Thai (or Tai) ethnic groups and not to Chinese, Malays, Mons, or any other minorities.

LEFT: King Bhumibol's coronation.
RIGHT: book showing 1932 coup d'état leaders.

World War II

When Hitler invaded France in 1940, the French hold over its Indochinese colonies was seriously weakened. Anticipating that Japan might make a claim, Thailand made its own by invading southern Laos and parts of western Cambodia, in November 1940. Stepping in as a mediator, Japan sided with Thailand. For the previous 50 years, Thai foreign policy had been coupled with Britain's, but these military ventures now meant that the (soon-to-be) Allies thought little of cooperating with Thailand.

On December 7, 1941, (December 8 in Asia) the Japanese bombed Pearl Harbor and launched

known as Seri Thai. Starting with overseas Thai students, Seri Thai linked up with a network in Thailand headed by Pridi. The resistance supplied Allied forces with intelligence, but it never quite reached the stage of operating a guerrilla army.

By 1944, Thailand's initial enthusiasm for its Japanese partners had evaporated. The country faced runaway inflation, food shortages, rationing and black markets. The assembly forced Pibul from office. When the war ended in 1945, Britain demanded reparations and the right to station troops in Thailand. The Thais argued that, due to the work of Seri Thai, they

invasions throughout Southeast Asia. Thailand was invaded at nine points. Despite a decade of military buildup, resistance lasted less than a day. Pibul acceded to Japan's request for "passage rights," but Thailand was allowed to retain its army and political administration.

Popular anecdote has it that the Thai ambassador to Washington, Seni Pramoj, single-handedly prevented war between Thailand and the United States by hiding the war declaration in a desk drawer. It's not true. Thailand in fact declared war against Britain and the United States. It is true, however, that Seni immediately offered his services in Washington to set up an underground resistance movement,

were in fact allies. The US supported the Thais, partly because it was trying to blunt British and French efforts to repossess their Asian colonies.

After the war

Following World War II, Bangkok began to develop its economy along the lines of European countries, with new industries, firm administration, and the first of many five-year plans. Bangkok began to change dramatically in response to the new prosperity. The last of the major canals were filled in to make roadways. The city began its big push to the east, as Sukhumvit and Petchburi roads changed from quiet residential areas into busy, business-filled thoroughfares. (But it wasn't until the arrival of American forces in the late 1960s that the city gained its present look. Large infusions of money resulted in a burgeoning economy, multistory buildings and a population that swelled in response to the new jobs that were on offer. The Thai military, which had steadily been gaining power in Thai politics, reached its peak of influence during these years.)

The first few years after the end of World War II were marked by a series of democratic

PRIDI IN EXILE

After fleeing into exile in 1949, ex-prime minister Pridi spent 20 years in China, and died in France in 1983.

After attempting a coup in 1949, Pridi fled into permanent exile. Pibul sealed Pridi's fate by convening an official inquiry that implicated him in the death of King Ananda. In 1946, on a visit to Thailand from school in Europe, the young king was found shot dead in his palace bedroom. (Pridi believed that the king accidentally shot himself.) The charge against Pridi now seems absurd, but with the mass media in Pibul's hands, many people at the time probably believed it.

Ananda was succeeded by his younger

civilian governments. Pridi served behind the scenes, drafting a constitution, and briefly served as prime minister. In 1948, under threat of military force, Pibul took over once again. In the early years, his power was contested. Two coup attempts, supported by the navy, resulted in fierce battles on the streets of Bangkok and along the Chao Phraya River. In the 1950s, Pibul's grip grew tighter. Police power was abused, newspaper editors were beaten, and government critics mysteriously disappeared. Pibul had also rid himself of his nemesis, Pridi.

LEFT: soldiers at a ceremony. **ABOVE:** Bangkok's Democracy Monument, a popular rallying point.

brother, Bhumibol Adulyadej (Rama IX), the present monarch, who returned to Switzerland to complete law studies. He did not take up active duties until the 1950s. By then, Thailand had been without a king for 20 years.

Anti-communism

In addition to renewed anti-Chinese campaigns, Pibul vigorously hunted out communists. Many of the leaders of the small, outlawed Communist Party of Thailand were Sino-Thais. Pibul's anti-communist credentials helped win both economic and military aid from the United States. American largesse, with too few strings, has been blamed as cause for the corruption that permeates the police and military to this day. Another cause was Pibul's practice of placing military officers to run state enterprises. Many private firms were also encouraged to appoint officers as directors.

In 1957, a clique of one-time protegés overthrew Pibul. The leader, General Sarit Thanarat, and two cohort generals, Thanom Kittikachorn and Prapas Charusathien, ran the government until 1973. While Pibul had retained some trappings of democracy, such as a constitution and legislature, Sarit employed

> **WESTERNIZATION**
>
> Many Thais were exposed to Western values in the late 1960s and early 1970s due to the resident population of 45,000 American servicemen.

facilities proliferated. From here, US aircraft bombed Vietnam and Laos. The Northeast was also the Thai base for forays into Laos. Thousands of Thai soldiers died fighting in allegiance with the Royal Lao Army against Lao communists. Meanwhile, Thai communists had turned to armed conflict in 1965. The original strongholds were in the impoverished Northeast, but by the early 1970s, there were communist areas throughout, including the Muslim south. Sarit, Thanom, and Prapas used their power to accrue

martial law. Labor organizations were banned, and even educational and cultural groups found it difficult to associate. The Buddhist *sangha* was coopted to promote anti-communism and other campaigns.

The Vietnam War

Unadorned dictatorship did not hinder official relations with the United States. By the end of the 1960s, the war in Vietnam was raging and Thailand was America's staunchest ally. A small Thai contingent served in Vietnam. Total aid was running at about $100 million annually. American funds built the first roads in the Northeast, where air bases and other military

enormous personal fortunes, but they also deserve credit for development. Health standards improved, the business sector expanded, construction boomed, and a middle class began to emerge, especially in Bangkok. Yet, the dictatorial trio did not anticipate that socio-economic changes would lead to new aspirations.

The October revolution

In 1969, in a mystifying burst of generosity, Prime Minister Thanom issued a constitution and held elections. His party naturally won most seats, but the general quickly grew bored of the slow parliamentary processes. In November 1971, Thanom and Prapas dissolved the parliament and reverted to their old ruling habits. Many Thai people felt betrayed, but only students kept up low-key protests, despite grave personal risk.

With reasonable demands for a constitution and popular elections, students were able to harness public support. The final straw was the arrest of 13 student leaders and professors who had made such demands.

On October 13, 1973, a demonstration to protest against the arrests attracted 400,000 people to Bangkok's Democracy Monument. The following day, the protest turned violent and at least 100 students were shot by riot

duced civilian governments, but the diverse parties could not work together for long.

The middle class was originally strongly supportive of the student revolution, as were parts of the upper class. But they came to fear that total chaos or a communist takeover was at hand. The 1976 return of Thanom, ostensibly to become a monk, sparked student protests and paramilitary counter-protests. On October 6, police and paramilitary thugs stormed Thammasat University. Students were lynched and their bodies burned on the spot. A faction of army officers seized power. Self-government had lasted but three years. Ironically, the civil-

police. The two generals then discovered that their army had deserted them. They fled to the United States.

Political parties, labor unions, and farming organizations sprang to life with very specific grievances. The press has never again been so unfettered as it was then. Right-wing and paramilitary organizations sprang up in response. Between 1974 and 1975, the new Farmers' Federation was decimated by the murder of 21 of its leaders. Two elections in the mid-1970s pro-

ian judge appointed to be prime minister, Thanin Kraivichien, turned out to be more brutal than any of his uniformed predecessors. Besides outlawing political parties, unions and strikes, he ordered arrests of anyone "endangering society." A curfew was strictly enforced. Teachers suspected of left-wing leanings were required to attend anti-communism indoctrination. Many students and other dissidents joined the communists in the countryside.

Yet another military coup ousted Thanin in October 1977. For the next decade, two relatively moderate generals headed the government. Both endorsed amnesties for communists. Ex-students returned first, but by the

FAR LEFT: honoring pro-democracy protesters killed by the army, 1992. **LEFT:** military officers.
ABOVE: waiting for election results.

mid-1980s, most guerrilla soldiers had also given up. For the Thai communists, one disillusioning factor was the arrival of thousands of refugees from Laos, after the communists triumphed in 1975. Perhaps the final blow was the cut-off of guns and support from China to the Thai communists by the early 1980s. The governments and armies of Thailand and China had joined together to become partners in the face of a shared historical enemy, Vietnam. To thwart Vietnam's ambitions in Cambodia,

> **GRIDLOCKED**
>
> Bangkok has fewer roads for its size than any other capital city; traffic congestion during peak hours – plus the pollution and lost worker productivity – is thought to be the worst in the world.

Since the early 1980s, various government officials hoping to gain points with the public – or their superiors – have put forward solutions to Bangkok's traffic problem. Eventually the ideas evaporate, only to be recycled a year or two later.

The only substantive success – that is, successful completion of an idea – is the 20-km (13-mile) long Bangkok Expressway, opened in 1993. In early 1996, a grand traffic-signal synchronization attempt only compounded the gridlock.

the two countries actively aided and encouraged the Khmer Rouge army.

High-rise development

The 1980s and 1990s saw the vertical growth of Bangkok. Its skyline changed dramatically as 30- and 40-story buildings sprouted throughout the city. Development peaked during the early 1990s, but construction in the inner city has not slowed down: middle-class commuters are opting for residences near the center of town to reduce the amount of time spent in Bangkok's notorious traffic jams. (Surprisingly, too, new hotels continue to be constructed, despite a glut in this kind of property.)

Fragile democracy

The prospects for sustained democracy are uncertain. A former general was popularly elected in 1988, but was deposed two years later in a bloodless military coup. To the junta's surprise, the caretaker businessman installed as a prime minister exhibited an independent streak. In fact, Anand Panyacharun earned plaudits for running the cleanest government in memory. As expected, the junta's new party won the most parliamentary seats in the 1992 elections. Unexpected, however, was the public discontent when the coup leader, General Suchinda Kraprayoon, assumed the prime ministership without having stood for election.

With eerie echoes of the mid-1970s, professionals, lawyers, social workers, and the curious public, mostly middle-class people, began gathering at rallies in Sanam Luang and near Democracy Monument, in Bangkok. More than 70,000 met at Sanam Luang on May 17. Late in the evening, soldiers fired on unarmed demonstrators. Killings, beatings, riots, and arson attacks continued sporadically for the next three days. Thai broadcast media are controlled by the government, and so were able to carry out a news blackout of the events. But owners of satellite dishes, along with viewers around the world, watched coverage of "Bloody May."

carrying out the crackdown. Military influence in banks and state enterprises remained undiminished. Most important, Chuan was deflected in his efforts to push through a law that would have delegated more power to local government.

Chuan battled constantly to keep his coalition working together. It finally disintegrated when some members of Chuan's own party were implicated in a land reform scandal. Elections in July 1995 brought an old-style politician, Banharn Silpa-archa, to the premiership. As the Thai press phrased it at the time, both Banharn and his party, Chart Thai, had a strong

Unrepentant, Suchinda bowed out. The Democrat Party and other prominent Suchinda critics prevailed in the September elections.

Prime Minister Chuan Leekpai, who was personally not corrupt, persisted for almost three years, a record for a civilian government. Setting another record, he was not toppled by a coup. But by the end, Chuan had lost much of the goodwill of the pro-democracy groups that had lifted him to power.

Neither Suchinda nor anyone else was prosecuted, punished, or held responsible for

LEFT: a much-loved form of transport.
ABOVE: Constitution Day parade.

"reputation" for corruption. Regardless, military leaders reaffirmed that they had no plans to intervene in politics.

Economic crisis

The Thai economy, which registered phenomenal annual growth rates for over a decade to emerge as one of the famous "Tiger" economies of Southeast Asia, suddenly saw the good times come to an end in 1997. Of course, signs that all was not well had been there for a while, though all concerned seemed loath to admit it. But by late 1996, inflationary pressures, a widening current account deficit, and slower economic growth led to a censure motion against the 14-month-old Banharn Silapa-archa government. Elections held in November 1996 saw a coalition headed by the New Aspiration Party come to power. NAP leader Chavalit Yongchaiyudh became Thailand's 22nd Prime Minister, but many of his partners in government were the same as in the previous administration and little was done to stem the economic rot that had set in.

By February 1997, Moody's Investors Service, an international ratings agency, downgraded Thailand's long-term credit rating, ringing alarm bells at home and abroad. By around the middle of the year, the government was

forced to order the closure of 16 finance companies that were in the red. The final straw came shortly afterwards, on July 2, when the Chavalit administration made the decision to let go of the basket of currencies to which the Thai baht had been pegged in favour of a "managed float." This had the disastrous double effect of sending the currency down a devaluation spiral and making the foreign debts of local corporations shoot up.

The pressure to float the baht had been contributed to by some aggressive attacks on it by foreign hedge funds, and enormous sums were spent in its defense from the country's foreign exchange reserves. The upshot of all this

was that the government had to ask for US$17 billion in support from the International Monetary Fund. And, in accordance with the IMF's dictates, it had to order another 42 finance firms to shut down on August 5, 1997.

The economic crisis was, in the final analysis, a fall-out of the so-called fast-track growth strategy that had been pursued for many years, which relied on high interest rates to attract foreign funds and finance cheap exports. Unfortunately, not enough attention was paid to ensure the money was used productively and to promote development of human resources or infrastructure. Instead, the bulk of the funds pouring in went into speculative activities, real estate being on top of the list, and towards expanding domestic credit.

New constitution

The crisis saw companies and businesses go bankrupt and many thousands lose their jobs, either due to closures or downsizing. Amid all this, September 27, 1998, turned out to be an important day because a censure vote on the Chavalit government was scheduled to be held an hour before the vote on the draft of a new, more open constitution. Despite fears that the new charter would not be passed, it sailed through Parliament after some acrimonious wrangling. Yet, later in the year, as the economic crisis deepened, Chavalit had to bow to pressure from the public, especially the business lobby, and step down.

This brought in a Democrat government, headed by Chuan Leekpai, a former premier and a moderate with a clean image. After over a year of hard work, the economy, which had bottomed out, began showing gradual signs of recovery. The process was helped along by a banking reform package in August 1998 that helped boost confidence in the country among foreign investors. The government also pushed forward business laws to help speed up corporate debt restructuring.

An economic stimulus package introduced in March 1999 was designed to speed up recovery, and the stock and debt markets soon began to respond. The baht, too, stabilized at around Bt37.5 per US dollar after having plunged to an all-time low of Bt56.9 in early 1998. ❑

LEFT: the future for Thailand is far from mapped out.
RIGHT: family on moped.

Bangkok Traffic

Many visitors ask: is Bangkok traffic always this bad? The answer is no – sometimes it's worse. It's especially bad in the middle of a heavy rainy season when small, low-lying streets and *sois* may be under water for days. But the worst traffic is, without doubt, after a sudden rainy season downpour when commuters and schoolchildren don't even attempt to struggle home until midnight. Even on "normal" days, many Bangkok children have to get up at 5am in order to take a string of buses to school.

entering the street dramatically dropped, but car sales soon picked up again in 1999. Regardless, with about 2½ million cars registered in the city, it has long been true that if everyone were on the roads at once, there simply wouldn't be enough road space to contain them.

Economists estimate that traffic congestion results in economic losses of Bt447 million (US$12.5 million) every day, due to wasted time and health costs. But that doesn't take into account the potential foreign investors who automatically shelve any plans for joint ventures after a single confrontation with the city's traffic jams.

No one seems to want to contemplate the future

Bangkok has less than half the density of similarly sized developed cities. According to the latest available figures, only 8 percent of Bangkok's land area is road space, compared to 20 percent in other major cities. And the traffic continues to get worse – that is, slower – because there are no restrictions on buying, registering or driving new vehicles. The speed of traffic during morning and evening peak periods continues to drop. It's somewhere below 2 kmph (about 1 mph), which is equivalent to walking speed. Evening peak period runs from about 4pm to 9pm. The number of new vehicles entering the roads varies from between 300 and 500 registered each weekday. Thanks to the economic crisis in 1997, the number of new cars

health costs. A few Chinese cities could challenge claims that Bangkok is the most polluted city in the world, but it is securely among the top 15.

Of course, motor vehicles are not solely to blame for the city's air pollution. Exhaust fumes from diesel vehicles and motorcycles remains the chief culprit. These spew out levels of carbon monoxide, lead, dust particles, benzine and toulene that would unnerve and shock even the most cynical of Western environmentalists.

The health risks are also considerable for the traffic police. About one-third suffer from respiratory problems and another one-quarter have damaged hearing from horns and the rumble of the engines. Exposure to lead hits children hard and can cause permanent nerve damage, but there are no official estimates of the number of pre-school children who spend whole days beside their parents at sidewalk stalls or shops.

So what is Bangkok doing to solve this mess? The city is, finally,overseeing the construction of the new alternatives of commuting. The new century's first improvement is an elevated train service, dubbed the Sky Train, to run 23.5 km (nearly 15 miles) across downtown Bangkok. And in 2004, the citizens will at last experience the country's first underground transportation after a long discussion with the authorities that has taken more than 40 years to come to fruition. The underground

enforced, such "Band-aid" methods wouldn't be enough to alleviate the crisis. They say that traffic won't improve until a comprehensive approach to car ownership is adopted. Contrary to the promises of politicians, they say that a rail or subway system won't miraculously cure congestion. The real solution is an inevitable one: the number of cars allowed on the roads must be severely restricted.

At least a half-dozen city and national agencies have claims over transit, construction and vehicle ownership, and they are far more concerned about protecting turf than co-operating with traffic solutions. Finally, there are the social factors of restricting the number of cars for citizens who have had

service runs over a greater area than the Sky Train, but both will complement each other in several connecting stations.

That few Bangkokites seem to know or care about these new advances may seem odd, given that they say in surveys that traffic is the city's number one problem (the environment is second). But residents have observed so many ballyhooed mass-transit plans collapse and fail.Traffic engineers, both foreign and Thai, say that, even if

the run of the road for so long. Not only this, but Thailand is a very hierarchical society, where the only badge is conspicuous wealth. Car ownership is perhaps the most important symbol of status.

The "middle class" wealthy boast constantly of the number of imported Mercedes they own. Hungry to emulate the elite, members of the new middle class think nothing of sinking US$20,000 in a domestically assembled car, even though the price-tag is two or three times their annual salary. A person who can afford to commute by car and nonetheless chooses to take a taxi or an air-conditioned bus to get from A to B isn't considered either sensible or environmentally-conscious in Thai society. On the contrary: he is considered "stingy." ❑

LEFT: the longest traffic jam in Bangkok stretched for over 200 km (124 miles) and took place during the Thai New Year festival celebrations.
ABOVE: two of Bangkok's long-suffering traffic police.

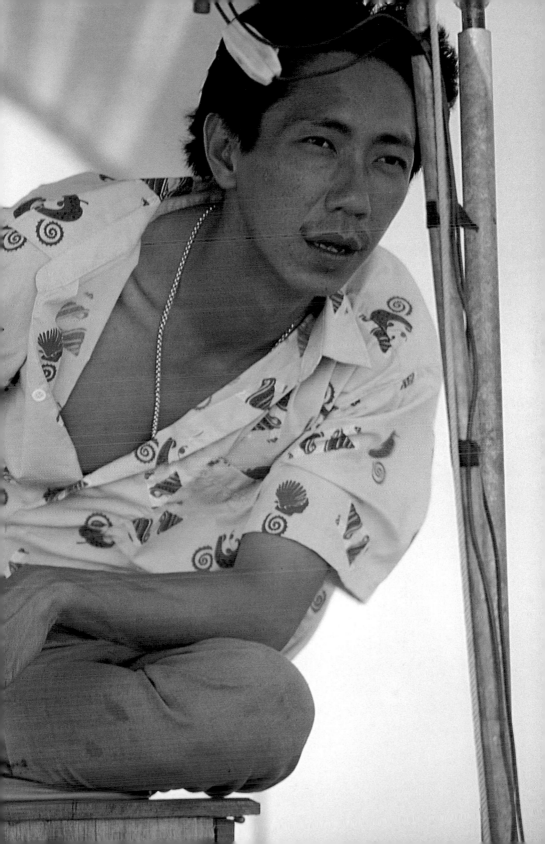

PEOPLE AND SOCIETY

The attitude of "cool heart" not only makes the Thais delightful to meet, it has also helped them survive as a sovereign nation

U nderlying the distinctive Thai warmth, to visitors and to life in general, is *sanuk*, a word that can be translated as "fun" or "enjoyable." The quantity – and quality – of *sanuk*, whether in work or play, determines if something is worth pursuing.

Thailand's culture and society has traditionally been centered on agriculture, an activity that nurtures a sense of community, especially during the planting and harvesting seasons. The shift to urban life has changed much of the countryside's ways, but it is a rare Thai who does not enjoy getting together with friends. Most are puzzled by westerners who dine or holiday alone, as they do not understand the need for occasional solitude. In general, Thais consider such singular experiences as *mai sanuk* (not fun).

An easygoing charm

The sense of family about Thai activities does not exclude outsiders. The community spirit extends to the workplace, where it is not unusual at the end of the day for a group of co-workers to gather together into a small party, with the attendant music, snacks, and alcoholic drinks to relax and release the day's tensions.

When a visitor encounters a tense situation, it is usually because of language difficulties. In this instance, it is best to adopt another Thai attitude, *jai yen*, or "cool heart," to deal calmly with a problem. Thais believe expressions of anger only exacerbate the situation. A smile or apology work better at defusing conflict.

Indeed, it is difficult to stir a Thai to real anger in public. But touching a Thai, on top of the head, threatening their strong sense of independence, or speaking disrespectfully of the monarchy will effect a hostile response. Visitors should also be aware that pointing their feet at Thais is considered a great insult, as they consider the feet to be unclean.

PRECEDING PAGES: the royal family at Wat Phra Kaeo; river boatman.
LEFT: girl at Wat Arun. **RIGHT:** novice monk.

Closely allied with *jai yen* is a concept that provides the answer to all life's vicissitudes: *mai pen rai*, a phrase that eludes precise translation, but usually rendered as "never mind." The Thai would rather shrug shoulders in the face of adversity than to escalate a difficult situation. Solutions that re-establish calm are

welcomed. In fact, the Thais have survived intact as a sovereign nation by adopting a superb sense of compromise, putting trifling matters in perspective, or else ignoring them.

A stable monarchy

The three colors of the Thai flag are revered as symbols of stability amid changes – values evoked in 1992 when Thais rose up against the military's grip on political power with massive street demonstrations that sometimes turned bloody. King Rama IX (Bhumibol) ended the political crisis between the prime minister and his chief opponent, which had threatened civil war. The two men prostrated themselves at the king's feet, on live television, as the king lectured them to bring the country back to a peace. Within hours, life returned to normal.

Thailand is a constitutional monarchy therefore King Bhumibol does not rule the country. But his influence on government and society cannot be overlooked, as he has earned the respect, trust, and admiration of the nation by keeping to the words he spoke at his coronation, "We will reign with righteousness for the benefit and happiness of the Siamese people."

Bhumibol came to the throne in 1946, the latest king of the Chakri dynasty that has produced several fine monarchs over the past 100 years. He was born in Massachusetts, USA, in 1927, where his father, Prince Mahidol of Songkhla, was studying medicine at Harvard University, and his mother, nursing. His father, a son of King Rama V and later regarded as the father of modern medicine in Thailand, was a minor member of the royal family. At his birth, there seemed little chance of Prince Bhumibol becoming king. Between him and the throne, according to the laws of succession, stood his father and elder brother, Prince Ananda. (Rama VII had borne no sons to take the throne.)

However, the abolition of the absolute monarchy in 1932 had exerted unprecedented

COLORS OF THE FLAG

Thailand's national flag is raised at 8am and lowered at 6pm in every Thai town and village, accompanied by the playing of the *King's Anthem*, which replaces radio and television during the ceremonies. The modern flag – introduced in 1917 to replace the earlier red flag of the absolute monarchy emblazoned with a white elephant – is composed of five horizontal bands of white, red, and blue. Outer bands of red, representing the nation, enclose equal inner bands of white, evoking religion. The blue band, the central third of the total area, symbolizes the monarchy. The design reflects the complementary nature of these three pillars of the Thai nation.

strain on the system; royalty seemed to lose contact with the people, along with their confidence. There were doubts if the monarchy could survive the turmoil of World War II, when 18-year-old Bhumibol ascended the throne unexpectedly after the fatal shooting of his elder brother, King Ananda (Rama VIII), in the Grand Palace. The king's death was never fully explained, but much later, two royal servants were executed for his murder.

King and country

In the five decades since his coronation, King Bhumibol has proved himself a worthy successor to his celebrated ancestors.

His Majesty has devoted himself to public service and has made enduring contributions to Thailand's development, initiating vital projects in areas such as crop rotation, fish breeding, irrigation, dairy farming, reforestation, road building, and the establishment of self-help villages.

His involvement with rural people began as an effort to find new crops for the hilltribes, to wean them away from opium cultivation. He incorporated this into programs to aid farmers in each of the country's four regions.

ROYAL RESIDENCE

The Grand Palace in Bangkok is only used for ceremonial and state occasions. The Thai monarch actually resides in Chitralada Palace.

also respect him as a man, a fact that makes the Thai monarchy stronger now than at any period since the reign of King Bhumibol's grandfather, Chulalongkorn (Rama V).

A royal family

The king's wife, Queen Sirikit, often accompanies the king when he visits country areas, and shares his concern for the wellbeing of rural Thais. The queen has helped establish foundations such as SUPPORT, which assists Thailand's rural population to produce and sell traditional crafts.

He has also turned over his palace grounds to agricultural purposes. Behind the walls of Chitralada Palace, the king has transformed gardens into an agricultural research station, with a dairy farm, rice fields, and orchards.

King Bhumibol has traveled throughout the country – by helicopter, jeep, train, and on foot, often to the remotest areas of the kingdom – in pursuit of his projects, and is the first Thai monarch to visit some parts of the country. If the Thais revere their king as a symbol, they

LEFT: King Bhumibol Adulyadej at the crown prince's investiture.
ABOVE: Royal Plowing Ceremony (Raek Na), Bangkok.

The king's mother, known to Thais as Mae Fah Luang, which translates as "mother who came from the sky," never forgot the mission of her husband, Prince Mahidol, and devoted her time to bringing better health care to the people of Thailand. In 1968, she founded the Volunteer Flying Doctors Foundation as a center to help rural people in need of medical treatment. With her team of volunteers from all medical specialties, she flew into isolated areas, many of which had no modern health care, and provided much-needed medical treatments. Although the Princess Mother died in 1995 at the age of 95, her long dedication to the people of Thailand keeps her memory alive.

Choice or Fate?

Thailand has a prostitution problem which is neither recent nor imported. Contrary to common belief, prostitution has been illegal for over 30 years. Social scientists and non-governmental organizations (NGOs) estimate that there are between 300,000 and 2 million Thai prostitutes both in the country and overseas in places like Japan. In Thailand, no truck stop or town with a population of 20,000 would be complete without a brothel.

According to a Thai newspaper editor, except for the area surrounding the Grand Palace, there is

not a single neighborhood in Bangkok where sex is not for sale. Venues include brothels, hotels, nightclubs, massage parlors, bars, barber shops, parks, karaoke lounges, tea houses and even golf courses. At the top are private member clubs, advertised in glossy magazines. At the bottom are locked brothels, where women and young girls are virtually enslaved. As measured by compensation and working conditions, the tawdry bars serving foreign men are somewhere in between.

There is no single reason why Thailand has more prostitutes than many poorer countries. The traditional explanation of poverty carries less and less weight. While it's true that the wealthy chiefly profited from the economic boom that lasted for

most of the 1990s, benefits also trickled down to the poor. Even after the subsequent economic crisis many Thais assumed prostitution would diminish with the gradual increase in prosperity over the years. Instead, the business is booming.

While most patrons of Thai prostitutes are Thai men, foreigners also contribute to the demand. Besides the infamous sex tours from Japan, Germany, Australia and elsewhere, there is also a sizable community of Western men, notably in Pattaya and Phuket, who live in Thailand solely because of the cheap sex, child sex or their "marriages" to teenage wives.

Agents kidnap young girls or trick them (with offers of factory jobs) from remote provinces. These girls often end up in locked brothels, from which they may eventually be smuggled to other Asian countries.

It's hard for poor families to resist. Particularly at April "harvest time," when 12- and 13-year-old girls finish the customary six years of schooling, agents flock to villages, where they offer parents hundreds of dollars or dazzling electric appliances in exchange for pretty daughters. Typically, a girl has to work off a debt that is twice her sale price, although she may have to start over if she is resold before reaching her goal of freedom.

When asked why she became or remains a prostitute, a young woman will usually talk about luck or fate. Yet true Buddhists do not subscribe to predestination. And Buddhism, of course, doesn't sanction prostitution at all.

NGOs working in Thailand no longer focus their primary efforts on extricating women from prostitution. They have found that regardless of how women were originally lured into prostitution, few are motivated to get out. The work is easy, the money too good, the family pressure overwhelming. Instead, they concentrate on prevention, trying to teach marketable skills and initiating scholarships to help keep vulnerable girls in school beyond the sixth grade. But, despite an enhanced government program, only a few thousand girls are reached this way every year.

Prostitution is the principal reason why the HIV epidemic is extensive in Thailand. Random blood testing indicates that just under 1 million men, women and children are infected with the virus in Thailand. It is neither a Thai nor a *farang* (foreigner) problem. It is a human problem. ❑

LEFT: the sex industry earns 50 billion baht in foreign exchange a year but wages for workers are poor.

King Bhumibol and Queen Sirikit have four children: Her Royal Highness Princess Ubol Ratana, Crown Prince Maha Vajiralongkorn, Crown Princess Maha Chakri Sirindhorn, and Her Royal Highness Princess Chulabhorn. Traditionally, succession to the throne has been restricted to male relations. However, the elevation of the respected technocrat, Maha Chakri Sirindhorn, to Crown Princess, and the change in existing laws pave the way for the possibility of a female monarch.

IN ROYAL ATTENDANCE

Among the annual royal ceremonies attended by the king and queen are the seasonal robing of the Emerald Buddha, various Buddhist holy days and the opening of Parliament.

During the economic crisis that engulfed Thailand in 1997–98, some segments of society cried out for a military coup. However, the military refused all such calls and their public statements added credence to the idea that democracy is here to stay.

Yet high-ranking military officers continue to sit on the boards of state enterprises and private banks, own hotels and restaurants, and otherwise participate in business even as they actively pursue military careers – a practice that contributes to

The Thai military

After ousting General Suchinda Kraprayoon, perhaps the only lasting effect of the May 1992 demonstrations and killings was an amendment to the constitution mandating that the prime minister be an elected member of parliament.

In the years since, there has been a steady decline in the role of the military. The Thai people no longer want a military dictatorship in charge of the country, and they have even accepted, albeit grudgingly, a non-military man as Minister of Defense.

ABOVE: military academy cadets on parade at Sanam Luang during bicentennial celebrations.

corruption. If a golf course is encroaching on a national forest, for example – which is common – villagers and forest rangers are afraid to complain if a high-ranking officer sits on the board, assuming that such an influential person guarantees the resort protection. The much-publicized logging deals between the Thai military and their counterparts in Burma (Myanmar) and Laos (and at one time the Khmer Rouge in Cambodia) are another example. Thailand has now lost most of its forests.

The Thai soldier, like the civil servant, belongs to a sprawling and secretive organization with activities that extend far beyond defense. The army runs national television and local radio stations. Basic services, such as ports and airports, are also the fiefdoms of a military which has fiercely resisted efforts to increase civilian oversight in these areas.

Parliamentary government

Since the 1950s, Thailand has largely been ruled by military dictators. But in the 1980s the far-sighted General Prem Tinsulanonda willingly shared power with an elected parliament. Since 1992 the country has been governed by an elected parliament and prime minister.

In successive elections, no party emerged with a majority, so fractious coalitions were

by former Prime Minister Anand Panyarachun, and the committee actively sought opinions from mass media, academics, NGOs, and people from all walks of life; a process unprecedented in Thailand's history.

This new constitution brought with it a more democratic system that emphasizes transparency and accountability, and the principles of decentralization and local participation. Until the new constitution, the way the bureaucracy worked had remained virtually unchanged since the turn of the 20th century. It is now recognized that the chief role of the central government should be to plan and monitor, and that

formed. The trappings resembled British parliament, with an upper house (senate) appointed by the prime minister every five years .

Thai political parties do not pretend to have political platforms. They revolve mostly around the personality and purse of a single man, and it is normal for politicians to jump from one party to the next. Most Thais only hear from their MPs at election time. In between, they resort to protest rallies, which can turn violent.

A healthy constitution

This all began to change in 1997, when the country embraced a new constitution. The constitutional drafting committee was chaired

this is impossible unless responsibility is delegated down to the departments and local administrations that will be actively involved in implementation.

The new constitution also addressed the issue of political reform. The Senate, as well as the House, are elected and Members of Parliament are unable to serve as Cabinet Ministers.

An end to corruption?

The constitution also created a new counter-corruption commission that will be responsible not to the Ministry but to the Senate. Furthermore, this new commission establishes administrative courts through which charges of bureaucratic or political corruption can be tried expeditiously. The constitution also permits Thai citizens to force an investigation into suspected corruption, if 50,000 signatures are affixed to a petition.

The constitution is clearly in step with the changing attitude of the Thai people, who have become increasingly intolerant of wide-scale corruption. They are no longer willing to sit back with a *mai pen rai* attitude. Since 1997, misuse of educational funds, traffic policemen taking bribes, Health Ministry officials over-pricing drugs, misuse of

A FAIR VOTE

The past practice of vote-buying has been changed by the supervision of elections by independent commissions.

a result of their reporting, uncovered highway policemen accepting bribes.

The second factor at play is the economy. Thailand's vibrant economy suffered from recession in 1997–98 and businessmen are now less willing to make payments when they are suffering from a reduced bottom line.

While there is a long way to go before Thailand is rid of corruption, these are certainly steps in the right direction. The people are no longer going to sit back and let corruption squeeze the economy.

educational funds, unusual school admissions schemes, and logging scandals have all been exposed, not by the government, but by "whistle-blowers" coming forward.

In addition to the new constitution, there are two other factors at play, the first of which is media freedom. While Thailand is renowned for having one of the freest presses in the world, the army has long controlled television and radio stations. However, a license was given to create an independent television station and, as

LEFT: Thai children start school at the age of six, and many remain in education for just six years.
ABOVE: Thai women don't have legal parity with men.

The role of women

The status of Thai women is also undergoing change. In the past, women were not entitled to the same legal rights as men in matters of land ownership, marriage or citizenship, despite the fact that women obtained the right to vote at the same time as men, in 1932.

In the past few years, changes have been made to permit a woman monarch, and many of the land restrictions, such as forbidding a Thai woman married to a foreigner to purchase land, have been overturned. Historically, Thai women have enjoyed more power and liberty than, say, their counterparts in India, Japan or China. They worked by the sides of men in the fields, could inherit property and had considerable freedom of movement. Although noble men acquired scores of concubines and the Chinese brought a penchant for prostitutes and, with vast additional wealth, the habit of collecting "minor wives," for the majority of the population, consisting of peasants in rural villages, one wife was the norm and prostitutes were unavailable.

SCHOOL-LEAVING AGE

Schooling is only compulsory in Thailand for six years, from the ages of six to 12; at this age many children leave education forever.

Thai women have been at the top of big businesses for generations, especially the service industries. Thai businesswomen often joke

about the difficulties of convincing Japanese businessmen that a woman really *is* in charge.

Women also are involved in the public sector and have reached the upper echelons of many government agencies. They flourish as market vendors, cooks, and storekeepers; more than half of factory laborers are female and, at the very bottom, women work alongside men on construction sites, albeit on lower wages.

Yet much still needs to be done before women achieve legal parity. For example, while a man can divorce his wife on grounds of adultery, a woman must prove that her husband was maintaining another woman as a "minor wife." In Theravada Buddhism, a woman cannot take the same vows or perform the same duties as monks. At home, a girl must sacrifice so that her brothers can get the better education.

The paradoxes are probably explained by differences in class. Girls born into the upper and middle classes, have much the same options as their brothers. The university population is equally divided between male and female, and the elite now are just as likely to send daughters as sons abroad for an education.

Women in the lower ranks (the majority of the population) don't have any choice but to work. From a young age, girls are instilled with a sense of responsibility responsibility to the family, and women often end up as the family's sole support, even at the age of 12 or 13. Too often, that's the age that brothel brokers seek when they descend on villages with dazzling offers for young flesh.

The Chinese

When King Rama I selected Bangkok as his new capital, the site on which he wanted to build the Grand Palace was occupied by Chinese shops. He moved the owners a kilometer down the river to "Sampeng," where they settled in what is today Bangkok's Chinatown. Throughout the 19th and early 20th centuries, Chinese immigrants were denied land ownership and participation in government, so they naturally drifted towards trade and commerce.

The Thai Chinese, however, unlike their counterparts in other Asian countries, have been assimilated to a remarkable degree into the life of their adopted land. Chinese and Thais have intermarried freely and there is no deep-rooted anti-Chinese bias in Thailand, nor have there been the racial conflicts marring the histories of neighboring countries.

Only among the older generation do people speak of themselves specifically as "Chinese" or "Thai." The younger generation think of themselves as Thai, speak Thai as their only language, voice loyalty to the Thai monarchy, and have only a cursory interest in Chinese affairs or culture. ❑

LEFT: from their early teens, working-class girls are often the main source of support for their families.
RIGHT: community worship in Chinatown.

LIFE ON THE CHAO PHRAYA RIVER

Bangkok's notorious traffic problem drives most visitors into taking river transport during their stay; few return to the roads willingly

Tourists enjoy traveling on the Chao Phraya River more than the average Bangkok resident. This is no surprise as the city grew up around the banks of the Chao Phraya and many of its oldest and most spectacular buildings are best seen from the vantage point of a river craft. River travel also has some very obvious benefits in a city choking with traffic. Speeding in an express boat from one *tha* (pier) to another with the wind cooling your face it's hard to imagine, as you pass under a bridge packed with cars, why anyone would travel any other way in Bangkok. The answer is the same all over the world: people love cars, public transport is thought to be inadequate and in Bangkok no one walks anywhere if they can help it.

EXPRESS BOATS

Reua duan (express boats) have numbers which denote which *tha* (piers) they stop at (maps of express boat stops are available). The most well-known service is the Chao Phraya Express which starts out from Krung Thep Bridge and ends at Nonthaburi, a route which takes about 90 minutes. Express boats don't stop at piers unless requested. Some "special express" boats with either green, red or orange flags only make a few stops along the route. Before your stop go to the back of the boat and attract the attention of the person with the whistle who signals to the skipper to either stop or start. Getting on and off the boat takes a bit of practice but no one ever falls in the river. Take your time; other passengers will help you on board if necessary.

▷ **FLOATING FOOD**
Small boats appear along the river and *khlongs* at lunch-time laden with tasty piping hot curries and noodles.

▽ **LONGTAIL BOATS**
Reua hang yao, operating on a shared taxi basis cost from 5–13 baht but visitors can also hire individual boats to tour the canals of Thonburi.

▽ **KHLONG SEN SEB**
This cross-town longtail boat route is good for visitors since it has many useful stops along the way. The canal is smelly but the trip is fast.

△ **CROSS-RIVER FERRY**
Cross-river ferries (*reua kham fak*) are the sedate craft which chug back and forth from one side of the river to the other. Pay your 1–2 baht fare at the pier.

◁ HALLMARK IMAGE
The truly authentic Thai floating market is more or less a thing of the past. Head for the market at Damnoen Saduak and try to avoid an organized tour.

△ INSIDE OUT
Life on the river is lived outdoors; most domestic and social activities take place on wooden decks outside the house, creating close-knit communities.

△ WASH DAY
There was a time when the Chao Phraya provided drinking water for river dwellers; today, most people only do their washing in the river and occasionally have a swim.

HOW THE *KHLONGS* DEVELOPED

When Ayutthaya was founded in 1351, to protect the city Thai engineers diverted a river to turn it into an island and dug a canal across the neck of land to cut traveling time from side to side. Erosion widened the canal which became the main course of the river between Thammasat University and Wat Arun. The abandoned river loop became Khlong Bangkok Noi and Khlong Bangkok Yai, the principal canals that run through Thonburi. Rama I repeated this defensive pattern when he established Rattanakosin (Royal Bangkok) and dug three concentric canals to make it into an island. Houses were built on bamboo rafts that rose with the flood waters and travel was by boat (in the 19th century, more than 100,000 boats plied the river). In the mid 20th century, Bangkok abandoned boats for cars. Canals were filled in to make roads and houses were built on solid ground. The result? Congested streets in the hot season, flooded streets in the monsoon season. Some would say it was a bad trade, although with the reopening of Khlong San Seb, the canals seem to be undergoing a bit of a welcome renaissance.

△ RIVER RIVALS
The Chao Phraya's main competitor is the less-frequent Laemthong Express running from Pakkred to Krung Thep Bridge from 6am to 7pm.

▷ PADDLE POWER
It you live on the riverbank it makes sense to have a boat to get about in. Modest craft are still used on a daily basis by families living In Thonburi.

RELIGION

Buddhism is central to the lives of most Thais, as shown by the many rituals that are part of daily life. But Muslims, Hindus, Christians and Sikhs have their place too

In the pale light of early morning, a young saf-fron-robed monk walks with grave dignity along a city street, a metal alms bowl cradled in his hands. Silently, he opens his alms bowl to receive the offerings – not handouts – of rice and curries placed in it by ordinary Thais, who have stood before their homes, quietly await-ing his arrival. He says not a word of thanks, because, according to Buddhist tenets, he is doing them a favor, providing them a means to make merit so they can be reborn in the next life as higher beings. Turning, he continues to walk on bare feet to the next set of alms-givers, following the steps of monks who have gone before him over the last 2,000 years.

Buddhism – a philosophy, rather than a religion – has played a profound role in shaping the Thai character, particularly in the way in which people react to events. The Buddhist concept of the impermanence of life and possessions, and of the necessity to avoid extremes of emotion or behavior, has done much to create the relaxed, carefree charm that is one of the most appealing characteristics of the people. Tension, ulcers, nervous break-downs, and the like are not unknown in Thai-land, at least not in places like Bangkok. But they are remarkably uncommon, in no small way due to the influence of Buddhism.

Theravada Buddhism

Most of the Thai population are supporters of Theravada Buddhism, which is also the main Buddhist sect in Laos, Cambodia, Burma (Myanmar), and Sri Lanka. (Nevertheless, even a casual visitor to temples in these countries will quickly see differences between them. As they have done with most outside influences – Khmer temple decorations and Chinese food, for instance – over the centuries, the Thais have evolved a Buddhism of their own cast.) Ther-avada Buddhism is a mixture of Buddhist, Hin-

LEFT: blessing a commercial liner.
RIGHT: the glow of the Golden Buddha.

duist and animistic beliefs and, as the oldest of all Buddhist faiths, it is the only one to trace its origins directly back to the teachings of the Gautama Buddha in the 6th century BC.

The central doctrines are based on the tem-porary nature and imperfections of all forms of beings. Every existence is caught up in the

wheel of reincarnation and must be reborn in a new life after death. A new life in turn means new suffering. The root cause of the never-end-ing cycles of rebirth and life is desire, since all desire gives rise to fresh suffering. The total conquest of desire will end the suffering and lead to the final enlightened state of *nirvana*. The only way to achieve this goal is to prac-tice the so-called Noble Eightfold Path.

With the help of a complicated system of rules, each Thai, whether lay person or monk, tries to achieve spiritual merit in the present life so that it will favorably influence their next life, thus permitting an existence characterized by less suffering, until ultimately nirvana is reached. Almost all the religious activities that a traveler will experience in Thailand have to do with merit-making. A man who spends some part of his life as a monk will earn merit by living in accordance with the strict rules governing monastic life. So, too, a person who supports the monks on a daily basis by donating food, or visits a temple to pray for a sick person, gains merit.

The Buddha image in front of which the prayers are offered provides only a formal background for these activities. Neither the statue, nor the Buddha himself, is worshiped; after all the latter was only a mortal.

meditation is essential. But Chinese Buddhism, at least as practiced in Thailand, primarily consists of incense, lucky charms, and heaps of other practices. The visitor entering a *sanjao,* or inner shrine, of such a temple will have a chance to shake sticks out of a canister, from which a fortune can be told. At funeral times, paper money and doll-size cardboard houses (complete with paper toy cars) are burned to assist the deceased in his or her next life.

Temple complex

Most of Thailand's 300,000 monks live in *wats,* practicing and teaching the rules of human con-

Mahayana Buddhism

In addition to Theravada Buddhism, there is the Mahayana Buddhism practiced by those of Chinese descent. Their shrines can be found throughout Bangkok, and in most Thai towns.

Particularly in Chinatown, visitors are likely to spot Mahayana temples. Mahayana literally means "Greater Vehicle" and, according to this doctrine, those who have attained nirvana return to help others reach the same state. The various sects and practices that predominate in China, Tibet, Taiwan, Japan, Korea, and Vietnam are classified as Mahayana. It is taught that dissatisfaction is caused by insatiable desires, which the Eightfold Path can stem;

duct laid down by the Buddha more than 2,500 years ago. There are literally hundreds of Buddhist *wats* in the cities and suburbs, usually sited in serene pockets of densely packed neighborhoods and serving as hubs for spiritual and social life.

The term *wat* defines a large, walled compound made up of several buildings, including a *bot* or hall where new monks are ordained, and one or more *viharn* where sermons are delivered. It may also contain a belltower, a *ho trai* (library), and *guti,* or monk meditation cells, as well as stupa, called *chedi* in Thailand. *Chedi* contain the ashes or relics of wealthy donors, emulating the Buddha whose ashes and relics were placed by his instruction in a mound of earth. There may be a government school on the premises to educate the local children. If there is any open space in the grounds, it is a sure bet that it will be filled with happy kids playing soccer or *takraw*.

Temple life

Tradition requires that every Buddhist male enter the monkhood, for a period ranging from seven days to six months, or even a lifetime. Regulations require that government offices and the mili-

popular belief, and she can even reach nirvana. Even more alarming, to reformist monks and sects, such as Santi Asoke, is the preeminent belief in merit-making, which is sometimes simplified down to the making of donations to monks and temples. While making donations is perfectly admirable, reformers observe that too many Thais believe they can somehow "buy" earthly luck or eternal nirvana for themselves or their relatives by making these donations. At the same time, these gamblers neglect to

tary give a man time off to enter the monkhood; companies customarily grant leave time with pay for male employees who would like to enter the monkhood.

The entry of a young man into monkhood is seen as repayment to parents for his upbringing, and as bestowing special merit on them, particularly his mother. Unlike in other countries, women cannot be ordained in Thai Buddhism. It is thus popularly believed that a son, as a monk, can earn merit for his mother and other female relatives. Enough merit, goes the -

LEFT: morning offerings at Wat Benjamabophit.
ABOVE: prayer at the Erawan Shrine.

practice right living, loving kindness, moderation, and other fundamental Buddhist tenets.

Prior to being ordained, the would-be monk is shorn of all his hair. He then answers a series of questions put to him by the abbot, assuring that he is in good mental and physical health. He then moves to a monks' dormitory, or to a small *kuti* or meditation house.

While in the temple, he listens to sermons based on the Buddha's teachings, studies the *Tripitaka,* or Three Baskets (the teaching of Buddha in Pali), practices meditation, and learns the virtues of an ascetic life. He shares in the work of the monastery, including washing dishes and keeping the quarters clean. He goes out at dawn to receive his daily meals. The shaven-headed, white-robed women living at some *wats* are known as *mae chee*. They cannot correctly be called nuns, since they cannot take the same vows or conduct the ceremonies that monks do. They chant and meditate separately from the monks, consume the monks' leftover food, and help to maintain the grounds of the *wat*. Many elderly women retire to these *wats* as a sort of nursing home, and some eventually become *mae chee*.

A Buddhist monk must not only abstain from stealing, lying and idle talk, taking life, sex, intoxicants, luxuries and frivolous amusements,

schools were those run by monks), the *wat* has traditionally been the center of social and communal life in the villages. Monks serve as herbal doctors, psychological counselors, and arbitrators of disputes. They also play an important part in daily life, such as the blessing of a new building, or a birthday or funeral.

Except during the period of Buddhist Lent, from July to October, monks are free to travel from one temple to another at will. Moreover, the *wats* are open to anyone who wishes to retire to them. On *wan phra,* a day each week determined by the lunar calendar, Thais go to the *wat* to listen to monks chant scriptures and

he must also obey no fewer than 227 rules that govern the minutiae of daily conduct and manners. In practice, however, most monks observe 10 basic rules, including no possessions except the yellow robe, the alms bowl and a few personal necessities; two meals a day, the first early in the morning and the second before noon; no sleeping on a comfortable bed. Moreover, there should be no singing or dancing.

Communal center

For all its Spartan life, however, a Buddhist *wat* in Thailand is by no means isolated from the real world. In addition to the schools that are attached to most *wats* (for centuries, the only

deliver sermons. In addition to providing monks with food, the laity earns merit by making repairs on the temple or, even better, replacing an old and derelict building with a new one. At the end of the Lenten season, groups of Thais travel to distant villages to make donations, an occasion filled with as much riotous celebration as solemn ceremony.

Religious tolerance

A little over 90 percent of the Thai people are Buddhist, but religious tolerance is extended to other religions. Around 6 percent of Thais are Muslim, with the remainder Christian, Hindu, and Sikh. In Bangkok and areas to the south, there are hundreds of Muslim mosques, Islam being the second-largest religion in Thailand. The repair or construction of mosques is undertaken by the government.

Christian missionaries have struggled for more than a century to attain converts, without great success. Today, there are only 200,000 Christians in Thailand. King Mongkut, who welcomed missionaries in the 1860s and learned English and Latin from them, is said to have told them: "What you teach us to do is admirable, but what you teach us to believe is foolish." He sug-

ROYAL TOLERANCE

The Thai national constitution declares that the king is the "upholder" of all religions.

high school. Christians also started the first hospitals, which remain among the best in the country today. Christians also led the way in the provision of schooling, medical care and other valuable services to hilltribe people.

Spirits and amulets

When Buddhism started to spread across Southeast Asia during its early centuries of existence, the people in what is now Thailand still worshiped a world of gods and spirits who used to determine the course of their daily lives down to the last detail.

gested that Christianity succeeded only with a weak indigenous religion. There are pockets of Christians – notably in Chiang Mai – but few steeples can be seen amidst the *chedi* forest.

Christians have, nonetheless, wielded a greater influence than their numbers might suggest. They founded the first schools outside of temples, introducing secular subjects such as science. In Bangkok, Catholic high schools and one university (Assumption) are bastions of the elite. In fact, Queen Sirikit attended a Catholic

LEFT: monks' quarters at Wat Arun, Bangkok.
ABOVE: a Buddhist *malai*, made of jasmine flowers.
RIGHT: a spirit house.

Buddhism, the new religion of goodness and renunciation, offered promises of a better life, but for farmers, it provided little assistance with the unfathomable tragedies of daily life, and certainly no answer to the questions of the supernatural. They thus continued to worship their old deities or spirits to fill in what they saw as gaps in Buddhism.

The variety of *phi* (spirits) in Thailand is legendary, outnumbering the human population many times over. A seductive female *phi*, believed to reside in a banana plant, torments young men who come near. Another bothersome one takes possession of her victims and forces them to remove their clothes in public.

(For some reason, the most destructive spirits seem to be female.) To counteract the large numbers of spirits and potential dangers in life, protective spells are cast and kept in small amulets worn around the neck. Curiously, the amulets are not bought, but rather rented on an indefinite lease from "landlords," often monks considered to possess magic powers. Some monasteries have been turned into highly profitable factories for the production of amulets. There are amulets against accidents while traveling, bullet and knife wounds, or –

AMULET TRADE

Prices for particularly powerful amulets can run into millions of whatever currency one chooses.

very popular among sailors – those that transform sea water into fresh water. All this has no more to do with Buddhism, certainly, than the protective blue-patterned tattoos sported by some rural Thais to ward off evil.

Spirit houses

No building in Thailand, not even the humblest wooden hut, will be seen today without a "spirit house," or at least a house altar. In ordinary residences, the small doll-like house may resemble a Thai dwelling; in hotels and offices, it is usually an elaborately decorated mini-temple. In either case, these spirit houses serve as the abodes of the resident spirits. It is within their power either to favor or plague the human inhabitants of the real house or building, so the spirit house is regularly adorned with placative offerings of food, fresh flowers, and incense sticks. If any calamity or ill luck befalls the members of the compound, it may be necessary to call in an expert to consult the spirit to determine what is wrong.

One of the most famous spirit houses in Bangkok is the Erawan Shrine, at the intersection of Ratchadamri and Ploenchit roads. This shrine, honoring the Hindu god Brahma, was erected by the owners during the construction of the original Erawan hotel in the 1950s, after several workers were injured in mysterious accidents. The shrine soon acquired a widespread reputation for bringing good fortune to outsiders as well.

A less well-known shrine sits in the compound of Bangkok's Hilton Hotel. Its offerings consist entirely of phalluses, ranging from small to gargantuan, sculpted from wood, wax, stone or cement, and with fidelity to life. They are left by women hoping to conceive a child, or unable to do so.

Brahman beliefs

Many of the Thais' non-Buddhist beliefs are Brahman in origin, and even today Brahman priests officiate at major ceremonies. The Thai wedding ceremony is almost entirely Brahman, as are many funeral rites. The rites of statecraft pertaining to the royal family are presided over by Brahman priests. One of the most popular and impressive of these, the Plowing Ceremony (Raek Na), takes place each May in Bangkok.

To signal the beginning of the rice-planting season, a team of sacred oxen is offered a selection of grains. Astrologers watch the events carefully, as the grains that the oxen choose will determine the amount of rainfall to come, and the degree of success or failure of the crops in the year ahead. Afterwards, the oxen draw a gilded plow around the field and seeds are symbolically sown (and afterwards eagerly collected by farmers to bring them luck). The head priest makes predictions on the forthcoming rainfall and the bounty of the next season's harvest. ❑

LEFT: making merit is an important social activity.
RIGHT: nearly every Thai male spends time as a monk.

THE CULTURAL ARTS

The Thai people have combined a lively imagination, a superb aesthetic sense and great craftsmanship to produce some of the finest arts in Asia

In Southeast Asia, the symbols and aesthetics of Thailand's culture are perhaps the most widely recognized by outsiders. And in the performing arts, Thai dance dramas are among the world's most dazzling, with elaborate and colorful costumes, and graceful movements.

Dance-drama

When discussing Thai theater, one cannot use the word "drama" without uttering the word "dance" immediately before it. The two are inseparable, as the dancer's hands and body express the emotions that the silent lips do not. In effect, the actor is a mime artist, with the storyline and lyrics provided by a singer and chorus to the side of the stage. An orchestra creates not only the atmosphere, but also an emotive force.

It is thought that the movements of dance-drama originated in the *nang yai* (shadow puppet) performances of the 16th and 17th centuries. Huge buffalo hides were cut into the shapes of characters from the *Ramakien*. Against a translucent screen, which was back-lit by torches, puppeteers manipulated shadow puppets to tell complex tales of good and evil. As they moved the hide figures across the screen, the puppeteers danced the emotions they wanted the stiff figures to convey. These movements evolved into an independent theatrical art.

The most popular form of dance-drama is the *khon,* performed by dancers wearing brilliantly crafted masks. An evening's entertainment comprises several episodes from the *Ramakien*. (The entire *Ramakien* would take 720 hours to perform.) The expressionless masks focus the viewer's attention on the dancers' movements, where one sees grace and control of surpassing beauty – a dismissive flick of the hand, a finger pointed in accusation, a foot stamped in anger. The favorite character is Hanuman, in his white

monkey mask. Only the characters of Rama, Sita and Phra Lak appear without masks, but features are kept stiff and "mask-like."

The most graceful dance is the *lakhon*. There are two forms: the *lakhon nai* ("inside" lakhon), once performed only inside the palace walls by women, and the *lakhon nawk* ("outside" *lakhon*)

performed beyond the palace by men. *Lakhon nai* is the more popular form.

Garbed in costumes as elaborate as their movements, the performers glide slowly about the stage; even in the most emotional moments, their faces are impassive and devoid of expression. The heavily stylized movements convey the plot and are quite enchanting, though for most foreign visitors, 30 minutes is sufficient to absorb the essentials of the play. *Lakhon's* rich repertoire includes the *Ramakien*, and tales like *Inao* that have romantic storylines.

There have always been two cultures in Thailand: palace and village. The village arts are often parodies of the palace arts, but more like

---

PRECEDING PAGES: leather fan puppet.
LEFT: masked *khon* dancer.
RIGHT: young dancers in traditional costume.

burlesques with pratfalls and heavy-handed humor. *Likay* is the village form of *lakhon*. Bawdy humor is its mainstay, played out against gaudy backdrops to an audience that walks in and out of the performance at will, eating and talking, regardless of what takes place on stage.

It is possible to glimpse *likay* at a *wat* fair, or at Bangkok's Lak Muang, when a troupe is hired by a worshiper to give thanks for a wish granted or a lottery number that has won. A variant often seen in markets is *lakhon ling*, the monkey theater, where the roles are played, as the name suggests, by monkeys.

Puppetry

Puppet theater has also lost most of its Bangkok audiences to television, but a few troupes remain. *Hoon krabok* puppets, similar to Punch and Judy puppets, tell the story of Phra Aphaimani. Delicately crafted, they are intriguing to watch. Performances are often arranged by major hotels for their guests during the holiday season.

Over 100 exquisitely detailed puppets of characters from the *Ramakien*, commissioned by the Vice-Regent to King Rama III, have been lovingly restored and are now on display at the National Museum near Sanam Luang.

Theatrical venues

Although modern Thai drama has made great advances in recent years, it has yet to come into its own in a major way. Part of the problem is the capital's lack of a venue of international standard. The nearest Bangkok has is the Thailand Cultural Center on Ratchadaphisek Road.

However, Patravadi Mechudhon and her Patravadi Theater in Thonburi have won acclaim for their adaptations of classic Thai tales. The Moradok Mai and Crescent Moon Theater groups are similarly applauded for their innovative productions. The Bangkok Playhouse on New Phetchaburi Road offers opportunities for new playwrights and directors.

Established in 1998, the Company of Performing Artists brings together local and international dancers, choreographers and directors. Its production of *The Love Story of Kaki* in 1998 combined Thai and Japanese traditional dance, modern dance and ballet.

Classical music

Classical Thai music eludes many finely tuned western ears. To the uninitiated, it sounds like a mishmash of contrasting tones without any pattern. To aficionados, it has a very distinct rhythm and

MUSEUM OF DANCE

The first museum dedicated to the art of Thai dance was opened in March 1999 at Suan Pakkad Palace on Sri Ayutthaya Road.

instruments of the orchestra. A classical *phipat* music orchestra is made up of a single reed instrument, the oboe-like *phinai*, and a variety of percussion instruments. The pitch favors the treble, with the result that the music sounds airy rather than stentorian. The pace is set by the *ching*, a tiny cymbal, aided by the drums beaten with the fingers. The melody is played by two types of *ranad*, a bamboo-bar xylophone, and two sets of *gong wong*, tuned gongs arranged in a semicircle around the player. Another type of orchestra employs

plan. The key is to listen to it as one would jazz, picking out one instrument and following it, switching to another as the mood moves one. Thai music is set to a scale of seven full steps, but it is normally played as a pentatonic scale (the scale of "*Auld Lang Syne*"). The rhythm is lilting and steady, with speeds varying according to section. Each instrument plays the same melody, but in its own way and seemingly without regard to how others are playing it. Seldom does an instrument rise in solo; it is always being challenged and cajoled by the other

two violins, the *saw-oo* and the *saw-duang*, usually heard accompanying a Thai dance drama. A separate type of orchestra performs at a Thai boxing match to spur the combatants to action – the quartet comprises the *ching*, two double-reed oboe-like flutes, and a drum. It plays a repertoire entirely its own.

Long drums

Originating in the countryside, but having found a permanent home in the city as well, are the *klawng yao*, or long drums. They are thumped along with gongs and cymbals as accompaniment to group singing. Never played solemnly, they lend an exuberant note to any

LEFT: dance-drama students.
ABOVE: *phipat* ensemble, with oboe-like *phinai*.

Ramayana and Ramakien

One of the two great Indian epics informing Thai dance-drama is the *Ramayana*. (The other one is the *Mahabharata*.) From the Sanskrit meaning romance of Rama, the *Ramayana* is the basis for many of Southeast Asia's epic tales, including Thailand's *Ramakien*. It's a moral tale, full of instructions and examples on how to lead the good life. It praises the rectitude, wisdom and perseverance of the noble *satriya* or warrior

class, and stresses faithfulness, integrity and filial and fraternal devotion.

The *Ramayana* acknowledges that the trek along the path of virtue demands humility, self-sacrifice and compassion. It is a cautionary tale – less a battle between good and evil (in which evil must always lose) than a recognition of the perpetual ebb and flow of the spirits of darkness and light.

In India, the *Ramayana* has been known for 3,000 years. With the spread of Indian religions and culture through Southeast Asia, the *Ramayana* became part of the mythology of Burma, Thailand, Laos, Cambodia, Malaysia and Indonesia.

The epic is long and complex. Rama, Laksmana and their half-brother, Barata, are the sons of the king of Ayodya. An accomplished bowman, Rama wins the hand of beautiful Sita in an archery contest, but he is prevented from succeeding his father as king by Barata's mother. Rama, Sita and Laksmana go into exile, refusing Barata's entreaties to return. In the forest they meet a sister of Rawana, king of the demons (*raksasas*); she falls in love with Rama, is spurned, and then turns to Laksmana, who cuts off her nose and ears.

Rawana, determined to avenge this indignity, sends off a servant in the form of a golden deer. Rama stalks the animal and kills it. Its dying cries sound like Rama calling for help, and Laksmana, taunted by Sita, goes in search of his brother. In his absence Rawana appears as a holy beggar and confronts Sita, who refuses his appeals to desert Rama. Rawana abducts Sita, and flies off with her.

Searching for Sita, the brothers meet Hanuman, a general in the kingdom of the apes, who takes them to meet Sugriwa, his king. Sugriwa, who has been usurped by his brother, seeks Rama's aid in regaining his throne. Rama kills the errant brother, and the grateful monkey king places his army at Rama's disposal. They all set off and learn that Rawana has carried Sita across the sea to the island of Langka, Rawana's homeland.

Hanuman undertakes a reconnaissance of Langka and finds Sita in Rawana's palace garden. He gives her a token from Rama, and Sita gives Hanuman one of her rings, but Hanuman is discovered by Rawana's guards, captured after a fight, and is sentenced to be burnt at the stake. With the pyre blazing, he wrenches free, his tail a mass of flames, and sets fire to the palace before fleeing from Langka.

Hanuman carries Sita's ring to Rama, and the ape armies gather on the shore opposite Langka and build a causeway across the sea. On the island, a battle ensues. One of Rama's magic arrows eventually fells Rawana, and the victors return home with Sita to a boisterous welcome. Rama receives the throne from Barata.

On stage Rama is semi-divine (an incarnation of Vishnu), of noble birth and moves in a refined (*halus*) manner. Even in battle, he is graceful, using his mind as much as muscles. Rawana struts upon the stage, every step filled with menace. His head turns sharply with each movement. His face (whether a greasepainted human one, a mask, or a puppet head) is an impassioned, furious red in keeping with his aggressive, hostile nature. ❑

LEFT: characters from the *Ramayana*.

occasion – and for a Thai, it doesn't take much of an excuse to have an occasion. It may be a procession on the way to ordain a new monk, a trip upcountry, or a *kathin* ceremony in the late autumn, when groups board boats to travel upriver to give robes to monks at the end of the three-month Lenten season.

The *klawng yao* beat an infectious rhythm, inviting one to join in a *ramwong*, a dance that, despite its simple steps and body movements, eludes most foreigners' attempts to execute. (One's

BACKGROUND MUSIC

The *ja-kae*, a stringed instrument similar to a Japanese *koto*, sits flush with the floor and is often played solo in the lobbies of some of Bangkok's larger hotels.

comeback in 1997's post-IMF Thailand. *Luk thung*'s revival was helped by the fact that it is regarded as 100 percent Thai, and thus fitted in nicely with the nation's "Buy Thai" campaign. Headed by stars Monsit Kamsoi and Sodsai Rungphothang, the music now has its own radio station.

Classical literature

Thais have always placed a heavy emphasis on oral tradition, which is a lucky break. Aside from some inscribed steles and stones, most of the country's classical

participation, not skill, is important to a Thai; the rewards for joining in are laughter and warm acceptance.)

Country sounds

Get into any Bangkok taxi and chances are the driver will come from Northern Thailand and *luk thung* music will be blaring from his tape deck. The kingdom's country music, *luk thung*, reflects the rural Thai way of life. Immensely popular in the 1960s and 1970s, it was regarded as old-fashioned by the 1980s, only to make a

ABOVE: a temple mural: story-telling was both oral and visual.

written literature was completely destroyed when the Burmese burned Ayutthaya to the ground in 1767. Most of the classical works that survive are the product of late-night sessions during the reigns of Rama I and II when scholars delved into their collective memories and recreated a literature on palace verandas.

At the heart of Thai literature is the *Ramakien* (*see page 84*), the Thai version of the Indian *Ramayana*. The enduring story has found a home in the literature, dance and drama of every Asian nation. In Thailand, it is the basis of a dance-drama tradition. Familiarity with the *Ramakien* enables one to comprehend a variety of dramatic forms, its significance for the Thai monarchy, which adopted the title "Rama" for kings in the 1920s, and its role as a model for exemplary behavior.

The 547 *Jataka* tales are also of Indian origin. They tell of Buddha's reincarnations before he became enlightened, though some are probably based on tales that existed before Buddha lived. The first tales were translated from Pali to Thai in the late 15th century. They have generated many other popular and classic stories and are still retold like fairy tales to Thai children.

BOOK-EATING BUGS

As tropical insects relish the palm leaf paper on which stories were written, Thai books were manifest examples of the Buddhist tenet that nothing is permanent.

Modern literature

Although Thais began to translate and adapt Chinese sagas and mediocre Western novels in the late 19th century, it wasn't until the 1920s that genuine Thai novels were published. Running through the novel ever since has been a strong thread of social or political criticism. Novelists moved from trenchant attacks on the old existing elite to the rising military elite.

In the 1950s, however, censorship became so heavy and writers were so harshly persecuted

A classical work, pure Thai in its flavor and treatment, is *Khun Chang, Khun Phaen*, a love triangle involving a beautiful young woman with two lovers, one a rich, bald widower and the other, a poor but handsome young man. This ancient soap opera provides a useful insight into Thai manners and morals of the Ayutthaya period. Written by Sunthorn Phu, the poet laureate of the early 18th century, *Phra Aphaimani* is the story of a rebellious prince who refuses to study to be king. But after numerous adventures, the prodigal son returns home to don the crown. These stories or segments of them can be seen in Bangkok theaters or in restaurants offering cultural shows.

that quality fiction practically disappeared for 20 years. Those writers who were not exiled, jailed or silenced resorted to churning out pulp romance, which Thais dub "stagnant water literature." As the literati lament, Thailand is not a "reading culture" and if Thais read for pleasure at all, this is it.

The overthrow of military dictators in 1973 precipitated a heady three years in which burned books were revived and banned writers rediscovered. With Marxism in the air, a work was often judged by how well it advocated the interests of the Thai poor or furthered the way to revolution. Aesthetic merit was a secondary factor. This schism between "art-for-life" and "art-for-art" still lingers in the arts today, from literature to music to painting to sculpture.

After a brief return to the dark ages in the late 1970s, Thai writers since the 1980s have enjoyed almost total political freedom. While they remain social critics, they are striving to create work of literary merit. Probably the best writers under 50 today are of modest or dirt-poor origins.

WRITING FOR MONEY

The success of new Thai writers goes some way to contradicting the old Thai saying, "*Nakkien sai haeng*" – which roughly translates as "writing is a poor career."

Since 1978, the highlight of the literary calendar has been the SEAWrite awards, held every August/September. The awards alternate

Lives gives a good introduction to the Buddhist way of thinking. Also of note are Kampoon Boontawee's *Children of Isan* and Botan's *Letter from Thailand*.

Pongpol Adireksarn, a prominent political figure who has served as a government minister in several administrations, has penned half a dozen English-language adventure novels based in Thailand and Southeast Asia under the pen name Paul Adirex. More and more expat writers are giving a *farang* angle to life in the kingdom, such as Jim

every three years between novels, short stories and poetry. Work by several SEAWrite winners has been translated into English, including Naurarat Phongpaibool and Phaivarin Khao-ngarm.

Many of the main works of Thai fiction were translated into English in the early 1990s. Look for the names Kularp Saipradit (Seebooorapha), K. Surangkhanang, Chart Korpjjtti and Sila Khoamchai. The first was a courageous journalist who died at the end of a 17-year exile in China. The last spent more than five years as a Communist guerrilla. Kukrit Pramoj's *Many*

LEFT: early Thai painting.
ABOVE: mural in the Royal Palace.

Eckhart, Christopher Moore, Geoffrey Bracken and Roger Beaumont. Their ranks should swell in the near future, as a number of local publishing houses are actively seeking work by *farang* writers.

Painting

The inner walls of the *bot* (ordination halls) and *viharn* (assembly halls) are traditionally covered in paintings, usually displaying a high degree of skill. In the days before public education, a *wat* was the principal repository of knowledge for the common person. Monks were the teachers, and the interior walls of the temples were illustrated lectures. The principal themes are the life of Buddha and the Tosachat, the last ten of 550 *chadok* (incarnations) of a single soul before he was born as the Buddha, thus ending a long cycle of lives and passing into nirvana.

The back wall generally depicts the *Maravijaya* (Victory over Mara), in which all earthly temptations are united to break the meditating Buddha's will and prevent his achieving nirvana. He is guarded by the goddess Mae Toranee, who helps him by wringing out her hair with a torrent of water to drown the evil spirits.

The murals at Wat Buddhaisawan in Bangkok's National Museum are among the finest

examples of Thai painting. Others include the murals at Wat Suthat and the avant-garde 19th-century paintings at Wat Bowon Niwet. Although restored several times with less-than-perfect accuracy or regard for previous artists' efforts, the *Ramakien* murals in the cloisters that surround Wat Phra Kaeo include wonderful, whimsical scenes of village and palace life.

Lacquer and gold works

Among the most stunning minor arts are the lacquer and gold works that cover the shutters of most *bot* and *viharn*. Thai artists employ the technique of covering a plank of wood with seven coats of lac, the black sap of the sumac tree. A scene is drawn on a sheet of rice paper and a pin is used to prick holes along the outlines. The paper is then laid on the lacquered wood and a bag of ashes is tapped against the paper. When the paper is removed, lines of ash-white dots remain to indicate the pattern.

The artist then paints, with the yellow sap of the mai khwit tree, all the areas he wishes to remain black, much the same way a batik artist paints with wax those areas whose color he does not wish to change. When the paint has dried, he covers the surface with gold leaf. When the wood is gently washed with water, the gold over the mai khwit-painted areas washes away, leaving the gold figures to gleam against the midnight sheen of the lacquer.

The best examples of lacquer painting can be found on walls of the Lacquer Pavilion in the Suan Pakkad Palace. It also decorates the ornate manuscript cabinets found at Suan Pakkad and in the Buddhaisawan Chapel.

Mother-of-pearl

Mother-of-pearl, as executed by Thai artists, differs from its Chinese counterpart both in material and technique. Thai artisans use the Turban shell, which secretes nacreous material along its rim, so it will not peel with age. Also, Thai artists cut the patterns in small pieces, affix them to a wooden panel and fill the spaces with the same black lac used in lacquer and gold works.

Two fine examples are the 200-year-old doors of Wat Po, with scenes from the *Ramakien*, and the doors of Wat Ratchabophit, which depict the royal decorations awarded to nobles of old. ❏

THAI SCULPTURE

The focal point of the *bot* and *viharn* (ordination and assembly halls) of a *wat* is the Buddha image. The image is not considered a representation of the Buddha, but is instead meant to serve as a reminder of his teachings. The casting in bronze, or carving in wood or stone, of Buddha images constitutes the bulk of Thai sculpture. Buddha images epitomize the zenith of the sculpting art and employ some of the finest artistry (and some of the highest prices) of any arts. Superb examples of bas-relief sandstone carving can be seen around the base of the *bot* of Bangkok's *Wat* Po. Delicately executed, the dozens of panels depict scenes from the *Ramakien* drama.

LEFT: Buddha at Thonburi factory.
RIGHT: a lacquered window depicting foreign traders.

SHOPPING

From traditional craftsmanship to beautiful Thai silks and masterfully disguised

fake designer goods, Bangkok will satisfy the most serious shopper

With the artistry that 19th-century craftsmen lavished on temples, today's artisans now employ their talents in creating a wealth of beautiful products that have made Bangkok a place to seek out art, crafts, clothing and jewelry. The crafts of Thailand are a result of outside ingredients – Indian, Chinese and European – being stirred by skilled practitioners over the centuries to form something uniquely and clearly Thai.

Bargaining is meant to be fun, not a clash of wills, and it is generally accompanied by casual bantering. If the price doesn't suit you, smile and walk away. Chances are that you will be called on to return and that your offer will be accepted. If not, you may find the price you want just down the block.

Remember that when making several purchases at the same shop, bargain down the price for each item, and then try to bargain down the total; you can usually knock a little extra off the overall price. On the other hand, don't descend into the absurdities of trying to knock off a few baht just for the righteousness of it.

Thai silk

For decades, silk languished in the remote regions of the country, shunned by the Thai aristocracy who preferred imported cloths. In fact, silk production was a dying art when it was revived by American entrepreneur Jim Thompson (*see page 196*). He promoted it abroad, where it quickly gained wide acceptance for its nubbly texture and shimmering iridescence. Within a few years, silk had become a major Thai industry.

Thai silk is thicker and stiffer than Chinese and European silks, but it holds its own when transformed into a suit, for example. It tends to look better on women than men, but it can be turned into superb evening attire or a business suit by one of Bangkok's tailors. It is also

LEFT: bargaining can be an essential part of shopping at places other than department stores.
RIGHT: shimmering Thai tribal silks.

turned into pillow slips, scarves, ties, and bags.

Mudmee, a northeastern silk, is a form of tie-dye wherein the threads are dyed before they are strung on the loom. It is characterized by a very subtle pattern of zigzagging lines and tends to be made up in more somber hues such as dark blue, maroon and deep yellow.

Other textiles

Cotton is made into dresses and most of the items into which Thai silk is rendered. A surprising number of visitors arrive with measurements for sofas and curtains.

Northern hilltribes each have their own distinctive patchwork and embroidery designs, mainly in bright blues, magentas and yellows. The embroidery is either appliquéd on clothes, or else sold in short lengths. Although a major textile producer, Thailand imports a large amount of Chinese and Japanese silk, Chinese satin, denim, linen, poplin, wool (surprising for tropical Thailand), and polyester blends. Look for them in Pahurat market (Pahurat Road),

Sampeng Lane, Pratunam market, Chatuchak weekend market, the Naraiphand Shop on Rajdamri Road and major department stores.

Gems and jewelry

Thailand mines its own rubies and sapphires (with some also coming from Burma and Cambodia), and is the world's leading cutter of colored gems. Rubies range from pale to deep-red (including the famous "pigeon's blood" red); sapphires come in blue, green and yellow, as well as in the form associated with Thailand,

– the Star Sapphire. Many zircons have been heat-treated to change them from red to colorless, enhancing their beauty but lowering their overall value. Modern-pattern jewelry that is designed and crafted in Thailand has become one of the country's largest export products. Globally, Thailand occupies a place in the international jewelry market rivaled only by Sri Lanka and India. Thai craftsmen turn gold, white-gold silver, and platinum into handsome jewelry settings, and the standard of workmanship is

generally good. Local craftsmen can produce both traditional and modern designs.

However, on streets and in some small shops, the stones are often not of the quality and weight advertised, and some shopkeepers are less than scrupulous in ensuring that the gold content of the settings is of the carat stated. Shops offer guarantees of the authenticity of each piece, but these cannot always be believed. Once you have paid, it is difficult to get refunds or restitution. It is best to shop at a larger store or one that comes recommended.

Gold can be found in shops along Chinatown's Yaowarat Road. Gold shops are easily recognized – they seem stamped out of the same mold, with glass fronts, upswept ceilings, vermilion lacquer surfaces, acres of display cases and a security guard out front. Rings, earrings, bracelets, anklets and other items are sold with plain surfaces, etched with designs, set with precious or semi-precious stones, and as linked chains. The hallmark is generally accurate. Craftspeople in Chiang Mai make attractive silver necklaces, bracelets and other accessories that are sold in Bangkok shops. In addition, there are purses, boxes, betel-nut sets, teapots

TRIBAL JEWELRY

Thai hilltribe women are known for their elaborate jewelry. The pieces resemble American Indian jewelry, the flat parts being similarly etched with tribal patterns.

often passed as jade. Heavily-guarded farms off the island of Phuket produce fine cultured pearls. Pearl necklaces, earrings and other accessories are sold in Bangkok. Imported Mikimoto pearls are also sold.

Metalwork

Northern silversmiths pound out a variety of bowls, which they coat with an extract of tamarind to make them shine. They also weave stout silver strands into baskets. Among the more intriguing items are Cambodian silver

and much more made by Khmer, Lao, Shan, Burmese, and Chinese craftspeople.

A lot of Thai jade comes from Burma. Most of it is smuggled across the border, with very valuable pieces shipped abroad; the lesser grades are cut and sold in Thailand. Nephrite jade is rare and prized by the Chinese, while jadeite, the bright-green jade familiar to European buyers, is common along with the less expensive types of jade in a rainbow of earth colors. Beware of stones such as jasper that are

animals. Charming elephants, chickens, horses and others are, in fact, shells that can be pulled apart and small items, such as pills or earrings, stored inside. Most items are replicas of antiques, but their quaint beauty makes them perennially popular.

Bronze Buddha images cannot be taken out of the country because they are regarded as religious and sacred objects. But there are statues of classic drama figures that make handsome decorations. Most modern bronze pieces are designed to decorate a living room. Subjects range from recumbent deer from the *Ramakien* (*see page 84*) to modern figures of flowing grace. The bronze pieces are generally annealed

LEFT: gold, silver and gemstones are Thailand's sixth most lucrative export.
ABOVE: Chinatown has the most gold shops.

with a brass skin to make them gleam. Small bronze temple bells can be hung in house eaves to tinkle in the wind. The expensive and rare Laotian frog drums (rain drums) are often covered with glass and used as tables. Brassware includes items as elegant as the large noodle cabinets that vendors sling on bamboo poles. There are also brass lanterns and small cabinets. Brass items and bronzeware with brass coatings are generally protected by a silicon layer in order to preserve their sheen.

PEWTER PIECES

Thailand is one of the world's leading producers of tin, the prime constituent in pewterware. It is used to make vases, plates, tankards etc. with a matte or burnished silver finish.

For years, upcountry wooden temples and their art objects have been disappearing with alarming rapidity, sold by abbots tired of battling with leaky roofs and termites. The abbots are content to tear down the old structures and, with the proceeds from selling antiques, tend to the maintenance of their temples. The Fine Arts Department of Thailand maintains fairly strict control over the export of religious antiques. Thus, Thai Buddha images are allowed out of the country only under very spe-

Antiques

Thai and Burmese antiques are among the finest in Asia – if they can be found. Most of the good Thai pieces were snapped up long ago by collectors, but it is still possible to discover a treasure. Most things in antique shops are beautiful and even perhaps old, but rarely true antiques. Purchasers don't buy them for investment value, only aesthetic value. (Most of the so-called antiques are produced in "antique" factories in Burma, then smuggled across the border.) It is a rare dealer who does not know the value of the pieces he sells, so forget bargaining or trying to find a bargain. Dealers usually keep the best pieces in the back of the shop.

cial circumstances. As a result, most antique shops now deal almost exclusively in Burmese Buddha images, which for some undefined reason are not covered by the export law.

Antique dealers can clear the buyer's purchases through the Fine Arts Department, obtaining the export permits and shipping them abroad. Buyers can also handle all this themselves, but the process is lengthy and time-consuming (*see Travel Tips, page 289*).

Thai shopowners have been quick to recognize that while many people are interested in antiques, they are reluctant to the pay large sums of money required. Instead, they want "antique-looking" pieces as home decor items.

As a result, an entirely new industry has grown up to produce them. Centered in Chiang Mai and Ayutthaya, craftspeople turn out wooden art objects like deer, celestial deities and other items, most of them modeled on Burmese pieces. In Ayutthaya, cabinet-makers produce wooden cabinets with glass doors and old-style grandfather clocks. The craftsmanship of these fakes can be of a surprisingly high caliber. Reputable dealers, however, will not attempt to pass off these pieces as true antiques.

COLONIAL TREASURES

European antiques like Dutch lamps, old brass fans and photographs left from the 19th century, can be found in antique shops and in Chatuchak market.

where the lacquered doors have stood exposed to the weather for 200 years and not even begun to show signs of cracking.)

Thai craftsmen also excel at lacquerware, the art of overlaying wooden or bamboo items with glossy black lacquer, and on this black "canvas" painting scenes in gold leaf (*see page 88*). Many shops carry Burmese lacquerware, which is made by applying a matte red lacquer over bamboo or wicker items. Simple designs are painted on this with black lacquer. Handsome and often

Lacquerware

Thai craftsmen are supremely skilled at setting oyster shells aglow in black lacquer backgrounds to create scenes of enchanting beauty. Because Thai mother-of-pearl is made from the Turban shell, it does not separate and flake as the Chinese varieties do. Check to ensure that the lacquer is really lacquer and not black paint, as is sometimes used. The difference is in the sheen; if it shines, it is lacquer; if not, it's paint. (If the shopkeeper tries to claim that lacquer normally cracks with age, mention Wat Po,

LEFT: lacquerware at Wat Rajabobit.
ABOVE: painting a decorative umbrella.

large baskets and trays are the main items sold.

One of Thailand's lesser known arts is nielloware, which involves applying an amalgam of black metals to etched portions of silver or, to a lesser extent, gold.

Pottery and ceramics

If archaeological evidence is correct, Thais have been throwing pots for 5,000 years with a considerable degree of skill. Said to date from 3600 BC, the red whorl pottery of Ban Chiang, the prehistorical site in the northeast, is considered to be a historical artifact and its export is prohibited. Copies abound, however, and these can be taken out of the country.

Other historical items are Sangkhaloke ceramic plates, with their distinctive twin fish design resembling the Pisces sign, from kilns near Thailand's 13th-century capital at Sukhothai. Originally produced for export to China, they keep turning up in shipwrecks discovered on the Gulf of Siam. Few are now available on the open market, but there are numerous copies.

Various ceramic pieces are claimed to have been brought up by divers from the river that flows around Ayutthaya. Dealers insist that the pieces were dropped overboard from ships moored outside the city walls between the 14th and 18th centuries. Either the sailors were a careless lot or else they were the originators of the throwaway economy – judging from the number of pieces offered for sale, there seems to have been more pottery than water under the ship's hulls. Treat with a large degree of skepticism any claims to the contrary.

Among the most beautiful stoneware items are those with a light jade green or dark-brown glaze called celadon. Said to have originated in China and recreated in northern Thailand in the 13th century, celadon glaze, created from wood ash (no dyes are added), is characterized by a highly polished surface overlaying fine craz-

THE COUNTERFEIT CITY

Notorious as a red-light district, Patpong Road is also known as the place to shop for fake designer goods in Bangkok. The closed road, bordered by massage parlors and nightclubs, is filled during the evening with hundreds of vendors selling items all labeled with designer names.

The shopping usually begins around 7pm and bargaining is *de rigueur*. Language is no problem – a calculator will be handed over hearing the initial asking price. Punch in your counter-offer and the bargaining begins.

If you want to buy a fake watch, reproductions of timepieces by Rolex, Cartier, Omega, Tag Heuer and Gucci, are all sold at a fraction of their actual price. The quality of some pieces is good. In other cases, you may find your "Rolex" stops running three months later. Clothes are a safer purchase. Men's clothing comes adorned with the names Nike, Hilfiger, Armani and Polo Ralph Lauren. The quality can vary, so inspect each garment. Shoes bear the labels of Nike, Reebok, Adidas and Timberland. For women, popular brands are DKNY and Morgan. Reproduction of shoes by Prada, Gucci and Ferragamo proliferate. Purses gleam with names like Vuitton, Celine and Valentino.

Although fake goods can be found almost anywhere in Bangkok, the buzzing atmosphere of Patpong can provide a festive backdrop to an evening of bargain hunting.

ing. Pieces include dinnerware, lamps, serving platters, statuary and others.

Bencharong is a style of ceramics that originated in China and was later developed by Thai artists. Its name describes its look: *bencha* is Sanskrit for five, and *rong* means color. The five colors of Bencharong – red, blue, yellow, green, and white – appear on delicate porcelain bowls, containers, ashtrays and decorative items. There are a few, but not many, antique Bencharong pieces.

Although it originated in China, blue-and-white porcelain has been produced extensively in Thailand since ancient times. There aren't many antique pieces around, but craftsmen are prolific in turning out a wide range of replica items, with quality ranging from superior to the barely passable.

Dolls and masks

Dolls dressed in classical dance or hilltribe costumes, rag dolls in contemporary clothes, *Tukata chao wong*, the tiny, painted clay dolls belonging to royal daughters in former days, and generally sold as sets depicting everyday scenes, are all easily available in Bangkok.

Burmese puppets and *kalaga*, cloth wall-hangings usually copied from antiques, have gained wide popularity. The masks used in *khon* masked dramas are crafted both full-size and in miniature and make interesting gifts.

Ivory, wood and basketware

As the import and export of ivory is banned, "ivory" items found in shops are more than likely to be either bone or a plastic compound. Nonetheless, the workmanship on the fake ivory is superb. Long trains of elephants, classical Chinese scenes, globes within globes, snuff bottles, letter openers and other ornamental items can be found.

Most wood products made of teak or other woods have been crafted in Chiang Mai. Products range from practical items like breadboards, serving and cutting boards, dinner sets and salad bowls, to more decorative items such

as trivets and headboards. There are also statues of mythical gods, angels and elephants, some standing more than 1 meter (3 ft) high. Of the woods commonly used, teak is the heaviest; *mai daeng*, substantially inferior to teak and lacking the beautiful grain, is also cheaper and lighter.

Rosewood is usually employed in Chinese-style furniture (which is normally inlaid with mother-of-pearl). Its fine grain and satin sheen give it a warm glow in low light. Rosewood furniture is cheaper and

easier to find than teak items; hardwood and rattan furniture are the best buys and can be made to order then shipped home.

Objects of everyday rural life are popular and interesting purchases. Baskets, whose function was once strictly utilitarian, are now regarded as "folk art." Kitchen implements made from coconut shells and carved wood, large earthen water jars, baskets used to catch fish in the flooded rice paddies, and brightly-painted wooden "bells" or clappers that are hung around the necks of water buffaloes, are now in high demand. They can be purchased at very reasonable prices from markets and small shops in Bangkok. ❏

LEFT: Thai ceramics on sale at Chatuchak Weekend Market.
RIGHT: take your pick of pirated goods.

MARKETS

A trip to one of Bangkok's many markets is an essential city experience
and a good opportunity to pick up interesting gifts and bargains

Plunge into a Bangkok market and one is immersed into a vibrant and vigorous grassroots economy, a venue to bargain and feign. Haggling is an essential art, of course, but pursue it in a light-hearted fashion. Don't make an issue over a few baht. You won't win, and, in any case, you'll probably

sections for pets and books and magazines, both new and second-hand. On the south side of the market across Yan Paholyothin Road is the plant and flower section.

One of the best things about Chatuchak is the amount of food and drink stalls scattered around, where an iced-coffee or steaming plate

end up paying more than the locals to whom bargaining is the norm.

Day markets

Hugging Paholyothin Road, the Chatuchak Weekend Market (open Saturday and Sunday 8am to 8pm) is situated on over 12 hectares (30 acres) of land holding over 8,500 stalls. Shoppers flock to Chatuchak every weekend to pick up bargains from household goods to clothing. While the market is popular with collectors and antique hunters, it also attracts hordes of teenagers who buy locally designed clothing made by ex-art students, and funky accessories. The market is huge: there are also

of freshly-cooked food can restore the most exhausted of shoppers. Do be prepared for hot and quite stuffy conditions: the rows of stalls are close together and it is estimated that over 50,000 people visit the market on Saturday and more than 200,000 on Sunday. Some prices in the market are fixed, others are for bargaining, so try your hand.

The daily Pratunam Market, in the city center, at the intersection of Phetburi and Ratchaprarop roads, is Chatuchak on a smaller scale and one of the best places to buy trendy clothing. Bangrak Market on New Road, vastly reduced in size and relocated in a building behind the original, has lost some of its flavor but none of its spirit. It specializes in floral wreaths and garlands. A few kilometers from Bangrak is Khlong Thom Market, situated in one of the busiest areas in Bangkok. Bargain hunters come here to buy new and second-hand hardware and electrical appliances.

Located on the banks of Padung Krung Kasem canal on Krung Kasem Road, Thewes Market is one of the city's largest flower and plant markets. There are crotons and caladiums, dieffenbachia and dendrobia, creepers and climbers – not to mention varieties of the thousands of orchid species found worldwide.

Between Yaowaraj and New Road, near the western end of Chinatown, is Nakhon Kasem (Thieves Market). In the past, this run-down market had a reputation for selling stolen goods and later became an antique dealer's market. Today, however, the antiques have been nudged aside by more prosaic items like car parts and cement mixers.

Night markets

The most extensive night markets are at the railway tracks near Soi 1, Sukhumvit Road; on Sukhumvit itself between Soi 5 and Soi 11; on Gaysorn Road near Le Meridien President Hotel; along the upper end of Silom Road; and down the middle of Patpong Road.

Patpong Night Bazaar is one of the biggest and boldest bazaars in Bangkok. Here you can find watches, CDs, tapes, videos, clothing, and ethnic handicrafts. Most goods are imitations of designer items and hard and fast bargaining is part of the experience.

About five minutes' walk from Pak Khlong Talad, at the foot of the Phra Buddha Yodfa Chulalok Bridge, is the crowded Saphan Bhut Night Market (every evening except Wednesday). The market mostly consists of second- hand imported shirts and jeans and is very popular with Bangkok teenagers and trend spotters. Parking in this area is difficult.

Floating markets

Floating markets in Bangkok are a bit of a tourist cliché but it is possible to avoid the worst commercialized markets by traveling just outside the city. The Talat Nam Talingchan

LEFT: marble and jade plant pot holders at Chatuchak Weekend Market.
RIGHT: Sunday morning produce market.

(Talingchan Floating Market) located near Talingchan District, can be reached by cab from Sanam Luang (the fare should cost Bt100 and Bt150). This well-known fruits and food market gets very crowded over the weekend and it is best to get there as early as possible. A more authentic market is located at Khlong Bang Wiang in Thonburi. To get there, catch a boat from the pier at Wat Phra Kaew (first boat leaves at 6.15am). The market starts at 4am and is over by 7am, so once again, it is essential to get an early start. If you are near the town of Samut Songkhram, the floating markets of Damnoen Saduak are well worth visiting. ❏

THE ART OF BARGAINING

First, don't start bargaining unless you really want to buy. Stage One involves asking the price of the item. Stage Two opens the bargaining with a request from you to lower the price. The seller will then lower his original price, thereby signaling he's open to offers. Stage Three is when you offer your first price, which is always too low. From there the rally of bargaining bids begins until a price is agreed between you and the seller. Some experienced bargainers say you should always walk away from the seller and then return to get the best price. This sometimes works, but if you come back much later don't expect the same prices to be offered again.

FOOD AND DRINK

Thai food, with its careful blending of sweet, sour and spicy ingredients, has become one of the most popular cuisines in the world and is a highlight of any holiday

I t is probably best to diet before coming to Thailand, especially if harboring plans for a bikini-and-beach time. Once in Thailand, and especially in Bangkok, there is little chance of tending to one's vanity. The food is simply too tempting, and too available.

While it's true that Thailand's cuisine includes very spicy dishes – some Southern Thai regional specialties achieve a near-nuclear intensity – many are not hot at all. Generally, an authentic Thai meal will include at least one very spicy dish, a few that are less aggressive, and some that are positively bland, flavored with only garlic and herbs. Usually, purely Thai creations will take their place alongside adapted Chinese and Indian dishes, whose alien origins are quite easy to spot.

Each of Thailand's four regions has its own cuisine. Northern cuisine is strongly influenced by the cooking of Burma and Laos, while the cooking of the northeast is largely Lao. The rich central cuisine contains most of the dishes visitors are familiar with from their experience of Thai restaurants abroad, while southern food, combines Muslim influences with a fiery spiciness that is very Thai.

Table manners

At most Thai meals, dishes are placed in the middle of the table and shared by all, so it makes sense to eat in a large group so that there are more dishes to try.

Thai food is eaten with rice. Traditionally, the curries were a secondary element in the meal, a means of pepping up the tastebuds so that one would eat more rice and thus sustain oneself through the day. Even today, rural Thais eat large helpings of rice with nothing more than bits of dried or salted fish. Chilies are also a means of spicing up Thai rice, even though it is, on its own, one of the most flavorful rices in

Asia. (The Japanese say its taste is far too strong.) Try a few spoons of plain rice before you get into the meal and discover just how delicious it really is.

Thais eat with a spoon and fork, holding the spoon in the right hand and the fork in the left. The fork is used primarily to push food into the

spoon for transport to the mouth. Contrary to preconceptions, chopsticks are used only for Chinese dishes, especially the universally popular sub-cuisine of noodle dishes.

At the start of the meal, heap some rice onto a plate and then take a spoonful or two of a curry or some other dish, place it on top of the rice, and eat. It is considered polite to take only a little bit at a time, consuming it before ladling more onto the rice.

There seems to be some confusion among those who have sampled their first Thai meals abroad, in particular regarding the proper condiments to add to the food. Much to their surprise, they discover that peanut sauce, an

PRECEDING PAGES: eating alfresco at Lumpini Park.
LEFT: flower and produce market at Pak Klong Talad.
RIGHT: fresh chilies are an essential ingredient for most curries.

indispensable addition to every dish in many Thai restaurants in Western countries, is really of Malaysian and Indonesian origin; in Thailand it is used only for satay. Similarly, instead of salt, Thais rely on fish sauce, often mixed with small slices of high-firepower chilies, spooning a bit of these onto the rice and mixing them into the meal.

Thai curries

Gaeng (pronounced similarly to the English "gang") is usually translated as curry, although it covers a broad range of dishes ranging from bland vegetable soups to near-dry recipes, like

the northern Thai *gaeng ho*. It is the *gaeng* repertoire that includes some of Thailand's hottest dishes, so beware.

Curries can be divided into two basic types: those based on coconut cream and those made without it. The most popular curry in the central part of Thailand, where Bangkok is located, is *gaeng khio waan*, or green curry (although its color is often closer to gray). Among the green curries is *gaeng khio waan gai*, a spicy, coconut cream gravy filled with chunks of chicken, basil leaves, and tiny, pea-sized pieces of eggplant. The same type of curry is often made with pork, beef, or balls made from pounded fish meat.

Considerably milder is *gaeng karee*, a Thai-adapted, Indian-style curry, also coconut-based, that is most commonly made with chicken, although other ingredients can be used instead.

Spicy, red-colored *gaeng pet* ("red curry") is served in chicken, beef, and pork versions. Since it, too, contains coconut cream, it is quite rich, but less so than the ragout-like *panaeng* dishes which simmer the meats in a thick, creamy curry sauce.

Gaeng massaman is a rich but considerably milder curry containing beef or chicken combined with potatoes and onions in a fragrant brown gravy.

Muu thawd (pronounced similar to the English "taught") *kratiam prik Thai* is pork fried with garlic and pounded black pepper. When ordering the dish, ask that the garlic (*kratiam*) be fried crisp. The same dish is often made with chicken, fish, shrimp, or squid. *Muu pad prio waan* – sweet and sour pork – is probably of Portuguese origin and arrived in Thailand via Chinese imigrants. The dish can also be made with red snapper (*plaa krapong daeng*), beef (*nuea*) or shrimp (*koong*). *Nuea pad nam man hoi* is beef fried with oyster sauce, spring onions, and mushrooms. It's a mild, delicate dish, ideal for those who are sated on fierier fare.

Pat pet (pronounced "pot pet") *pad bai kaprao* ("pot by ka-prow") dishes are highly popular with Thais, but their extreme spiciness will put them out of range of some foreigners. They consist of meat, fish, or chicken stir-fried in a wok with very hot chilies, garlic, onions, and other herbal ingredients. *Bai kaphrao* means fresh basil in Thai, so *pad bai kaphrao* dishes have the flavour and aroma of that particular herb, which is added in abundant

---

THAI SOUPS

The mild T*om khaa kai*, a rich soup made from coconut cream, lime, lemon grass, mushrooms and chicken is a favorite with visitors. Among the fierier favorites is *tom yam goong*, a lemon-and-chili broth with shrimp, straw mushrooms, and herbs including lemon grass. Family-size servings come in tureens set in a mini charcoal furnace which keeps the soup hot. *Po taek* is a fishy cousin of *tom yam kung*, its spicy broth is filled with squid, mussels, crab, shrimp and other seafood. *Gaeng som* is hot and sour, balanced by a slight sweetness. It is usually made with fish or prawns. *Gaeng jued* are bland soups of glass noodles, pork, mushrooms and lettuce.

quantities. *Haw moke talay* is a delicious seafood casserole of fish, shellfish, crab, and squid in a spicy, curried coconut custard, steamed in a banana-leaf cup or, sometimes, a coconut shell.

Of Chinese origin, but having secured a place in Thai cuisine, is *plaa jalamet nueng buay kem*, steamed pomfret in sauce with Chinese salted plums and shreds of ginger.

Poo pad pong karee is made of pieces of whole, steamed crab slathered in an egg-thickened curry sauce with crunchy pieces of spring

HOT SALADS

The word *yam* is translated on menus as salads, but these are usually warm. Besides lime juice, chili, fresh vegetables and herbs, they contain, meat, fish or egg.

flour, and *ba mee*, made from wheat. Both can be ordered either wet (*sai naam*) or dry (*haeng*). Thus, an order for *ba mee naam* will produce a bowl of rice noodles in broth, while a request for *kui tio haeng* will bring dry rice noodles served without the soup. You'll also have to let the cook know whether you want broad or smaller noodles and which kind of meat or fish you prefer, but this can usually be done by pointing at the shop's selection.

The repertoire of noodle dishes available in

onion. *Hoi malaeng poo op maw din* is a dish of mussels in their shells, steamed in a clay pot with lime juice and various aromatic herbs.

Noodles and rice

At lunchtime, as Bangkok's teeming offices empty out for the midday meal, many workers head straight for the nearby noodle shop on virtually every corner. Noodles, originally from China, are now the lunchtime favorite of the Thais. Those served at street-side, open-front shops are of two types: *kui tio*, made from rice

LEFT and **ABOVE:** some of the tastiest food can be bought from street stall vendors – just point to what you want.

Thai restaurants is large and varied. A few of the many worth sampling are *kui tio raad naa* (rice noodles briefly pan-fried at high heat and topped with slices of meat and greens in a thick, mild sauce); *pat Thai* (narrow rice noodles pan-fried with a wide range of ingredients that can include egg, dried and fresh shrimp, spring onions, tofu, cashew nuts or peanuts, and beansprouts, among others).

Mee krawp is a dish of crisp-fried rice noodles tossed with a thick sweet-and-sour sauce and topped with sliced chilies, pickled garlic, slivers of the skin of a special type of Thai orange, and a range of other garnishes. Many rice-based lunchtime dishes are also of Chinese origin, and include *khao man kai* (rice cooked in chicken broth with seasonings, topped with slices of chicken meat and served with a spicy sauce); *khao moo daeng* (steamed rice with slices of Chinese red pork and sauce); and *khao kaa moo* (stewed pork leg meat with greens on rice).

Served late at night and early in the morning are two soup-like dishes based on boiled rice. The rice in *khao tom* comes in the water it was boiled in, and is eaten with whatever ingredients you choose. Garlic-fried pork, salted egg, pickled

> ### THAI STARTER
>
> *Mieng* – preserved, fermented tea leaves – are a Burmese import, eaten as an hors d'oeuvre.

and flavor to the meat. *Naem*, another local sausage, is made from fermented raw pork meat and skin seasoned with plenty of garlic. Beware of the *prik kee noo* chilies that lurk inside, waiting to explode on the tongues of the unwary. *Kao soi* is a dish that originated across the border in Burma. Fresh egg noodles share a bowl with chunks of beef or chicken, all cooked in a mild curried coconut cream sauce. Crispy noodles are sprinkled on top. *Nam prik ong* combines minced pork with mild chilies, tomatoes, garlic, and shrimp paste. It is served with

ginger, and various fish dishes are favorites. A close relative is *joke*, in which the rice has been cooked until the liquid becomes like a porridge. Into it is added seasoned minced pork, slivers of fresh ginger, and coriander. Crispy *pathongko*, pieces of fried bread, float on top as a garnish.

Northern cuisine

Northern dishes are generally eaten with *khao nio*, or sticky rice, which is kneaded into a ball and dipped into various sauces and curries.

Sai oua is a spicy dark-colored pork sausage that is one of the most famous northern Thai specialties. It is roasted over a fire fueled by dried coconut husks, which impart an aroma

crisp cucumber slices, parboiled cabbage leaves, and fried pork rind (the latter is also a popular northern snack).

Nam prik noom, a northern classic, is a thick dipping sauce made from grilled chilies, onions, and garlic. It is eaten with pieces of crisp-fried pork rind called *khaep moo*. It can be pretty potent, so take a small taste before dipping into the dish more deeply. *Laap* is a minced pork, chicken, beef, or fish dish that is associated more with northeastern cuisine. While northeasterners often eat it raw, northerners cook it thoroughly. It is usually served with long beans, mint leaves, and other vegetables that contrast with its mellow flavor.

Gaeng hanglay is another dish of Burmese origin. Made with large chunks of lean pork, it has a sweet and sour flavor that derives from the ripe tamarind fruit used in the cooking process. This curry is at its best when eaten northern-style – without utensils, but dipping in balls of sticky rice with your hands. It can be quite spicy, but not dauntingly so.

> **INSOMNIACS' CURE**
>
> *Isan* (the Thai word for the northeast) diners claim sticky rice weighs heavily on the brain and makes one sleepy.

Northeastern cuisine

Northeastern food is simple and spicy. Like northern fare, it is eaten with bowlfuls of hot

or Lao origin. The dish can be extremely hot, so take care. *Isan*-style *laap* is more assertive than the northern variety. It can be spicy, so take a small sample spoonful first. Even adventurous visitors should steer clear of some of the more challenging types, which are made with ingredients like raw meat and blood, and extremely bitter, half-digested grass removed from cows' intestines. Popular as they may be with customers in local restaurants, these exotica can make short work of an uninitiated digestive system.

sticky rice. *Kai yang*, or northeastern grilled chicken, has a flavor found in no other form of Thai chicken. Seasoned with herbs and plenty of garlic, it is roasted over an open fire and chopped into small pieces. Two dipping sauces, one hot and one sweet, are served with it.

Som tam is a salad-like dish made from shredded green papaya, garlic, chilies, lime juice, and various combinations of tomatoes, dried shrimp, preserved crab, fermented fish, and a few other ingredients that can quickly identify the recipe being used as being of Thai

LEFT: steamingly good food cooked in palm leaves.
ABOVE: dried fish on a market stall.

Southern cuisine

The south is the origin of some of the hottest dishes in the Thai repertoire, but there are also some popular specialties that pose no threat to those who prefer gentler culinary pleasures. *Kao yam*, for example, is an innocuous salad-like dish made with rice and vegetables, pounded dried fish, and a special southern fish sauce called *budu*. Slightly spicier is *phad sataw*, a stir-fried dish, usually made with pork or shrimp, where the challenge comes not from aggressive seasoning but from the *sataw* bean that gives the dish its name. This vegetable, which looks rather like a large lima bean, has a strong flavor and smell that has a pervasive quality, like that of garlic. *Kao moke kai* is like an Indian chicken biryani – roasted chicken mixed with highly seasoned yellow rice whose color comes from turmeric. It is often served with a topping of crisp-fried onions.

Gaeng tai plaa is said to have been created by bachelor fishermen who wanted a dish that would last them for days. Fermented fish innards (there is no nice way to put this), chilies, pieces of bamboo shoot, and optional vegetables are blended into an often intensely hot curry sauce and cooked to create a dish whose firepower can confound even the most jaded palates which are completely at home with Bangkok-style cuisine. *Gaeng lueang* ("yellow curry") is, if anything, even hotter than *gaeng tai plaa*, but lighter in consistency. A southern variant of central Thai *gaeng som*, it places pieces of fish, chunks of green papaya, and bamboo shoots or hearts of palm in a highly explosive, soup-like sauce. Delicious, but to be approached with extreme respect.

Thai desserts

In Bangkok, *khanom* – desserts and sweets – come in a bewildering variety, from light concoctions served with crushed ice and syrup through custards, ice creams, and cakes to an entire sub-category of confections based on egg yolks, cooked in flower-scented syrups.

The heavier Thai confections are rarely eaten after a big meal. Desserts, served in small bowls, are generally light and elegant. *Kluay buat chee*, a popular after-dinner sweet, consists of slices of banana stewed in sweetened, slightly salted and scented coconut cream, and served warm.

Another favorite, *taap tim krawp*, is made from balls of tapioca flour, dyed red and shaped around tiny pieces of crisp water chestnut. These are served in a mixture of sweetened coconut cream and crushed ice.

Anyone walking through a large Bangkok market is bound to come across a sweets vendor selling anything from candied fruits to million-calorie custards made from coconut cream, eggs, and palm sugar. They are generally sold in the form of 8-cm (3-inch) squares wrapped in banana leaves. Such snacks are good for a quick energy boost or an afternoon treat. Many of these sweets are startlingly inventive, putting familiar ingredients in surprising surroundings. You might find yourself finishing off a rich pudding, for example, before realizing that its tantalizing flavor came from crisp-fried onions.

Excellent *khanom* of various types can be bought from roadside vendors, who prepare them on portable griddles. One such sweet is *khanom bueang*, translated as "roof-tile cookies", which consists, in one version, of an extremely thin, crispy shell folded over taco-style, and then filled with coconut, strands of egg yolk cooked in syrup, spiced and sweetened dried shrimp, coriander, and cream.

In buying Thai sweets, picking what looks good to eat is usually disappointment-proof.

CHINESE CUISINE

Most of Thailand's ethnic Chinese are of southern Chinese descent, and many still speak the Taechiw dialect. Most Chinese restaurants therefore serve Taechiw food, which strongly resembles Cantonese cuisine. Especially famous are thick shark's fin soup, goose cooked in a soya sauce, and a wide variety of steamed and fried fish dishes. Fruits and teas are an integral part of every meal. Poultry, pork, and seafood are essential, as are a variety of mushrooms and other fungi. Other Chinese cuisines are represented in Thailand, from garlic-intensive Taiwanese dishes to stuffed dumplings from the north to Shanghainese specialties.

Sangkhaya ma-prao awn is a magnificent custard made from thick coconut cream, palm sugar, and eggs, that is steamed inside a young coconut or a small pumpkin. *Kao laam* is glutinous rice mixed with coconut cream, sugar, and either black beans or other goodies, all of it cooked inside lengths of bamboo, which are split open and the rice eaten.

Taeng Thai nam kati consists of pieces of Thai melon cut into small cubes and mixed with ice and sweetened, flavored coconut

ESSENTIAL FRUITS

Bananas and coconuts grow everywhere in Thailand, and their proliferation makes them the major ingredients of *khanom* – Thai dessert cookery.

Time for tea

In Bangkok, drinking tea often seems to be associated with nostalgia. Certainly, many of the most fashionable places where people gather to enjoy it are decorated in a way that suggests a bygone age.

The lobby of the Regent of Bangkok hotel is ornamented with elaborate murals that evoke the Siam of an earlier era, and the Oriental Hotel's Authors' Lounge is an unabashed throwback to the days of Joseph Conrad. This is not to say it isn't authentic; it

cream. *Khanom maw gaeng* is another custard-like sweet, again made with coconut cream and eggs, but this time with mung bean flour added to thicken it before it is baked in an oven in square metal tins.

Kluay kaek uses bananas sliced lengthwise, dipped in coconut cream and rice flour, and deep-fried until crisp. If you sample nothing else while in Thailand, don't miss out on trying a refreshing dish of *i-team kati* (the first word is a corruption of the English "ice cream"), a rich and heavenly coconut ice cream.

LEFT: a selection of Thai desserts.
ABOVE: the delicate art of food presentation.

was the courtyard of the original Oriental Hotel, and one can easily imagine a 19th-century gentleman and his escort enjoying the air while sipping a cup of piping-hot Darjeeling or Earl Grey tea. Many famous writers have stayed in the Author's Lounge including Somerset Maugham, Noel Coward, Graham Greene and John le Carré.

Today, the Authors' Lounge is chilled by air-conditioning and the open sky is shut out by a fiberglass canopy, but the atmosphere is still something to savor. Tall, slender bamboo trees reach high along whitewashed stucco walls that are covered with photographs of Thai royalty at the turn of the 20th century. In the colonial-style wooden building, guests sit on wicker sofas to sip a variety of teas and filtered coffees, and to snack on pastries under the shade of brightly-colored parasols.

In the Dusit Thani Hotel, Library 1918 offers similar fare and elegant surroundings as one sits in high-backed Regency chairs to enjoy the view of the gardens, and of the waterfall that tumbles down through them.

The Regent of Bangkok was originally called the Peninsula Hotel, and its lobby was modeled on that of the incomparable Peninsula Hotel in Hong Kong, one of the classic establishments of Southeast Asia. The present management has maintained the traditional tea hours of its predecessor, when a string quartet on the balcony provides soft music.

Other refreshments

Locally-brewed beers include Singha and Leo, both made by the same brewery, and Chang. Singha (pronounced "sing") has been a favorite with Thais for several decades, although it is capable of leaving a fearsome hangover. Leo, by comparison, is a gentler brew. Chang, a comparative newcomer, is also popular with locals and foreigners alike. Foreign brands like Kloster and Carlsberg find more favor with some visitors.

The most popular brand of the local cane whiskey is Mekong, and it packs a wallop for the unsuspecting. A little sweeter than Western varieties, it is drunk neat or, more popularly, mixed with club soda and lime.

Iced tea is always sweetened in Thailand, and even the tempting-looking blender drinks made from fresh fruit and ice will get a splash of syrup unless you request otherwise.

Cocktail hour

Daytime Bangkok is hard on the nerves and by the time the (approximately) four-hour rush hour descends, many people are ready to sit down and wait out the horror while sipping a long, cool drink.

The breezy terraces of major hotels along the banks of the Chao Phraya River are the best places to watch the sun go down. In the cool of the evening, order a colorful tropical drink or a tall glass of beer, sit back, and watch the drama taking place on the river before you. At this hour, ferries shuttle commuters between the banks, tugboats cruise up- and downstream, and barges are towed homeward in the glow of the setting sun. The terraces of six hotels offer superb views of river life: the Montien Riverside, the Marriott Royal Garden Riverside, the Menam, the Shangri-la, the Oriental, and the Royal Orchid Sheraton.

During the monsoon season, step in out of the rain for a late afternoon drink in the lobby of the Oriental, the Regent of Bangkok, or the uniquely elegant Sukhothai and listen to soothing music as you watch Bangkok's elite meeting to discuss business or exchange gossip. ❑

CAFÉ SOCIETY

Coffee connoisseurship is just beginning to take shape in Thailand. Affluent coffee drinkers who made do with instant coffee a few years ago now order up an espresso, latte, or cappuccino at international coffee emporia like Starbuck's and Coffee World. Traditional Thai coffee is still brewed, but you'll have to visit a food stall to get it. Compounded of coffee beans and burnt tamarind seeds, it is brewed at maximum strength. In serving it, vendors fill the bottom of a glass with two fingers of sweetened condensed milk and then pour the coffee over it. You can also sample it as *oliang* – the same brew sweetened with lots of sugar and poured black over ice.

LEFT: cocktail waiter.

A Calendar of Fruits

Bangkok is fortunate to have a variety of fruits coming in and out of season throughout the year and a number, such as bananas (*gluay*), oranges (*som*), pomelos (*som-O*) and watermelons (*daeng mo*), that are available year-round.

There are over 100 varieties of banana, which are eaten fried, boiled, roasted, and raw. Watermelons are small but seductively sweet and juicy. Pomelos are often mistaken for grapefruits, but their sweet juices soothe on a hot Bangkok day. Any fruit that can be peeled is a great street snack.

Here's what to look for in different seasons:

MARCH–JUNE: Papaya (*malagaw*). Especially tasty after the advent of the hot season. Thais like to squeeze lime juice on them to add a bit of tang. Shredded papaya is the main ingredient in *som tam*, a fiery salad popular in the northeast.

MARCH–JULY: Sapodilla (*lamood*). A surprisingly sweet, soft pulp fruit eaten peeled or halved and sampled with a spoon. Beware of the black seeds.

APRIL–MAY: Lichee (*linchee*). Only a decade ago, this small fruit with its thin, hard shell was regarded as sour and unpalatable. It is now grown to nearly twice its former size and sweetness. Resembling, the rambutan, the whitish flesh conceals a big black seed.

APRIL–JUNE: Mango (*mamuang*). Mangoes have yellow flesh which is sweet, often bordering on tart. There are many ways of serving them but the old standard *khao niew mamuang* (mango and sticky rice) reigns supreme. They enjoy a strange relationship with the durian: if it is a good year for mangoes, the durian crop will be bad and vice versa.

Durian. The durian is either hated or loved. The most expensive of Thai fruits, it is recognized by its hedgehog skin, the heavenly aroma (or disgusting stench to some) of its flesh, and by the rather mushy consistency of its meat. Try it in a coconut milk sauce on sticky rice. The durian has a reputation for producing gas, but it is a small price to pay. Persevere and you will be rewarded.

APRIL–JULY: Pineapple (*saparot*). Thailand is a top exporter of tinned pineapple and for good reason: its pineapples are sweet, with low acidity. Thais eat it sliced and garnished with a little salt and ground chilies which, odd as it sounds, enhance its natural sweetness.

RIGHT: citrus fruits are not the only fruits to try in Bangkok.

Rose Apple (*chompoo*). The pink- and green-skinned *chompoo* is pried apart with the fingers to reveal a crisp white meat with the texture of a pear.

MAY–AUGUST: Custard Apple (*noi-na*). This light green hand-grenade with its knobby surface, can be pulled apart by hand. The pulp is soft, very sweet and very tasty. The fruit conceals long black seeds.

JULY–AUGUST: Longan (*lamyai*). A relative of the lichee and rambutan, it resembles the langsard with its yellow skin, but has the lichee's sweetness.

JULY–SEPTEMBER: Rambutan (*ngor*). Similar to the lichee, its skins is covered in red hairs. Any Thai can demonstrate the technique to squeezing it open. The flesh is translucent and sweet.

AUGUST–SEPTEMBER: Jackfruit (*khanoon*). Dividing this fruit into its myriad sections is best left to the experts. The yellow sections resemble buttercup blossoms, are waxy-textured and semi-sweet.

AUGUST–OCTOBER: Langsard. A slightly bitter fruit that breaks into sections like garlic cloves.

Mangosteen (*mangkut*). The hard red shell conceals pulpy sections that ooze with sweetness. A favorite Thai game is to ask visitors to guess the number of sections it contains without breaking it open. (Count the number of "petals" in the woody flower on the bottom of the fruit.)

OCTOBER–FEBRUARY: Green Plum (*putsa*). Shaped like a plum, *putsas* resemble green apples in color and pulp texture. ❑

ON THE TOWN

The choice ranges from traditional attractions such as dance-drama and
Thai boxing to local folk-rock and unrestrained karaoke

Bangkok is a city made for night-owls. Aside from its less savory reputation as a center for Southeast Asia's sex industry, it has much to offer those in search of a more innocent evening in the capital, from traditional dance-drama performances to more Western-style jazz and disco venues.

Thai dance-drama

Dance-drama shows (*see page 81*) are performed at about half a dozen hotels and restaurants every night in Bangkok. Most hotels and guesthouses sell tickets that include transportation and a traditional Thai meal. Travel agencies can do likewise. If you are looking for something a bit more authentic, the National Theater (Ratchini Road, tel: 224 1342) has weekend shows including masked *khon* performances of stories based on the *Ramakian* (*see page 84*). The Chalerm-krung Royal Theater (intersection between Charoen Krung and Triphet roads tel: 222 0434) is a beautifully restored Thai Deco building which holds stylish twice-weekly *khon* performances.

Thai boxing

At Thai boxing matches, visitors are easily outnumbered by raucous Thai fans. With origins as a battlefield martial art (*see page 119*), Thai boxing (*muay Thai*) employs not only fists, but elbows, feet, knees and almost every other part of the body.

A high-pitched orchestra accompanies the fight. A *ram muay* (stylized dance) precedes each bout on a 10-fight card. The fighting inside the ring may be violent and fast-moving but this is matched in pace by the frenetic betting of the audience and lively atmosphere at the ringside. Whether watching the crowd or the sparring in the ring, attending a Thai boxing match is an enthralling experience and one which should not be missed out on.

PRECEDING PAGES: the city at dusk.
LEFT: eating out at Silom Plaza.
RIGHT: traditional Thai dancer.

Nightclubs and pubs

Bangkok's venues for music and dancing emerge and evaporate with the blink of an eye as one place falls out of fashion while another becomes the next "in thing." Bangkok has nightclubs to suit all tastes and age groups, from the ultra-trendy, celebrity-spotting mega

discos to the younger, hipper music-orientated clubs off Silom Road. One of the oldest and flashiest discos in town is the Nasa Spacedrome, on Ramkamhaeng Avenue. Novotel Siam Square and the Grand Hyatt Erawan (Rachapasong intersection) also have two of the greatest dancing venues in town.

The area of Silom Soi 2 and Silom Soi 4, is the site for hipper DJs and clubbers, as well as accomplished drag shows after midnight – an East-meets-West male hangout area, where gays cruise each other in a cozy atmosphere. The area of Suthisarn, off Vibhavadi Rangsit Road, is up-and-coming. If go-go bars are what you are after, then head for the two lanes of

Patpong between Silom and Surawong roads (Patpong 1 is straight; Patpong 2 is gay); Soi Cowboy between Sois 21 and 23 on Sukhumvit Road or Soi Nana Tai, just off Sukhumvit Road.

Live music

If live music is more your scene, there are a string of music bars featuring Thai jazz bands with foreign vocalists on the northern edge of Lumpini Park, along Soi Sarasin. Another dependable stand-by is the Saxophone Pub and Restaurant, at Victory Monument, which has both blues and jazz. Soi Thonglor at Sukhumvit 55 is another upmarket and long-term venue.

At the southeastern intersection of Petchburi and Phyathai roads are yet another clutch of clubs featuring a strong favorite among young Thais: heavy metal bands. The British-style Bobby's Arms Pub, on Patpong Soi 2, has for many years hosted a popular Dixieland band on Sunday evenings. The Oriental Hotel usually has a pianist and jazz singer from the US as its nightly entertainment.

Still intriguing to Thais, who have usually moved into the city from the provinces, as well as to many foreigners, is "songs-for-life" music. The sound can be described as folk-rock incorporating traditional Thai instruments; the lyrics are socio-political critiques. Again, venues change rapidly and may be far-flung.

Karaoke

One of the most recent trends in Bangkok for night-time activities is karaoke. Originally from Japan, the craze has taken the city by force and if you've ever wondered what your singing voice sounds like over a microphone, karaoke clubs offer you a chance to find out. Some clubs offer the opportunity to record your efforts on disk. Choose between singing on stage, in the lobby, or renting one of the private VIP rooms with a group of friends.

Movies

Bangkok has seen a blossoming of new movie theaters in recent years, most of them multiplex cinemas in new shopping centers. English-language movies are either subtitled or dubbed in Thai; check before buying a ticket. Siam Square and the World Trade Center have several cinemas, mostly screening Hollywood block-buster imports.

Second in the running for popularity in Bangkok are Hong Kong Chinese films. The themes are similar to the Hong Kong variety – mostly body language with lots of karate kicks and jabs – very easy to follow even if you don't speak the language. Slightly more refined are the movies shown at the Alliance Française (Sathorn Tai 29 Rd; tel: 213 21223) and the Goethe Institute (Soi Attakarnprasit, off Sathorn Tai Rd; tel: 287 09424) which regularly run high-quality French and German films, with English subtitles. ❏

LEFT: Silom village entertainment.
RIGHT: movie poster.

SPORTS

Many of the skills and rituals of Thailand's traditional sports have been passed down for generations, but still provide spectacular entertainment

Thailand has a long sporting history and it has become one of the major powerhouses in the Southeast Asian region. A large proportion of the most popular sports, however, are the traditionally Thai events which may not be familiar to those visiting the country for the first time. Many of the following are popular local sports that may have been founded centuries ago, but are still avidly practiced today.

Thai boxing

Thai boxing, or *muay Thai*, is the local martial art and is the most popular traditional sport in Thailand, as well as being the fastest-growing full contact sport in the world. It is also one of the most dangerous martial art forms and it is commonplace for a present-day *muay Thai* fight to end with blood all over the ring, occasionally splashing the clothes of unlucky ringside spectators.

The history of the sport dates back to the 1500s and the reign of King Naresuan, when it was taught mainly to soldiers and troops as a form of bare-hand combat. The soldiers of Siam would practice and compete with each other locally and regionally.

The aim of *muay Thai* is to use the whole body as an offensive weapon. Unlike Western boxing, practically all parts of the body are used, including the fists, elbows, knees and legs. Equally all parts of the body are legitimate targets except for the groin. The most popular place for knock-out blows is the head.

Before the sport was standardized, fighters did not wear protective equipment such as boxing gloves. In fact, ancient fighters used strips of canvas to wrap their fists in order to harden their punches; even if the target was missed, a slight touch of the canvas caused cuts and burns to the skin. By the 1700s, *muay Thai*'s popularity had reached all levels of the population with schools and training camps being set up all over the country. Earlier in the 20th

century, *muay Thai* was considered to be an art form and was usually performed for entertainment at large temple festivals. Having shaken off its associations with open combat, the practice of *muay Thai* was handed down either from father to son or from teacher to student.

As *muay Thai* developed into a more orga-

When Ayutthaya was conquered by the Burmese in 1767 its people became prisoners. Nai Khanom Tom, a skilled Thai fighter, was among the captured. When the King of Burma held a festival in Rangoon which included boxing displays, Nai Khanom Tom was picked as an opponent from a group of prisoners. In the contest that followed, he defeated 10 Burmese opponents in a row and was granted his freedom as a reward. Another famous boxer, Phra Chao Sua (King Tiger) was head of state and also a skilled *muay Thai* fighter. He was known to travel to the countryside disguised as an ordinary man, testing his skills at festivals and sporting events around the country.

LEFT: a *muay Thai* boxer prays before a bout.
RIGHT: aerial pirouettes during a game of *takraw*.

nized sport, rules were introduced in the 1930s to standardize it, which were based on the international rules of boxing. Weight limits were imposed and matches were divided up into 10 bouts a session each consisting of five three-minute rounds with a two-minute rest period for the contestants between each round. Fighters were also required to wear either blue or red shorts and use gloves. Some traditions remain: even today, although boxers don't wear shoes, they are required to tape their feet.

PLACING BETS

Although gambling is illegal in Thailand, *muay Thai* and horse-racing, are exceptions. Gamblers at the stadiums create as much excitement as the boxers.

ful movements, which also serve as body-stretching exercises. Each fighter has his own dance which incorporates some ritualized movements from the dance of his training camp.

Although not often seen today, Thai boxers traditionally wrap a *mongkol* (small rope or cord) around their head. According to ancient beliefs, the *mongkol* can be removed in the ring only by the mentor or trainer of the fighter, who also blesses him before starting the fight. Fighters still wear armbands which

The fighting ritual

Muay Thai is a spiritual and highly ritualized sport. Boxers are given a name by their trainers which incorporates the name of his training camp. Before the fight starts the competing boxers perform the *Wai Khru* (ritual dance), in which they give thanks to their mentors, parents and ancestors. Contestants bow first in the direction of their birthplace, and then to the four points of the compass to honor their teachers and the spirit of the ring.

To the accompaniment of a *phipat* (a four-piece ensemble made up of the Thai *phinai* (oboe) and percussion instruments they dance slowly around the ring in controlled and grace-

have a small Buddha image attached to them for divine protection.

All parts of the body used in *muay Thai* – fists, elbows, knees, legs – can cause a knock-out blow. Although the fist seems to be the most convenient weapon for pounding an opponent, more points are awarded by the judges for the use of the knee.

The spectacular elbow shots are intended to open a cut on the opponent's forehead, preferably above the eyes, so as to weaken him. Kicks can be deadly, especially if they land on the opponent's neck, and it is common for a fight to end as the result of a well-placed kick to this delicate area.

Widespread appeal

There are two main *muay Thai* stadiums in Bangkok – Rajdamnoen Stadium (near Democracy Monument; open 6pm Mon, Wed, Thur; 5pm Sun; tel: 281 4205/281 0879), which is the oldest, and the Lumpini Stadium (Rama IV Road open 6pm Tue, Fri and Sat; tel: 251 4303; admission fee). Other highly regarded venues are the Omnoi, Rangsit and International Muaythai Channel 7 boxing stadiums.

Muay Thai became increasingly popular in the 1990s and today, large number of foreigners practice *muay Thai* in Thailand and abroad. The sport has become popular in France and Belgium, as well as in the US where several schools have been set up and professional-standard fighters have emerged.

International tournaments have also begun to be held regularly in which local Thai fighters take on foreign counterparts in televised matches. The recent Asian Games held in Bangkok included *muay Thai* as a demonstration sport. Whether one likes violence or not, *muay Thai* is an incredibly exciting experience and it's easy to see why it is the nation's favorite sport.

Takraw

The 500-year-old sport of *takraw,* or Siamese football, has slowly cultivated an international following with its aggressive and acrobatic attacking style of play and fast-moving action.

A simple *luk takraw* (a ball of woven rattan) embodies the spirit of this national pastime, played throughout the country by men and boys who gather together after work in a field or vacant lot. With the exception of the hands, all body parts – the feet, knees, elbows, shoulders and head – are used to keep the ball in the air with displays of extraordinary grace.

There are two main forms of *takraw*. Net *takraw* (known as *sepak takraw*) is the competitive form, which is very similar to the principles of volleyball. Two *regus* (teams of four) compete against each other – three players battle it out while the fourth player is kept as a substitute. The main difference between net *takraw* and volleyball is that each side is allowed three contacts with the ball, which can be taken consecutively by any player.

A 1.5-meter (5-ft) high net separates the two teams while the service of the ball involves two players. The server stands 3 meters (9 ft) away from the center line of the court while the *takraw* "placer" – standing with his back turned to the net – feeds the ball with unbelievable precision in order for the server to swing his kicking leg in a swift pendulum-like motion.

Aerial attacks with foot smashes are executed in an almost upside-down, scissor-like maneuver, while the player's head points down to the floor before momentum brings his feet to cushion the fall in cat-like fashion.

Returning the opponent's thunderous smashes is achieved by using the player's back as a shield to rebound the ball which, again, is similar to a block in volleyball without the use of hands.

Thailand and Malaysia dominate the regional field in the lightning-fast pace of international *sepak takraw*. They have battled each other for supremacy in the sport for many years with Thailand just gaining the edge over Malaysia

LEFT: raucous atmosphere at a boxing bout.
RIGHT: points are scored during *takraw* for the style and difficulty of maneuvers.

in a nail-biting final contest in the recent Southeast Asian championships .

The second popular version of *takraw* is *takraw-lod-huang* or hoop *takraw*. This involves a team of no less than six players whose sole aim is to kick the rattan ball into a hoop positioned high above the ground with no back board. Each game lasts for about an hour during which time each team is given a set time in which to score as many points as possible before it is the opposing team's turn.

RAIN GODS

Longboat racing is a celebration of the rainy season, where offerings and festivities are thought to help appease the mythical spirits and gods that brought rain for the harvest.

from generation to generation. It takes anything from six to 60 sinewy male rowers with incredible determination and great gusto to power the graceful boats through the water. It is a great honor to be selected to take part in the longboat races and rowers are treated as sporting heroes in their hometowns.

A drummer controls the pace of the rowers by beating out a pounding rhythm by which to row. The rowers slice their heavy wooden oars (which measure up to 1 meter; 4 ft in length)

Longboat racing

Longboat racing traces its origins back to when waterways formed the principal means of transportation and communication in the Kingdom of Siam. Provincial communities rich in culture and tradition – Phichit, Ayutthaya, Phitsanulok, Bang Sai, Nakhon Ratchasima, Narathiwat and Bangkok – staged these colorful races each year.

Long, low-slung wooden boats are shaped by master craftsmen under the watchful eye of mystical spirits. A traditional Thai longboat is the result of painstaking time and attention to artistic detail and the highest standards of craftsmanship which have been passed down

through the water in unison. The frantic cheers of the spectators lined up along the river banks, and local people standing on the piers of their Thai-style wooden houses, increase the tension between the boats. The drum beat, which reaches a state of frenzy at times, often seems to overpower even the strongest of rowers at the climax of the race as every last ounce of strength is put into taking the boat first over the finishing line.

The annual longboat regatta falls on September 18–19 and is staged at Wat Phra Sri-rattanamahathat Maha Voraviharn in Phitsanulok province. The Phichit longboat races, held a couple of weeks earlier on September 4–5, start at the Wat Tha-Luang temple and run through the provincial capital. Smaller-scale events are held in Bangkok and throughout Thailand at this time of year.

Siamese fighting fish

Siamese fighting fish or any of the genus *betta*, are brilliantly colored freshwater fish with long fins, found primarily in Southeast Asia.

Small in stature with sizes ranging from 2.5–5 cm (1–2 inches) long, they have a fighting spirit larger than the fiercest of the Indian Shatriya warriors of the past. The male *betta* is striking in color, while the female's shade is somewhat duller. Once a confrontation between two *bettas* has developed, both sides of a gill-like structure flip outwards and the angry *betta* change color as they prepare for war.

Found in the wild, the fish used for fighting are usually raised domestically. A wounded *betta* can often be seen recuperating from a fierce attack in a liter-sized bottle filled with muddy water. *Betta* experts believe that the mud concoction in the water accelerates the healing process.

A basic *betta* fight involves the opposing fish facing off in their respective "bottles." This process enrages them just like a pre-fight scenario between heavyweight boxers. The *bettas* flash their bright colors and flap out their gill-like structures to show aggression. At any given moment the two *bettas* meet. Swift bites alternate with the locking of their jaws and fights can take anywhere from five minutes to an hour, depending on the strength and courage of the individual fish.

European sport

Football is without a doubt the most popular of foreign sports, but most Thais support foreign teams rather than step out on the field themselves. The European sport that seems to be practiced by the majority of male Thais is snooker, with close to 1,000 clubs in Bangkok alone (most hotels have their own facility). The popularity of the sport escalated in the late 1980s and early 1990s, thanks to Thai snooker sensation Wattana Phu-ob-orm who became the first Thai professional to play in England.

Golf is also very popular and Thailand has the greatest number of golf courses in the region, and nearly 50 beautifully-designed courses in Bangkok to choose from. Mountain biking is also growing in popularity, with tourist destinations offering bike-hiring services, while the increasing number of bowling centers is evidence of the spread of this sport.

It would be difficult to mention all the sports popular in Thailand since there are so many. The chances are that the sport you're interested in can be found somewhere in the country. Even winter sports have a look in – there are skating rinks operating in Bangkok. ❑

LEFT: kites at Sanam Luang.
RIGHT: golf is just one of many European sports played in Bangkok.

KITE-FIGHTING

The sport of kite-flying was popularized in Thailand by the Thai aristocrat Phraya Bhiromphakdi, the founder of the Singha Beer company. Kite-fighting is an aerial battle of the sexes best enjoyed at Sanam Luang during March and April due to the dependable breezes at that time of year. *Chula* kites are huge male kites which require a sizeable team of flyers, while female kites are called *pakpao* kites. The *chulas* snare the *pakpaos* by precise movement of the kite-flyers, aided by a string smeared with a mixture of glue and smashed glass. Other kite-flying areas are the National Stadium, Rama 1 Rd and the Hua Mark Stadium near Ramkamhaeng University.

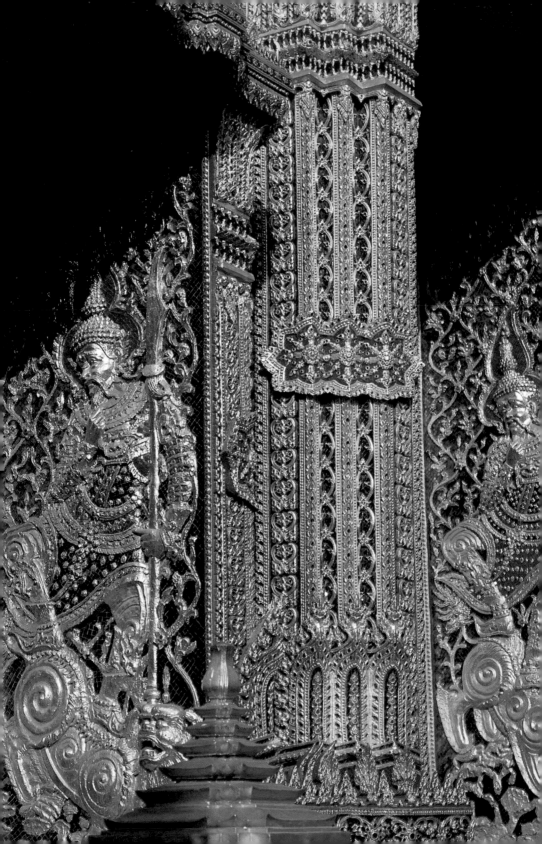

ARCHITECTURE

From traditional temples to the exuberance of its modern buildings,
Bangkok is a riot of architectural styles and influences

In 1782, at the beginning of the Rattanakosin era, when Bangkok became capital, many new buildings were erected. These were very similar in style to the ones that had existed in Ayutthaya before the Burmese sacked the old capital. Even the bricks used to build the city wall were transported from fortifications around Ayutthaya. Architectural concepts to do with planning, design, decoration, construction materials and function were thus pretty much the same as those in the old city.

Traditional Thai style

Most of the structures that were built during the first 70 years of the new reign were in traditional Thai style. These were mainly palaces, temples and other religious buildings, and houses. The time of public buildings had not come as yet because temples served not only as places of worship but also as schools, workplaces, hospitals and venues for community gatherings (*see Temple Architecture, pages 132–3*). Palaces were also important because, in addition to housing royalty, they were centers for the arts and culture, with the most talented people often working for the king.

Weather and environment were important factors in dictating the style of traditonal architecture. Like in Ayutthaya, typical Thai buildings had only one story. They had to survive floods in the rainy season and so they were built on wooden piles. Roofs with big eaves afforded protection from the rain and the strong rays of the sun. Wood was the favored material of construction, both because it was plentiful and because tropical hardwoods were highly durable. Thai construction methods did not use iron nails; all the wooden parts were dovetailed together and held in place with wooden pegs.

Thai architectural styles also reflected the social hierarchy. The palace, the king's residence, came at the apex of this architectural

pyramid, and featured a high, multi-tiered roof which was lavishly decorated with gold, stained glass or ceramics. Temples, too, stood tall with golden *chedi* (relic chambers) and *prang* (spires) because they merited importance as religious places. Traditional houses, on the other hand, were very simple in comparison.

But their roof decorations were a key indicator of the rank of the owners. For instance, a carved eave indicated the occupant was a high-ranking official or someone with an equally high social status.

Foreign influences

Foreign tastes in architecture began to exert a strong influence during the reign of King Rama III (1824–51), who was keen on promoting trade, especially with China.

Thai architecture began adapting many Chinese styles, and the porcelain and ceramic decorations of Wat Pra Chetuphon and Wat Po in Bangkok are good examples of this.

PRECEDING PAGES: Wat Arun, (Temple of Dawn), Thonburi. **LEFT:** gilded stucco at Wat Ratchabophit. **RIGHT:** old and new: Suan Pakkard Palace.

In 1855, King Rama IV (1851–1868) signed the Bowring Treaty of Friendship and Commerce with Britain, opening the doors of Siam to the West. The king was determined not to yield to any Western power but was eager to learn from the Occidentals. As a result, a new architectural style developed that combined Thai and Western features. The Khao Wang and the Phra Nakorn Khiri in Petch Buri province illustrate this fusion of styles well. The Chakri Maha Prasat in the Grand Palace, built in the

---

ANCIENT CITY

For the traveler with an interest in traditional Thai architecture but with limited time a visit to the Ancient City (*see page 212*), half an hour south of Bangkok, is a worthwhile day trip.

---

public buildings. Outstanding examples of this period's architecture include the Hua Lampong Train Station, the Government House, the Anantasamakom Throne Hall or the Old National Assembly, and the Defense Ministry next to the Grand Palace.

Post-1930s

Bangkok continued to become more Westernized in its architecture and lifestyle in the years between the World Wars. Temples gradually lost their importance as social centers, and pub-

reign of King Rama V (1868–1910), also mirrors this trend. Jocularly called a *farang* (foreigner) wearing a *chada* (a Thai headdress), this building has a European-style ground floor and a top floor in Thai style.

With the expansion in foreign investment and trade, Thai lifestyles began to change. New roads were constructed in Bangkok and some people moved their homes away from the river and canals. The so-called Chinese shophouse attained a degree of popularity, but traditional Thai wooden houses were still the norm.

As the decades went by, buildings sprang up in the city which adopted Western styles such as art deco, and neo-classic. Most of these were

lic buildings such as schools, hospitals, and offices were constructed. Chinatown emerged as the new hub of trade and commerce as also some areas along the new roads. The shophouse, where the ground floor was used for commerce while the upper floors served as a living quarters and became the predominant architectural form.

After World War II, Western influence waned, giving local architects more room to experiment with their own styles. The architecture of this time showed strong traces of both foreign and Thai styles. The buildings along Ratchadamnoen Avenue, meant to be a Thai version of the Champs Elysées, exhibit a mix of

Thai and Western styles, with the Thai flavor dominant. However, the trend now was to build with cement, not wood, or using a combination of both. Traditional buildings like temples retained their forms and patterns, but the construction materials changed. At the same time, the Thai aesthetic was overpowered by the innovations of the industrial age, making the architecture of this period look quite characterless.

A few decades later, there came another turning point. The oil crisis drove fuel prices up

> ### THAI DECO
>
> Thai Deco emerged in the 1920s as a blending and toning down of European Art Deco. Examples include the General Post Office and the Royal Hotel.

1960s on Sukhumvit Road, was one of the first high-rises in the city. This was followed by office buildings, shopping centers, banks and hotels, all at least 10 stories high. It was sai that many of them looked like concrete and glass shoeboxes made to stand upright. When a new building excited comment it led to a proliferation of "copycat" structures.

The Eighties' boom

Hand in hand with the country's economic boom in the 1980s went the real estate and

drastically and the worldwide economic recession in the 1970s changed the face of Bangkok one more time. Cost constraints forced developers to use the fruits of construction technology to lower costs. Curtain walls, fins and other new inventions made their appearance. Coupled to this was the fact that there was now a new generation of architects on the scene who had graduated from universities in the United States and Europe. Bangkok began to expand, not horizontally, but vertically. The 24-story Chokechai International Building, built in the

---

LEFT: mural of classical palace architecture.
ABOVE: buildings on the Chao Phraya River.

construction booms. High-rise buildings became out of date as rising land values led to skyscrapers becoming the in thing. The golden spires of the Grand Palace and temples that had been Bangkok landmarks for well over a hundred years were now surrounded by towering concrete skyscrapers in a multitude of modern designs.

New trends, driven by an increasingly prosperous middle class and the new rich who liked to be "different," dictated that architectural styles declare the superiority or "identity" of the owners or developers. Since many leading architects and developers were educated abroad, the designs were influenced by Western concepts. So it's not surprising that one now sees homes and offices in classic, Tudor, Bavarian or neo-classical styles all over Bangkok, especially in business districts like Silom, Sathorn, Rajdamri, Rajtavee, Payathai, Pathumwan and Khlong Toey.

The Amarin Plaza Shopping Center on the corner of Ploenchit and Rajdamri roads is designed in a unique classical style that makes the building look like a glass tower on a Greek temple. When it was completed, it spawned many imitations, and classical Greek columns appeared on buildings and homes of every sort, including, rather inappropriately, shophouses.

In the Chidlom area, the Jareemart Apartment building is more like a Greek temple sitting on top of a glass tower while the Thaniya Plaza building in Silom is more Thai in concept.

Today, there is no single identity or unity of architectural styles in the buildings of central Bangkok. There have, in recent times, been some architects who have tried to break out of the characterless mold with more imaginative designs. The buildings that fall into this category include the Robot Building on South Sathorn Road, the headquarters of Asia Bank; the Nation Tower on the Bangna-Trat Highway, which houses the offices of the Nation Multimedia Group; and the more recent and hi-tech Tuk Chang or Elephant Building on Paholyothin Road, which plays on the elephant motif with a sense of humor.

Although Bangkok's soil is very soft and sinks every year, thanks to advanced engineering techniques, the city is also home to one of the tallest buildings in the world, the Bai Yoke Tower II (470 meters/1,540 ft, including an antenna) in Pratunam.

Bangkok today

The 1990s have witnessed a back-to-the-roots trend with architects and builders looking back for the Thai aesthetic and wisdom that had been lost for half a century. Before the recession, new buildings were being designed that were more in tune with Thai concepts than any other influences.

The Siam Commercial Bank Park Plaza on Paholyothin Road incorporates a number of traditional Thai features, including a golden top that is reminiscent of ancient temples. The Sukhothai, a hotel on South Sathorn Road, is another example. Some official buildings such as the Ruan Thai (Thai House) of Chulalongkorn University, the Southeast Asian Cultural Research Centre of Mahidol University, and several new housing estates, such as the Baan Suan Rim Khlong housing estate, can also claim to be true to the Thai style.

Another noticeable trend is the borrowing of Japanese and Chinese styles and architectural beliefs. Japanese gardens, stone lanterns, and curved Chinese-style doors are just some of the many innovations now making their presence felt. Also noteworthy is the fact that many of the new designers pay heed to the counsels of Feng Shui, the Chinese system that prescribes rules for harmonious buildings in order to bring their owners health and prosperity. The Bangkok Bank office near Hua Lampong train station, which resembles a resting lion, is an example of this contemporary trend.

Modern architecture in Thailand today tends to incorporate concepts, beliefs and foreign architectural styles into an overall design rather than copy it directly from the original source. This would seem to indicate that Thai architecture has finally come of age and found an identity of sorts. ❏

LEFT: modern condominium.
RIGHT: Ratchadamri Road, Bangkok

TEMPLE ART AND ARCHITECTURE

The wat plays a vital role in every community, large and small, and for many visitors Thailand's temples are the country's most memorable sights

A typical Thai wat (which translates as either monastery or temple) has two enclosing walls that divide it from the secular world. The monks' quarters or dormitories are situated between the outer and inner walls. This area may also contain a bell tower (hor rakang). In larger temples the inner walls may be lined with Buddha images and serve as cloisters or galleries for meditation. This part of the temple is called buddhavasa or phutthawat (for the Buddha).

Inside the inner walls is the bot or ubosot (ordination hall) surrounded by eight stone tablets and set on consecrated ground. This is the most sacred part of the temple and only monks can enter it. The bot contains a Buddha image, but it is the viharn (assembly hall) that contains the principal Buddha images. Also in the inner courtyard are the bell-shaped chedi (relic chambers), which contain the relics of pious or distinguished people. Salas (pavilions) can be found all around the temple; the largest of these areas is the sala kan prian (study hall), used for saying afternoon prayers.

POPULAR TEMPLE ICONS

During the 10th century, the Thai Buddhist and Khmer-Hindu cultures merged together, and Hindu elements were introduced into Thai iconography. Popular figures include the four-armed figure of Vishnu; the *garuda* (half man, half bird); the eight-armed Shiva; elephant-headed Ganesh; the *naga*, which appears as a snake, dragon or cobra; and the ghost-banishing giant Yak.

SINGHA HEAD ▷
Fierce-looking bronze *singha* (mythical lions) stand guard outside the ordination hall of Wat Phra Kaeo in Bangkok.

△ **WAT PHRA KAEO**
The Temple of the Emerald Buddha is one of the most impressive Thai temples, and one of the world's great religious buildings.

THE ART OF MURAL PAINTING

Thai murals are found on the interior walls of *bot* (ordination halls) and *viharn* (assembly halls). Usually painted in solid colours without perspective or shading, the murals are used by monks as meditation and teaching aids. Not many murals over 150 years old remain intact in Thailand, as they were painted straight onto dry walls and therefore could not survive the Thai climate. The mural above comes from Wat Phumin in Nan, northern Thailand. It was painted in the mid-19th century as part of restoration carried out by Thai Lu artists. The murals depict *jataka* (Buddha's birth) tales and also illustrate aspects of northern Thai life. Murals dating from this period commonly contain scenes from everyday life, local myths, birds, animals and plants, as well as religious themes. Mural painting was at its peak during the reign of Rama III (1824–51), who started a program of building and restoring Buddhist temples. Of special note from this period are the murals in Wat Thong Thammacht in Thonburi, painted in 1850.

△ **SYMBOLIC ROOF DECOR**
The *bot* (ordination hall) roof of Wat Po in Bangkok is adorned with a carving of a mythical *garuda* (bird-man) grasping two *naga* (serpents) in its talons.

CHEDI ▷
Wat Po's 95 *chedi* contain the ashes of royalty, monks and lay people. Four large *chedi* are memorials to kings.

◁ **THE CLOISTERS**
The cloisters of Wat Po are lined by 394 seated bronze Buddhas dating from the reign of Rama I.

PHRA MONDOP ▷
Phra Mondop, Wat Phra Kaeo, was built by Rama I to house Buddhist scriptures. Libraries (*hor trai*) are built high up in order to protect the scriptures from floods.

NATURAL HISTORY

By traveling from Bangkok to one of Thailand's national parks, visitors can experience some of the country's unique flora and fauna

A visit to one of Thailand's national parks is high on the agenda for most travelers. Even if you are only in Thailand for a short while, or have no plans to travel far outside of Bangkok, the Wang Takrai Park and the Khao Yai National Park are in easy reach of the capital (*see chapter on Northeast of Bangkok, page 223*). Not only do Thailand's national parks offer a break from the frenetic pace of the city, but they contain areas of rainforest, tumbling waterfalls and many rare species of indigenous flora and fauna.

Topography

Roughly the size of France, Thailand covers 513,115 sq. km (198,115 sq. miles). The most conspicuous landscape features are striated mountains enclosing cultivated valleys, but there are great contrasts between the six geographical regions. In the north, extending along the borders of Burma and Laos, parallel mountains run north to south, generally reaching over 2,000 meters (6,500 ft) in height. The valleys have been cultivated for centuries, but until 50 years ago - with the proliferation of slash-and-burn farming – there was considerable forest cover in the higher altitudes.

To the south, the vast valley called the Central Plain stretches 450 km (300 miles) to the Gulf of Thailand. The overflowing tributaries traditionally deposited rich silt that created an agricultural rice bowl. The farms nowadays are supported by intensive irrigation, courtesy of a network of highly controversial big dams. The western region consists mostly of mountain ranges, the source of tributaries of the Mekong, Chao Phraya and Salween rivers. Sparsely populated by humans, this region is the richest repository of wildlife.

The northeast encompasses the broad shallow Khorat Plateau, which lies less than 200 meters

(650 ft) above sea level. This is a land of poor soils, little rain, too many people, and a bit of grass and shrub. The sandstone base has weathered into strange shapes.

The small, hilly southeast coast is bordered on the north by the Cardomom Range, which protrudes from Cambodia. It includes 80 rocky,

forested islands. Intense heat and violent underground pressures created the rubies and sapphires mined here. Endowed with the heaviest rainfall and humidity, the south covers the isthmus down to the Malay peninsula. The coastal forests were cleared to make way for rubber and palm plantations. But 275 islands, most of which are in the western Andaman Sea, support unique species and coral reefs.

The limestone rock so common in the western region was once seabed. Soft and easily eroded, it is limestone that is the basis of the crumbly mountains and jutting islets. Underground streams in limestone also created the many spectacular caves in this part of the country.

PRECEDING PAGES: a water buffalo feeds in the cool of a central plain dawn.
LEFT: yellow bittern fishing from lotus leaf.
RIGHT: waterfall in Khao Yai National Park.

Flora

Sixty years ago, forests covered about 70 percent of Thailand's land area. In 1960, the figure had dropped to 50 percent. Today, probably only about 15 percent of undisturbed forest remains, although perhaps another 15 percent of it has been replanted, often with non-indigenous species, or else turned into plantations growing palm-oil trees or eucalyptus. Aside from tiny Singapore, the scale and rate of forest loss in Thailand is the greatest in Southeast Asia. Following fatal landslides, logging was finally outlawed in 1989, but trucks ferrying contraband logs are still a common sight.

> ### I-SPY INSECTS
>
> Most insect species haven't been identified yet, but there are 1,200 variegated butterflies. Beetle species may number in the tens of thousands, but have been so little studied that amateurs occasionally discover a new one.

The nation's forests can be classified as either evergreen or deciduous. There are many subcategories and a single habitat may contain both types of trees. Evergreen forests are most abundant in the uplands of the south and southeast, where rainfall is plentiful and the dry season brief. Rain forests are among the evergreens.

Contrary to many preconceptions, all tropical forests are not evergreen, and all evergreen forest is not rain forest. A rain forest is a four-layered forest harboring the world's densest concentration of species. Herbs, shrubs, ferns and fungi form the bottom layer. A relatively open layer of palms, bamboos and shrubs is above ground level. Mid-level trees, festooned with vines, mosses and orchids, create a 25-meter-high (80 ft) canopy.

The well-spaced trees of the upper-most canopy soar as high as 60 meters (200 ft). Healthy rain forests can be found in the Khao Luang, Koh Surin, Tarutao and Thale Ban national parks, all in the south.

More common than rain forest is the broad-leaved evergreen forest, which grows at higher elevations. Here are found temperate-zone laurels, oaks and chestnuts, along with ferns, rhododendrons and the yew-like podocarps. Varieties of orchid proliferate. Usually the ground level consists of shrubs and grasses that attract larger mammals. The leaves of the taller dipterocarps turn yellow and red before shedding in the dry season. A few weeks later, they burst into purple, pink, orange and red flowers.

One hundred years ago, deciduous forests of the north were thick with teak trees, but virtually all were cut long ago.

Fauna

Of the world's 4,000 species of mammals, 287 can be found in Thailand: 13 species of primates, 18 hoofed species, nine of wild cats (including tigers and clouded leopards), two of bear, two of wild dogs and eight of dolphins. Bats are abundant, with 107 species identified so far. Tigers and the larger deer could soon join the list of mammals that have vanished this century – rhinoceros, several species of deer, two otter species, and the kouprey, wild cattle that was discovered in Thailand in the 1930s.

Declared the country's first protected species back in 1921, the Asian elephant is the national mascot, but nonetheless perilously close to extinction. From well above 20,000 a century ago, fewer than 8,000 survive in Thailand today. Khao Yai National Park offers the best chance of observing some of the few thousand remaining wild elephants.

Thailand also harbors four types of reptiles and three types of amphibians. Among the 175 species of snakes are deadly cobras, kraits and vipers. Visitors to national parks and sanctuaries may not see large animals, but they will be compensated with sightings of birds. There are around 900 species that are permanent residents. In the north are the colourful montane birds with Sino-Himalayan affinities. In the south the birds are similar to those of Malaysia. There are also about 240 wintering and non-breeding migrants species.

Marine life

Off the west coast, the flora and fauna of the Andaman Sea are characteristic of the Indian Ocean. Off the east coast, in the Gulf of Thailand, they are characteristic of Indo-Pacific seas.

ENVIRONMENTAL LAW

The country does have environmental and wildlife protection laws, but they are poorly enforced.

species of flora and fauna could also disappear, not only from Thailand, but from the world.

The Forestry Department, which includes the Parks Service, is underfunded and understaffed. In the past few decades, at least 40 rangers have been murdered in the line of duty. Earning less than a factory worker, many rangers also collude with poachers of logs and animals. The country's poorest people inadvertently contribute to the degradation by farming on protected lands. The demands of Chinese-Thais and Chinese visitors, for both

Coral reefs off both coastlines have been little surveyed, but they support at least 400 species of fish and 30 of sea snakes. The corals themselves come in almost 300 species, with the Andaman Sea containing a far greater diversity.

Environment at risk

Thailand's is an environment in danger of irreversible damage. With the destruction of habitats, be they forests or coral reefs, many more

LEFT: *Burmannia disticha*, a flower endemic to Khao Yai National Park.
ABOVE: the Asian elephant is decreasing in numbers, but they can still be seen.

medicinal purposes and gourmet "jungle" dining, further threaten the endangered populations of tigers, bears and deer.

Tourism undoubtedly plays a part in the degradation of Thailand's ecosystems, most visibly when seaside hotels spew untreated sewage. There are also signs that tourism might conceivably become a positive force in the preservation of what remains of Thailand's ecology. There are encouraging signs that a few Thais – among them trekking guides and local green groups, and even a few progressive politicians – are becoming aware that environmental caretaking will sustain tourism longer than continued destruction. ❑

PLACES

*A detailed guide to the entire city, with principal sites
clearly cross-referenced by number to the maps*

At first glance, this metropolis of over 10 million people seems a bewildering melding of new and old and indeterminate, and of exotic and commonplace and indescribable, all tossed together into a gigantic urban fuss. Years after that first glance, it usually still appears that way. More so than most metropolitan areas, navigation around Bangkok requires a few anchors for the traveler's – or resident's – mental map of the city.

Most obvious for such an anchor is the Chao Phraya, the river that Thai kings throughout the centuries have used to define their royal cities, first to the north and eventually Bangkok itself. In part for the symbolism and in part for defensive concerns, the kings would take a twist in the river, dig a canal or two between two of the river's bends and thus slice off a parcel of land into an artificial island. In Bangkok, the royal island became known as Rattanakosin. An essential part of any tour of the city, its highlights are many, including the Grand Palace, Wat Po, and the National Museum.

As outside threats diminished, the kings often established palaces in the suburbs, which were just beyond Rattanakosin. Dusit to the north and the regions to the east – rural countryside at the time – were popular. Today, one finds the current king's residence, a number of parks and the zoo in Dusit. To the east are the main boulevards and shopping malls of modern Bangkok.

South of the royal city are the several enclaves where foreigners settled, such as Chinatown, or Sampeng, and the Silom Road area. This is where the Oriental Hotel and several other luxury hotels now hug the Chao Phraya's waters. Silom Road itself, at one time girdled by swamps, is an important business and corporate center. At its eastern end, near the green oasis of Lumpini Park, *soi* (side streets) lead to the not-so-humble rumble and tumble of Patpong.

All of this is on one side of the Chao Phraya. On the other side is Thonburi, the royal capital before Krung Thep. Thonburi hasn't been paved over as much. Canals still thread through the neighborhoods, old wooden houses clinging to the canals. The growth that intrinsically defines Bangkok to the east of the Chao Phraya lacks the same intensity in Thonburi.

Growth in most of Bangkok has left a confusion, most clearly demonstrated by the city's world-class traffic snarls. But, like cities anywhere, Bangkok in no way represents the country as a whole. Bangkok is a distinct entity unto itself, and that is its unique and compelling interest to travelers.	❑

PRECEDING PAGES: long-tailed boat, Chao Phraya River; dusk over Silom; detail of Wat Phra Kaeo. **LEFT:** trading at the floating market at Damnoen Saduak.

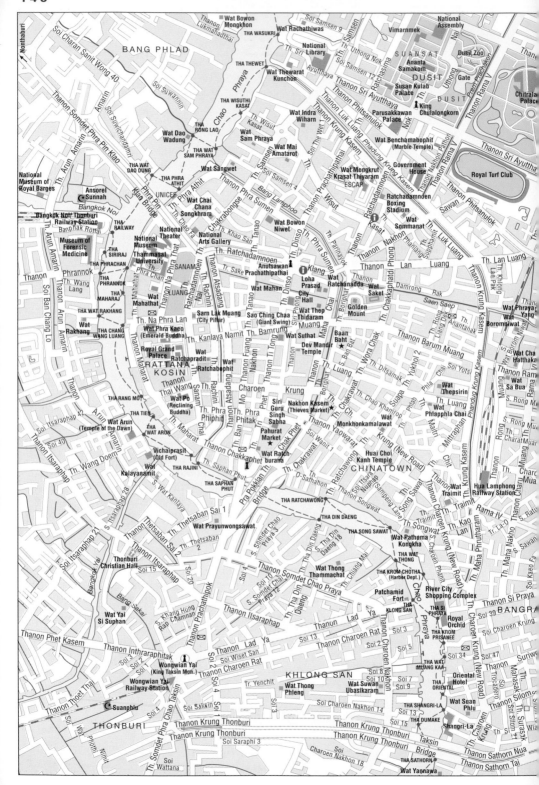

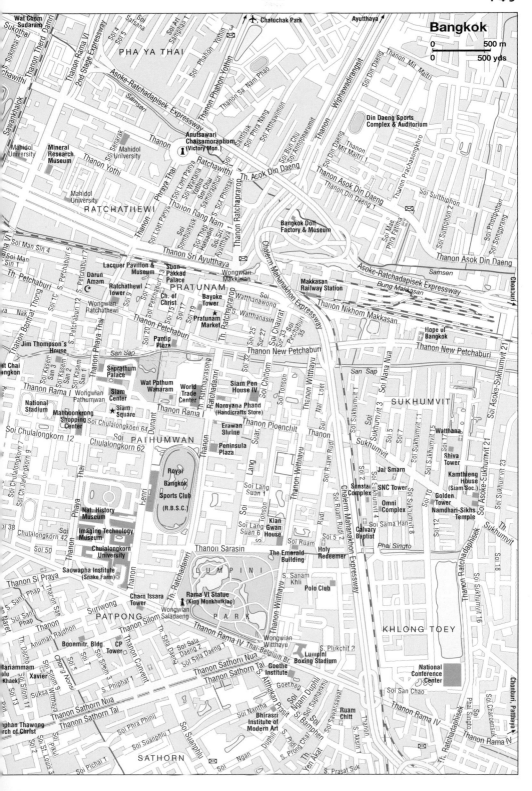

RATTANAKOSIN: ROYAL BANGKOK

Map on page 152

When Bangkok became the national capital in the 18th century, the monarchy began to construct ornate palaces and temples in the inner city to reflect its royal connections

T he heart of Bangkok is the royal center, Rattanakosin, an artificial island with most of the principal royal and religious buildings of the city. **Rattanakosin**, literally meaning "resting place of the Emerald Buddha," became the capital of the kingdom when King Rama I ascended the throne in 1782 and decided to shift the seat of royal power from the Thonburi Palace on the west bank of the Chao Phraya River to the opposite side for strategic reasons.

Search for the Chao Phraya River on the left-hand side of any map of Bangkok. To its right is Khlong Koo Muang Derm, more widely known as Klong Lawd, the city's inner moat. The canal runs north from Pak Khlong Talad market to Phra Pin Klao Bridge. It defines the boundary of Rattanakosin Island, or the "inner city." Any exploration of Bangkok should begin here.

Heart of Bangkok

Approach the island from the Democracy Monument on Ratchadamnoen Avenue (Chulalongkorn's version of the Champs Elysées). The lawn of Sanam Luang will appear ahead. At its far end is Wat Phra Kaeo, a sight so majestic that it will stir even the most jaded traveler.

LEFT: detail of Dusit Maha Prasad.
BELOW: Lak Muang.

The official center of Bangkok is **Lak Muang ❶** (City Pillar), a gilded pillar erected by King Chakri (Rama I) in the late 1700s, joined later by a second pillar, blessed with the city's horoscope and placed there by King Vajiravudh (Rama VI). Similar to the Shiva lingam that represents potency, the Lak Muang is regarded as the foundation stone of the capital, where the city's guardian deity lives and the point from which the power of the city emanates. Distances within Bangkok are measured from this stone.

Sheltered by a graceful, renovated shrine, Lak Muang and its spirits are believed to have the power to grant wishes. Floral offerings pile high around the pillar, and the air is laden with the fragrance of incense. Devotees bow reverently in front of the pillar before pressing a square of gold leaf to the monument.

In an adjoining *sala*, a performance of Thai *lakhon* classical dance and music is usually underway. The troupe is hired by suppliants whose wishes have been granted; for spectators, the performance is free.

The Grand Palace

The 1.5-sq. km (1.8-sq. yd) grounds of the **Grand Palace ❷** (Grand Palace complex open daily, 8.30–11.30am and 1–3.30pm; entrance fee includes admission to Coins and Royal Decorations Museum, Vimarnmek, and Abhisek Dusit Throne Hall) are open

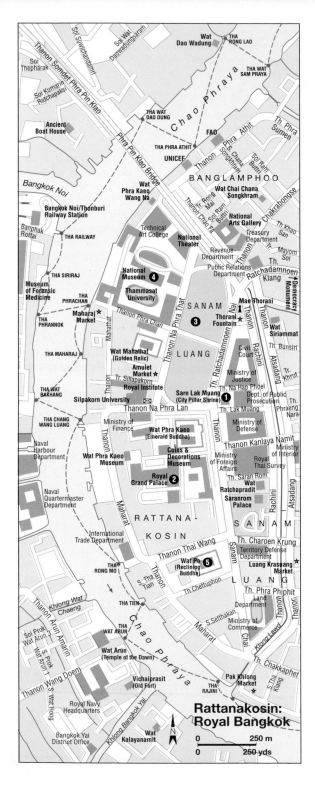

Rattanakosin:
Royal Bangkok

0   250 m
0   250 yds

to visitors who are suitably dressed (*see Tip, page 153*). They occupy part of a larger compound that also includes the Royal Chapel, the Royal Collection of Weapons, Coins and Royal Decorations Museum and a small museum containing Grand Palace artifacts.

Similar in layout to the royal palace in Ayutthaya, the palace compound embodies Thailand's characteristic blend of temporal and spiritual elements. Surrounded by high, crenellated walls and entered by a huge double gate, the Grand Palace was begun by King Chakri in 1782. Almost every king since then has added to it, so that today the complex is a mélange of architectural styles ranging from traditional Thai and Chinese, to French and Italian Renaissance.

After the palace death of King Ananda in 1946, his brother, the present King Bhumibol, moved to the more modern and comfortable **Chitralada Palace**, a short distance away in the Dusit area. Today, the Grand Palace is used only for state banquets and other royal and state ceremonies.

The Grand Palace complex

The grandest of the buildings in the complex was actually the last to be built. The triple-spired royal residence that commands the courtyard is the **Chakri Maha Prasad Ⓐ** (Grand Palace Hall), the audience and reception hall.

This two-story hall set on an elevated base, of which visitors are allowed to see only the reception rooms, was constructed during King Chulalongkorn's reign (1868–1910) to commemorate the 100th anniversary of the Chakri dynasty, in 1882. An impressive mixture of Thai and Western architecture (an influence resulting from the king's journeys to colonial Singapore and Java), the lower part of the building was designed by a British architect; the Thai spires were added at the last moment, following protests by purists that it was improper that a hallowed Thai site be dominated by a building with a European style. The top floor, under the tall central spire, contains golden urns with ashes of the Chakri kings. The pair of spires on either side hold the ashes of princes of royal blood. The large reception rooms are decorated with pictures of past kings, busts of foreign royalty (most of whom King Chulalongkorn met abroad), and a quantity of *objets d'art*, most of them European.

The central hall is the magnificent **Chakri Throne Room**, where the king receives foreign ambassadors on a niello throne under a nine-tiered white umbrella, originally made for King Chulalongkorn. Outside, the courtyard is dotted with ornamental ebony trees pruned in Chinese style.

To the left of the Chakri Maha Prasad, a door leads to the **Inner Palace** or **Women's Quarters**, where the king's many wives once lived. The king himself was the only male above the age of 12 allowed to enter the area, which led to the palace's lovely garden of cool fountains, pavilions and carefully pruned trees; it was guarded by armed women. Even today, this inner section is closed to visitors, except when the king throws a birthday garden party for diplomats and government officials.

North of the women's quarters lies **Borom Phiman Hall**, built in French style by King Chulalongkorn as a residence for the then Crown Prince Vajiravudh, later King Rama VI. It was in this building that the young King Ananda died in 1946.

The **Amarin Vinitchai Throne Hall ⑧**, just east of the doorway leading to the former Inner Palace, is another of the palace's few remaining original buildings. It is the northernmost of the three-building group known as the Maha Montien, and served as the bedchamber for Rama I; the three-room building originally served as a royal residence, the bedroom lying just beyond the main

Map on page 155

TIP

The dress code for the Grand Royal Palace is strict. Visitors must be dressed smartly – no shorts, sarongs, short skirts or revealing tops, sandals or flip-flops. Suitable clothing may be borrowed from an office near the Gate of Victory.

BELOW: drawing room, Chakri Maha Prasad.

audience hall. In the early days of Bangkok, the building was also the royal court of justice, where cases were heard and adjudicated by either the king or his ministers.

Today, the audience hall is used for coronations and special ceremonies. During these ceremonies, the boat-shaped throne is at first concealed by two curtains, called *phra visud*. The king takes his seat unseen by those in the hall. A fanfare on conch-shell trumpets precedes the parting of the curtains, with the king appearing resplendent in royal regalia. By tradition, each new king also spends the first night after his coronation here.

The building just to the west of the Chakri Maha Prasad is the **Dusit Maha Prasad** ⊙ (Dusit Hall), built by King Chakri (Rama I) in 1789 to replace an earlier wooden structure, the Amarindrabhisek, which was struck by lightning. As the flames crackled and brought down the building the king ordered the officials to carry out the heavy teak throne. A splendid example of classical Thai architecture, its four-tiered roof supports an elegant nine-tiered spire. The balcony on the north wing contains a throne once used by the king for outdoor receptions; the last occasion was when King Vajiravudh (Rama VI) received the oath of loyalty from his court after his coronation in 1911. Deceased kings and queens lie in state here before their bodies are cremated on Sanam Luang, called more formally for these occasions the Phramane Ground (*see page 157*).

Just in front of the Dusit Maha Prasad is Thailand's most exquisite pavilion, the **Arporn Phimok Prasad** (Disrobing Pavilion). It was built to the height of the king's palanquin, so that he could alight from his elephant and don his ceremonial hat and gown before proceeding to the audience hall. It was reproduced by King Chulalongkorn at Bang Pa-in, the summer palace just to the

BELOW: Dusit Maha Prasad, Grand Palace.

south of Ayutthaya. Nearby, a superb collection of small Buddha images made of silver, ivory, crystal and other materials can be seen at **Wat Phra Kaeo Museum** (open daily; entrance fee), north of the Dusit Maha Prasad.

Map on page 155

The Royal Chapel

Wat Phra Kaeo O (Temple of the Emerald Buddha) adjoins the Grand Palace and serves as the royal chapel. Unlike the rest of the kingdom's 28,000 *wats*, no monks live here. Wat Phra Kaeo ranks among the world's great sights: a dazzling, dizzying collection of gilded spires, sparkling pavilions and towering mythological gods, both awesome and delightful. It is what most foreigners expect to see when they visit Thailand, and it is the single most powerful image they take away when they leave.

The *wat* deserves at least two visits if possible. The first should be made on a weekday, when the compound is relatively uncrowded and one can inspect its treasures. Try to make the second visit on a Thai public holiday, when ardent worshipers fill the sanctuary, prostrating themselves on the marble floor before the golden altar. The air is alive with the supplicants' murmured prayers and heavy with the scent of floral offerings and joss-sticks. Bathed in an eerie green light, high on its pedestal, the small Emerald Buddha looks serenely down on the congregation.

Strict dress codes apply at Wat Phra Kaeo. Dress smartly and remove your shoes when entering the wat.

The Emerald Buddha

Wat Phra Kaeo was the first permanent structure to be built in Bangkok. Begun by King Chakri in 1782, in imitation of the royal temple of the Grand Palace in Ayutthaya, it was created to house the 75-cm-high (30-in) and 45-cm-wide (18-

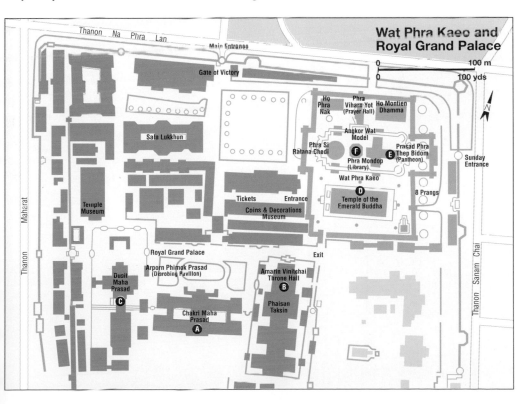

Wat Phra Kaeo and Royal Grand Palace

in) jade **Emerald Buddha,** apparently found in Chiang Rai in the early 1400s and the most celebrated image in the kingdom. It was moved around a lot in the subsequent decades, including a 200-year stop in Vientiane. King Chakri retrieved the image during battle and it was placed in the *wat* in 1784.

Today, the Emerald Buddha sits atop an 11-meter-high (36-ft) gilded altar, protected by a nine-tiered umbrella. Crystal balls on either side represent the sun and the moon. Three times a year, at the beginning of each new season, the king presides over the changing of the Emerald Buddha's robes: a golden, diamond-studded tunic for the hot season; a gilded robe flecked with blue for the rainy season; and a robe of enamel-coated solid gold for the cool season.

Glittering exterior details at Wat Phra Kaeo, one of the most important temples in Bangkok.

The walls of the cloister that surround the temple courtyard are painted with murals telling the *Ramakien* epic, the Thai version of the Indian *Ramayana* epic. They were originally painted during the reign of King Rama III (1824–50), but have been restored several times. The story begins on the left as one walks around the cloister. Epic battles, processions, consultations and other elements from the *Ramakien* epic crowd the murals, along with depictions of daily life. Marble slabs set in pillars in front of the paintings are inscribed with poems relating each episode of the story.

Pantheon and library

On a broad, raised marble terrace are the **Prasad Phra Thep Bidom E** (Royal Pantheon), the Phra Mondop (library), and a golden *chedi* erected by King Mongkut. The Royal Pantheon contains life-sized statues of the Chakri kings and is open to the public only on Chakri Day, April 6. In front of it stand marvelous gilded statues of mythological creatures. The original pantheon was built

in 1855, but was destroyed by fire and rebuilt in 1903. Behind the Pantheon to the west is the **Phra Mondop** (library), surrounded by statues of sacred white elephants. (The white elephant, which once roamed the kingdom, is the symbol of royal power.)

The library was erected to hold the *Tripitaka*, the holy Buddhist scriptures. The original library was also destroyed by fire, ignited by fireworks during festivities to celebrate its completion. It is a delicate building rising skyward, and its glory is the multi-tiered roof fashioned like the crown of a Thai king.

Nearby is a large, detailed model of the famous Khmer temple of Angkor Wat in Cambodia. The model was built by Mongkut to show his people what the temple looked like during the 16th century, when Thais ruled it. On the way out of the complex is the **Coins and Royal Decorations Museum** (open daily; entrance fee). It has a collection of coins dating from the 11th century and also royal regalia, decorations and medals made of gold and precious stones.

Beyond the Wat

North of Wat Phra Kaeo is a large oval lawn known as **Sanam Luang** ❸ (Royal Field), and, more formally, as Phramane Ground (Royal Cremation Ground). Originally, the palace (now the National Museum) of Wang Na, the so-called Prince Successor – a deputy king of sorts – occupied the northern half. In the early Rattanakosin period, rice was grown in the field. In more recent times, the ground has been used for state ceremonies. It has also served as the cremation site for high royalty, most recently the 1996 funeral for King Bhumibol's mother. In a significant departure from tradition, the bodies of those killed in the 1973 revolution were given a royal-sponsored cremation in the field.

Map on page 155

Map on page 155

TIP

The annual Plowing Ceremony, an ancient Brahmanistic ritual, is held at Sanam Luang each May (on an astrologically-auspicious date) to mark the official beginning of the rice-planting season.

BELOW: view toward the Grand Palace, from Sanam Luang.

Lavish exterior detail of 18th-century National Museum building.

Stately tamarind trees, which have been standing for nearly a century, surround Sanam Luang, which is also a place for recreation. Thais come here to *pai dern len* (take a leisurely stroll). Impromptu soccer games are played and children chase each other around the trees. From around mid-February through to April, vendors set up racks decorated with dozens of styles and sizes of kites. The annual kite-flying competition organized here attracts contestants from all around the country and abroad. Sanam Luang is also the place where people head to on festive occasions such as royal birthdays and New Year's Eve.

Off in the northeast corner of Sanam Luang is the intriguing statue of Mae Toranee. A key figure from the Buddha's life, Mae Toranee's image was erected by King Chulalongkorn at the turn of the 20th century as a public water fountain. In the stories of Buddha, the goddess wrings torrents of water out of her hair to wash away evil spirits threatening the meditating Buddha. It is an apt symbol, perhaps, in a city that is often submerged beneath the monsoon-swollen Chao Phraya's overflowing waters.

National Museum

To the northwest of Sanam Luang is the **National Museum** ❹ (open Wed–Sun; 9am–4pm; entrance fee; guided tours start at 9.30am); 4 buildings housing art and ethnology exhibits. (There are more than 30 branches of the museum throughout the country.) Besides housing a vast collection of antiquities, the museum has an interesting history of its own.

The oldest buildings in the compound date from 1782 and were built as the palace of the Prince Successor, a feature of the Thai monarchy until 1870. Originally, the palace included a large park that went all the way to Wat Mahathat

BELOW:
National Museum.

Map on page 152

and covered the northern half of the present Phramane Grounds. The first building to the left of the entrance is the **Sivamokhaphiman Hall**, which was originally an open-sided audience hall. It now houses the prehistoric art collection, in particular, the bronzes and some of the handsome painted earthenware jars found in northeast Thailand. The front of the building is the Thai History Gallery which narrates the country's history, from the Sukhothai period (13th century) to the Rattanakosin period (1782 to present).

Directly behind the entrance is the **Buddhaisawan Chapel**, built in the late 1700s by the Prince Successor as his private place of worship. It contains some of Thailand's most beautiful and best-preserved murals depicting 28 scenes from the Buddha's life and dating from the 1790s. Above the windows, five bands of *thep* (angels) kneel in silent respect to Thailand's second most-sacred Buddha image, the famous *Phra Buddha Sihing*, a bronze Sukhothai-style image which legend says came from Ceylon, but which art historians attribute to 13th century Sukhothai. The image is paraded through the streets of Bangkok, for once empty of cars, each year on the day before Songkran.

Also in the museum compound is the **Tamnak Daeng** (Red House). Originally located across the river in Thonburi, it was the residence of an elder sister of King Chakri and was formerly located in the grounds of the Grand Palace. It has a fascinating collection of early royal furniture.

The finely-proportioned old palace of the Prince Successor, which formerly held the museum's entire collection, is now reserved for ethnological exhibits of elephant *howdah*, ceramics, palanquins, royal furnishings, weapons and other objects. The Buddhist art collection in the new wings, includes sculptures from Asian countries, but its main exhibits are of Thai art and sculpture.

BELOW:
Buddhaisawan Chapel.

The Tuk-tuk

The tuk-tuk, a motorized tricycle rickshaw, or carriage as it is sometimes more glamorously described, has become an integral part of the Thai experience. Its origins can be traced to the rickshaws that made their debut on the streets during the celebrations marking the end of absolute monarchy and the introduction of a new constitution, at the Suan Amporn in 1935.

The tuk-tuk, which derives its name from the sound its two-stroke engine makes, has, however, had a checkered history. To begin with, it wasn't even called a tuk-tuk, but a *samlor* (three-wheeler). It looked quite unlike the ones seen now and it was pedal power that propelled it.

Three years after its first appearance, Luan Ponsophon, a local inventor, decided the *samlor* had to be made more energy-efficient. He redesigned it to make things easier on the drivers who had to pedal fast and furiously in the hot sun. Later on, he further modified the vehicle by fitting a motorcycle engine to it. This not only saved drivers from being pulley and chain-assisted beasts of burden, but also made journeys faster. These motorized rickshaws were christened *samlor krerng* (*krerng* means engine).

But during World War II, higher fuel prices made *samlor krerng* rides pretty expensive affairs. Most people shied away from hailing them and by the time the war ended, they had all but disappeared from the busy streets of Bangkok.

But the *samlor* wasn't destined to die that easily, given the demand in the city for cheap transport over short distances. In the late 1940s, motor scooters enjoyed a great vogue because their two-stroke engines were very fuel-efficient and people hadn't yet begun thinking about air pollution.

Sensing a ripe business opportunity, a Japanese automobile company designed a tricycle rickshaw that ran on a two-stroke engine. This vehicle was the direct ancestor of the tuk-tuk of today.

The *samlor krerng* acquired the new name tuk-tuk during the late 1970s. The tuk-tuk now is open on the sides, often brightly coloured and as noisy as it always was. It still provides great service at an affordable price to locals, especially in Bangkok's residential suburbs. And in areas downtown, it's become a very popular carrier with tourists wanting to try something different and catch the sights in a leisurely fashion. The only caveat, if one were needed, is this: tuk-tuks are not the most ideal way of getting around when it's wet.

Surprisingly, the noisy-engined tricycles have become as much a symbol of Thailand as much as orchids and Siamese cats. Tiny wooden and plastic tuk-tuks make good souvenirs for visitors who are charmed by this motorized rickshaw. Postcards featuring tuk-tuks are also best sellers.

The vehicle's potency as a symbol of Thai culture was confirmed at the 13th Asian Games held in Bangkok in December 1998. Tuk-tuks were used as the official transport for athletes and visitors who wanted to travel between stadiums and sports grounds or athlete residences. ❏

LEFT: take a tuk-tuk for a spin.

Thailand's universities

Adjoining the National Museum is **Thammasat University**, a very prestigious campus. The site was once a part of the Prince Successor Palace compound. Opposite the Prince Successor Palace, across a small road, is Wat Mahathat, which means "The Great Relic Monastery." The temple also houses the Mahachulalongkorn Buddhist University, one of the two highest seats of Buddhist learning in the country.

Another university in the area, opposite Wat Phra Kaeo, is Silpakorn University (University of Fine Arts). This area earlier had three palaces where the king's relatives resided until the fifth reign (1868–1910). Trok Petch, behind Silpakorn University, turns into an "Artists' Street" every weekend afternoon, with art students displaying and selling their art and craft works, while art activities such as painting classes are held. Going further along the same route, there is the Ratchaworadit Royal Pier and Ratchakit Winitchai Throne Pavilion which are exclusively used for royal ceremonies. The pavilion is the only one remaining of four similar structures that were built in the mid-19th century.

Wat Po

Wat Po ❺ (Temple of the Reclining Buddha; open daily, 8am–5pm; entrance fee), is the popular name for Wat Phra Chettuphon. The oldest and largest temple in Bangkok, it is located just south of the Grand Palace and is divided into two sections, one containing the living quarters of 300 resident monks and the other, a variety of religious buildings. The two sections are separated by the narrow and easy to miss Chettuphon Road. There are 16 gates in the massive walls of Wat Po, but only two of them, both on Chettuphon Road, are open to

Map on page 152

One of the many statues keeping guard in the compound of Wat Po.

BELOW: Wat Po: one-stop shopping and entrance.

Map on page 152

The traditional massage school at Wat Po (open until 6pm) offers hour-long full massages.

BELOW: anatomical diagrams, Wat Po. **RIGHT:** detail of the Grand Palace.

the public. Each of the 16 gates is guarded by giant demons. While the temple compound can seem dauntingly large, it is crammed with a multitude of fascinating buildings, pavilions, statues and gardens. The first temple building on this site was built in the 16th century, but the *wat* did not achieve real importance until the establishment of Bangkok as the capital. Wat Po was a particular favorite of the first four Bangkok kings, all of whom added to its treasures. The four large *chedi* to the west of the main chapel are memorials to them, the earliest being the green mosaic *chedi* built by King Chakri, and the last being the blue one built by King Mongkut in the mid-19th century. Around the chapel are 91 other *chedi*. The *wat* contains 1,000 bronze Buddha images, retrieved from ancient ruins in Sukhothai and Ayutthaya.

Acclaimed as the kingdom's first university, Wat Po was also the fountainhead of many branches of learning. Objects were placed in the compound as a way of letting people acquire knowledge, and not necessarily connected with Buddhism. Murals illustrated treatises on such diverse subjects as military defense, astrology, morality, literature and archaeology. Twenty small hills around the compound serve as a useful geology lesson, displaying stone specimens from different parts of Thailand.

Wat Po's *bot* is considered to be one of Bangkok's most beautiful. Girdling its base are sandstone panels superbly carved and depicting scenes from the *Ramakien*. The striking *bot* doors are also devoted to *Ramakien* scenes, brilliantly rendered in some of the finest mother-of-pearl work found in Asia. The surrounding cloisters contain some of the best Buddha images in the city.

Wat Po's great attraction is its gigantic **Reclining Buddha**, commissioned by King Rama III. The largest in Thailand, the 46-meter-long (150-ft), 15-meter-high (50-ft) image is covered entirely with gold leaf, and it depicts the dying Buddha entering nirvana. The soles of the Reclining Buddha's feet, just over 5 meters (16½ ft) high, are inlaid with mother-of-pearl designs, illustrating the 108 auspicious signs for recognizing Buddha.

Thai medicine and massage

Wat Po is also a center for traditional medicine. The building to the left is the headquarters for traditional medicine practitioners. The dozen stone statues of hermits were used as diagnostic tools by herbal physicians. In the late afternoon people still flock here for herbal treatments.

A traditional Thai massage is based on reflex massages, yoga and acupuncture, and originated from 1,000-year-old Indian therapies. Strong thumbs dig deep into tense muscles and work at the body's energy points. The masseurs bring their full body weight to bear as they rub vigorously up and down on either side of the spinal column. When the pressure from hands, feet and elbows ceases, the pain (the massage is vigorous) gives way to relief. The massage school at Wat Po offers hour-long massages.

Rattanakosin, the heart of the city, also has within its confines the National Theatre, Ministry of Justice, Ministry of Defense, the Royal Institute, and the Saranrom Royal Garden (now a public park). ❑

HIGHLIGHTS OF THE NATIONAL MUSEUM

The National Museum, one of the biggest in Southeast Asia, is a good place to start learning about the history and culture of Thailand

▽ SPIRITUAL BELIEFS
Ceramic figures were used both for decoration and religious tribute within the home and designed in accordance with people's belief in spirits.

The National Museum's three main galleries are spread over a handful of old and new buildings. Thai history from the Sukhothai period (13th–14th centuries) to the Rattanakosin period (1782–the present) is covered in the Sivamokhaphiman Hall, while behind the hall, the Prehistoric Gallery has 5,000 year-old exhibits from the Ban Chiang archeological site in the Northeast. The south wing exhibits Buddha images and artifacts from the Srivijaya and Lopburi periods, while the north wing displays exhibits from the Lanna, Sukhothai, Ayutthaya and Rattanakosin periods. The rooms in the old palace display fine art masterpieces, mostly from the Rattanakosin period. One can find treasures in gold, carvings, enamelware, ceramics, clothes, weapons and palanquins.

In front of the old palace is the Bhuddhaisawan Chapel, once the private chapel of the Prince Successor and a good example of Rattanakosin architecture. Today, it houses the second holiest image in Thailand, Phra Buddha Sihing, a Sukhothai-style Buddha image. The delicate 200 year-old murals inside the chapel depict the story of the Buddha's life.

△ BRONZE BUDDHA
This Buddha image reflects the outstanding features of Lopburi-style arts and is one of the most complete images remaining.

▷ DVARAVATI ROOM
This 12th–13th century head of Buddha, found in Khon Kaen, shows a combination of Dvaravati and Lopburi art styles.

△ INSTRUMENTS
Bandoh (drums) are used in Brahmin religious ceremonies. Room 23 has a collection of traditional musical instruments.

◁ DELICATE DESIGN
Sala Samarnmukkhamat pavilion was originally located in Dusit Palace, and moved to the National Museum during the reign of King Prajadhipok.

△ CARVING IN STONE
The subject of this 11th–12th century stone carving is the birth of Siddartha. It was used for decoration at Angkor Wat.

△ LOPBURI GOLD WORK
This gold square with flower design is part of a *luk nimit*, a metal ball used to mark important directions in a temple.

THE FIRST THAI MUSEUM

King Chulalongkorn (Rama V) established the country's first public museum in 1874 in the Grand Palace. The collections were based on those of his father, King Mongkut (Rama IV). In 1926 the museum was moved to what was the Wang Na, the palace of the second in line to the throne called the "second king" or the Prince Successor. This vast palace, dating from 1782, once extended across Khlong Lot and up to the Grand Palace and included a large park. When his heir-apparent attempted a violent overthrow, however, Chulalongkorn abolished the office in 1887 and tore down most of the buildings. The Wang Na is one of the remnants of the original palace and today it houses the *khon* masks, gold and ceramic pieces, weapons, musical instruments. Room 6 contains one of its highlights: a beautifully carved ivory elephant seat. Chulalongkorn's statue can be found in the Issaretracha Nusorn Hall which also exhibits the beds of Phra Pin Klao, the thrones of King Chulalongkorn and King Vajiravudh and intricate Chinese and European-style furniture.

△ CHARIOTS
Used in the elegant funeral ceremonies of high-ranking Royal Family members, funeral chariots are carved masterpieces.

▷ SANDSTONE FIGURE
Only a few Khmer-style female idols have been found in Thailand; this one is on display in the Dvaravati Room.

ACROSS THE RIVER

This small area of canals had a brief moment of glory as the country's capital in the 19th century; the royal connection has left behind exquisite temples and a quiet, regal atmosphere

Map
on page
168

After the second fall of Burma-battling Ayutthaya, a new capital was founded in the south by King Taksin, alias King Thonburi. His era was a brief transition of 15 years, until the present monarchy, the Chakri dynasty, began its rule in 1872. It took King Taksin most of his reign to conquer factions of rebels after his throne, leaving time only late in his reign to embellish his city. Thonburi is thus little to tourists, but still holds many charms.

Town of riches

Thonburi, as many residents understand, means "Town of Riches." It was not until 1971 that Thonburi was combined as a part of Bangkok Metropolis, presently reached by some 10 bridges; the oldest is **Memorial Bridge**. Most of the areas here were changed from agricultural farms and fertile orchards to residential areas; lowland Thonburi is still famed for various kinds of fruits. Pinklo-Nakorn Chaisri road is where upper-class houses are located. Large departments stores were also established here to draw in people who usually shopped in central Bangkok.

Commuting around Thonburi gives a view of low-rises and peaceful lives, with traces of the wonderful atmosphere of an old capital, distinct from the gleaming office buildings of modern Bangkok. Small houses along the banks of canals remain points of interest with people still commuting by boat. Wat Sai floating market, on Khlong Sanam Chai, is worth visiting in the morning to see gardeners selling their fruits and vegetables. Thonburi is not under Bangkok administration's plan to have elevated mass transit or underground trains. Still, the city is a gateway for people who want to travel to Nonthaburi in the north, Samut Sakhorn in the south, Bangkok in the east, and Nakhorn Pathom in the west. Thonburi has a coastline of 4.5 km (2½ miles) along the Gulf of Thailand.

LEFT: sunset at the Temple of Dawn.
BELOW: detail, Wat Arun.

River temples

One of King Taksin's attentive temples was **Wat Arun ❶** (Temple of the Dawn; open daily, 8.30am–5.30pm; entrance fee), on the Thonburi bank of the Chao Phraya River, opposite Wat Po. Wat Arun is probably the most-remembered image of Bangkok (aside from the traffic). It is reached by taking a ferry from Tha Tien pier just behind the Grand Palace.

Dating from the Ayutthaya period, this temple started as a short rounded spire (*prang*) next to an old temple called Wat Chaeng. In the early 19th century, King Rama II enlarged the temple and raised the central tower from 15 meters (50 ft) to its present 104 meters (345 ft) with a base of 37 meters (125 ft), making it one of the country's tallest religious structures.

But, at first, the soft earth defeated the royal engineers. It was not until the reign of King Rama III that a solution was found: hundreds of *klong* jars (earthenware water containers) were turned upside down and the tower was erected on this floating support. Wat Arun has stood to this day with only minor repairs, such as in 1971, after lightning split a portion of the upper spire. The latest renovation of the riverside temple was completed in 1999.

Wat Arun is featured on the silver 10-baht coin, and its silhouette is part of the Thai Tourist Authority's logo.

The great *prang* represents Mount Meru, with its 33 heavens. Its decoration is a mosaic of multicolored Chinese porcelain embedded in cement. The builders ran out of porcelain for this large edifice, compelling King Rama III to ask his subjects to contribute broken crockery to complete the decoration. Artisans fashioned the pieces into flowers, or used them to decorate the costumes of the small gods and mythical figures that ring each tier, guarding it from evil.

It's possible to climb about halfway up the central tower by one of four steep staircases for a fine view of the temple and river. The niches at the foot of each stairway contain images of the Buddha in the four key events of his life: birth, meditation (while sheltered by a seven-headed *naga* serpent), preaching to his first five disciples, and at death. The four outer *prangs* hold statues of Phra Phai, god of the wind. The entire complex is guarded by mythical giants called *yaksa* (giant guardians) similar to those that protect Wat Phra Kaeo. Some good murals cover the inside of the *bot*.

BELOW: Thonburi is divided from Old Bangkok by the Chao Phraya River.

A short distance upriver, opposite the Grand Palace, is **Wat Rakang ❷** (Bell Temple; open daily, entrance fee). It has a lovely collection of bells, which ring out each morning. Behind it are three wooden houses, now collectively called **Tripitake Hall**, which once belonged to King Rama I when he was a monk, and when Thonburi was the capital of Thailand. The *wat*'s treasure is its library,

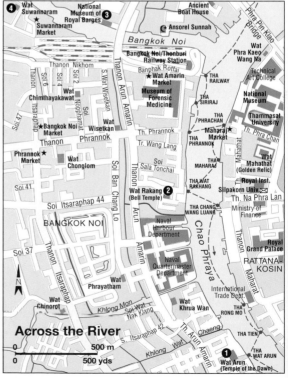

sitting directly behind the *bot*. Murals dating from 1788 depict scenes from the *Ramakien* and *Traiphum* (*Three Worlds*), the Buddhist cosmology.

Map on page 168

Canals and barges

A visit to Wat Arun can be combined with the **National Museum of Royal Barges ❸** (open daily, 9am–5pm; entrance fee). It is on the north bank of the winding Bangkok Noi canal, used as a main waterway during King Taksin's reign, which opens into the main river at Noi Station.

At the museum, eight of 53 splendidly carved barges are displayed. They are used during the annual Royal Barge Procession, when the king makes a royal offering of necessities (*kathin*) to monks at the end of the rainy season. He takes robes and gifts to the monks of Wat Arun, which is one of 16 temples across the kingdom to receive the Royal *Kathin*. His Majesty rides in the largest of the barges, the magnificent Sri Supannahong. Nearly 45 meters (150 ft) long, it requires a crew of 54 oarsmen, two steersmen, two officers, one flagman, one rhythm keeper and one singer, who chants to the cadence of the oars. Two seven-tiered umbrellas are placed in front of and behind the golden pavilion that shelters the king. The gilded bird's head that forms the prow of the barge represents a sacred swan (*hong*). It is a spectacle not to be missed, but one that is so costly that it is only rarely held, the last occasions being for the king's 60th birthday in 1987 and in 1996 for his grand jubilee.

A short distance away is **Wat Suwannaram ❹** (open daily, entrance fee). Erected by King Rama I in the late 18th century, it has been extensively renovated. The interior murals of the 10 lives of Buddha, commissioned by King Rama III, are thought by many to be among Bangkok's best. ❏

Lacquer hats of the Royal Barge oarsmen. Their last public appearance was in 1996 for the king's grand jubilee.

BELOW:
Royal Barges.

THE OLD CITY AND DUSIT

Map
on page
172

Bangkok's Old City is awash with temples, many with intricate and priceless decor. Further north, the area known as Dusit is the permanent residence of the Thai monarchy

This section of the "Old Bangkok" city holds temples whose beauty rivals those in the Grand Palace area (*see page 152*). Many of the principal administrative and religious buildings of the original center of Bangkok lie between the first and second canals, Khlong Lawd to the west and a canal with two names – Bang Lampoo on its northern half and Ong Ang on its southern half – to the east. Along the latter canal were 14 watchtowers; only two survive, at the canal's northern mouth on Phra Sumen Road, and at the intersection of Ratchadamnoen and Maha Chai roads, in the shadow of the Golden Mount.

Wat Ratchabophit

The temple **Wat Ratchabophit ❶** (open daily), located near the Ministry of Interior, east of Khlong Lawd, is easy to recognize by its distinctive doors, carved in relief with jaunty-looking soldiers wearing European-type uniforms. Built by King Chulalongkorn in 1870, the temple reflects the king's interest in blending Western art with traditional Thai forms.

The design of the principal structures is a departure from the norm, making it unique among Thailand's religious buildings. At the center of the courtyard stands a tall, gilded *chedi* enclosed by a circular cloister, like that encircling the Phra Pathom Chedi in Nakhon Pathom.

Built into the northern side of the yellow tile-clad cloister is the *bot* (chapel), itself covered in brightly-patterned tiles in a variety of hues. The windows and entrance doors of the *bot* are works of art. Tiny pieces of mother-of-pearl have been inlaid in lacquer, in an intricate rendition of the insignias of the five royal ranks. In a recess beside one of the doors is a bas-relief of a god named Khio Kang, or "Chew Hard – the one with long teeth," who guards this sanctuary. Four chapels, connected to the central gallery by small porticoes, further enlarge this colorful temple.

The doors open into one of the most surprising temple interiors in Thailand. Instead of the murals and the dark interior normal in Thai temples, this is rendered like a Gothic European chapel, with the light and delicacy of a medieval cathedral combined with a Versailles salon. Wat Ratchabophit was built before Chulalongkorn made his first trip to Europe so its design is all the more remarkable. He mixed the indigenous and foreign even further when, 30 years later, he built Wat Benjamabophit (*see page 179*).

Around Bamrung Muang Road

Bamrung Muang Road, beside the Ministry of Defense, heads east and, three name changes and several kilometers later, becomes Sukhumvit Road. Bamrung Muang Road is filled with shops selling

LEFT: Wat Benjamabophit during the Magha Puja festival.
BELOW: Wat Suthat.

religious objects for temples and homes. Before the second canal, directly ahead, is the tall, gate-like structure known as **Sao Ching Chaa ②** (Giant Swing).

The swing itself consists of two tall red poles in the center of a wide square, bounded on the north by the city hall and on the south by Wat Suthat. The "Swinging Ceremony," no longer held, was a popular Brahmanist ritual held in honor of the god Phra Isuan, who was believed to visit the earth for 10 days every January. Teams of men pumped back and forth to set the swing in motion, struggling to catch a bag of gold hanging from a tall pole. Miscalculations sent many plummeting to the ground. The ceremony was suspended in the 1940s.

The Brahman temple, the only one in Bangkok, is a plain building on Dinsor Road, just northwest of the Swing.

Temples of the Old City

Wat Suthat ③ (open daily), which faces the Giant Swing, was begun by King Chakri (Rama I) and finished during the reign of Rama III. It is noted for its enormous *bot*, said to be the tallest in Bangkok, and for its equally large *viharn*, both of them surrounded by a gallery of gilded Buddha images. Cast in 14th-century Sukhothai, the Buddha images' size and beauty so impressed King Chakri that he brought them down by river to Bangkok. The murals that decorate the walls date from the reign of Rama III; most intriguing are the depictions of sea monsters and foreign ships on the columns.

The *bot*'s doors, made of teak and 5.5 meters (18 ft) high, 15 cm (6-in) thick, are among the wonders of Thai art. Carved to a depth of 5 cm (2-in), they follow the Ayutthaya tradition of floral motifs, with tangled jungle vegetation hiding small animals. Accounts vary as to whether Rama II only designed the doors or

Since the 14th century, the long-haired, white-robed Brahman priests have been a fixture in Thai royal life. They are in charge of royal statecraft and rite-of-passage ceremonies. They have also introduced the Hindu gods, such as Shiva, Brahma, Indra and others who reappear in Thai art and architecture.

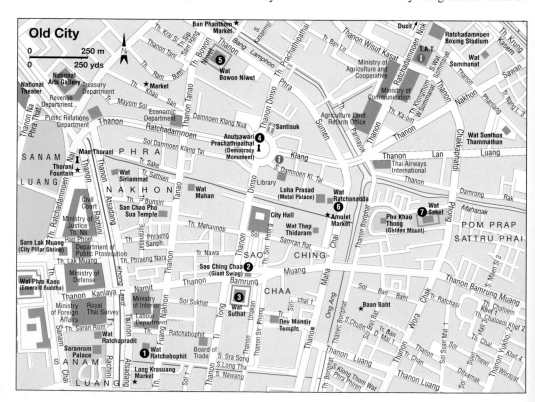

actually carved them himself, but when they were finished, he ordered the chisels to be thrown into the river so that no one could duplicate them.

The courtyard is a museum of statuary, with stone figures of Chinese generals and scholars. They came as ballast in Thai ships returning from rice deliveries to China. Given to merchants who had no space for them, they were in turn donated to temples, including Wat Po and Wat Arun. Even more beautiful are the bronze Chinese horses.

The **Democracy Monument** ❹ (Anutsawari Prachathipathai) was erected to commemorate the Thai nation's first constitution, in 1932. It has been a rallying point for public protests, including the civil demonstrations of 1992.

Almost due north of Wat Suthat, past the Democracy Monument, is **Wat Bowon Niwet** ❺ (open daily). It was built by Rama III for King Mongkut (Rama IV) when he was still a monk, and it was here that he reformed many of the Buddhist texts, ridding them of their superstitious elements. Since then, it has served as the temple where kings are ordained as monks; King Bhumibol donned the saffron robes here after his coronation. (Interestingly, the Catholic theologian, Thomas Merton, also died here.)

Nothing of note marks the buildings, but the *bot* contains some of the most unusual murals in the kingdom. They were painted by an innovative painter named Krua In-khong, a man who had never traveled outside Thailand, but who perfectly understood the concept of Western perspective. Unlike the flat, two-dimensional paintings of classical Thai art, these recede into the distance and are characterized by muted, moody colors. Also interesting are the subjects: antebellum southern American mansions, race tracks and people dressed in the fashions of 19th-century America. Gilded Chinese carvings surround the

Map on page 172

BELOW: Democracy Monument.

entrances to the *bot* and *viharn* – wealthy Chinese opium dealers once hoped that the gods would ignore their earthly business. The mouths of the temple guards at the doors were smeared with pitch so that they could not gossip. Royal crowns on the gables refer to King Mongkut and confirm the temple's royal connections.

Inside, the Jinasri Buddha stands on a plinth beneath a gilded baldachin, one of the finest works of art from the Sukhothai period. Behind it, adopting the same pose in a mystical half-light, stands an even larger gilded Buddha figure, from Petchaburi. Hidden away in the two *viharn* on either side of the huge bodhi tree are more Buddhas. The site is dominated by a 50-meter (160-ft) golden *chedi*.

The paintings on the double row of columns running from the back to the front of the *bot* relate the progress of humanity from barbarous to exalted state, in accordance with Buddhist precepts. The murals are unique in Thai painting.

Across Maha Chai Road from the watchtower below the Golden Mount is **Wat Ratchanadda ❻** (open daily) and its thriving amulet market. Thais are believers in the protective powers of amulets, wearing them around their necks and taking great care in selecting precisely the right one.

The majority of images here, often pressed into terracotta, are of Buddha, but there are amulets imprinted with portraits of monks renowned for their wisdom. Other figures of deities and specific numbers and letters inscribed on the back of the amulets are supposed to protect the wearer from harm. A ten-eyed deity, for example, protects not only from the front, but from the back and both sides as well. On a less religious note, there are amulets that attract women to men, and vice versa, and amulets that ward off bullets and car accidents, and most forms of bad luck that one might encounter or imagine.

One of the best selling amulets at the amulet market at Wat Ratchanadda is for fertility and depicts a monkey holding a phallus in its hands.

BELOW: Wat Ratchanadda and Loha Prasad.

Old City monuments

Behind Wat Ratchanadda is one of Bangkok's most unusual and interesting structures, the **Loha Prasad**. Built by King Rama III, the multi-tiered building is modeled on a monastery in Sri Lanka. Rising to a height of 35 meters (110 ft), the iron spires crowning its towers lend it the name *Loha* (metal).

The most prominent monument in the area is the **Phu Khao Thong** (Golden Mount; open daily; entrance fee), for many years the highest point in the city. Ayutthaya had a large artificial hill, and Rama III decided to reproduce it in Bangkok. Because of the city's soft earth, however, he was never able to raise it to the desired height, and it was not until the reign of Mongkut that the hill and the *chedi* were completed.

Standing 78 meters (256 ft) high, the top level is reached by a stairway of 318 steps that ascends around the base of the hill. The gilded *chedi* contains relics of the Buddha given to King Chulalongkorn in 1877 by the Viceroy of India, Lord Curzon. The climb is fairly exhausting. Until World War II, it served as a watchtower, with guards armed with signal flags to warn of enemy invaders. During the war, sirens howled from its heights during air raids by British bombers, the Thais having sided with Japan (*see page 44*).

Temple of the plague

At the bottom of the Golden Mount stands **Wat Saket** ❼ (open daily). It was built during the Ayutthaya period and was originally called Wat Sakae. Upon returning from Laos in 1782 with the Emerald Buddha (*see page 30*), General Chakri stopped here and ceremonially bathed, before proceeding on his way back to Thonburi to be crowned King Rama I. The temple's name was later

Map on page 172

The tiers of Loha Prasad have passageways running through them with meditation cells at the intersections.

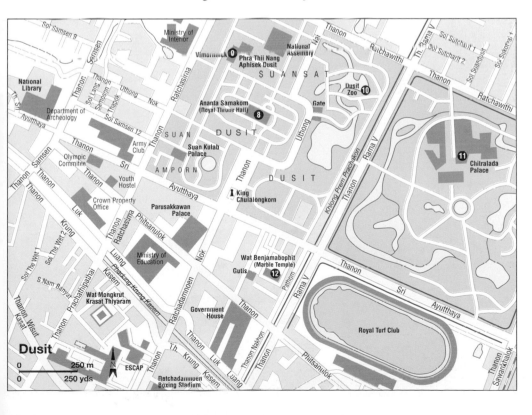

changed to Saket, which means "the washing of hair." The temple is also associated with a more grisly history, when commoners were once cremated here. An epidemic during the reign of King Rama II killed 30,000 people; their bodies were taken out of the city through the Pratu Pii (Ghost Gate), and laid here. Soon the sky was black with vultures. The scene was repeated during plagues in 1873, 1881, 1891, and 1900, each epidemic killing around 10,000 people.

Free guided tours are compulsory at Vimarnmek and start every half an hour. The dress code is strict; only smart dressers will be admitted.

North to Dusit

Crossing the khlong, Ratchadamnoen Avenue turns into a pleasant, tree-lined boulevard that leads to a square in front of the old National Assembly building. The square is dominated by a **statue of King Chulalongkorn** (Rama V) on horseback. Chulalongkorn was responsible for the construction of much of this part of Bangkok. On the anniversary of his death each October 23, the square is crowded with students and government officials honoring him by laying wreaths at the base of his statue.

To the left of the square is the attractive **Suan Amporn,** a spacious park filled with fountains and large trees. It is the regular setting for many royal social functions and fairs.

At the back of the square stands the **Ananta Samakom ❽** (Royal Throne Hall), the former National Assembly, which is an Italian-looking hall of gray marble crowned by a huge dome. It was built in 1907 by King Chulalongkorn as his throne hall, only later becoming the Parliament building. Special permission to go inside is only granted to state guests or school parties. The interior is decorated with huge murals depicting famous events in Thai history. In 1974, the Thai Parliament moved to new premises a short distance north.

BELOW:
Golden Mount.

Map on page 175

A royal hideaway

Behind the old National Assembly is **Vimarnmek** ❾ (Cloud Mansion; open daily; entrance fee or as part of Grand Palace ticket), billed as the world's largest golden teak building. Vimarnmek was built in 1901 by King Chulalongkorn as a cooler, rustic getaway home in what was then the Bangkok suburbs. The king lived here for five years and it was occupied on and off during the next two decades before it ceased being used as a residence in 1932. It remained a warehouse for the royal household until it was restored and given a new lease of life 50 years later.

Vimarnmek offers an interesting glimpse into how the royal family lived. A highlight is the king's bedroom, which has a European-style four-poster bed, and the bathroom, which houses what was probably Thailand's first bathtub and flushing toilet. However, the plumbing was a little primitive – the waste had to be carried out via a hidden spiral staircase.

While Vimarnmek's architecture is typically Thai, it has much that is Western within it including Thailand's first typewriter, portraits of Queen Victoria and china with the king's monogram in various styles.

There are guided tours of the residence every half an hour. Visitors dressed in shorts have to wear sarongs that are provided at the door. Shoes and bags have to be stowed in lockers.

To the right of Vimarnmek is the **Phra Thii Nang Abhisek Dusit** (Abhisek Dusit Throne Hall; open daily; admission fee or as part of Grand Palace ticket). Once a meeting place for high-ranking officials and a royal banquet hall, it became part of Thailand's modern history as well when the absolute monarchy ended in 1932. The king's half-brothers were detained here before he abdicated,

The impressive exterior of the Abhisek Dusit Throne Hall.

BELOW: the studio in Vimarnmek.

and the hall formed part of the new parliament until it was returned to the royal family in the 1970s. The Throne Hall now houses handicrafts – jewelry, wood carvings, silk and wicker boxes – produced by craftsmen under the patronage of the queen's SUPPORT Foundation.

The Vimarnmek ticket also allows access to the **Suan Si Ruedu** (Four Seasons Residential Hall; open daily). The building is modern but it is modeled on the Vimarnmek residence of King Chulalongkorn's queen. It houses gifts presented to King Bhumibol on the 50th anniversary of his accession to the throne in 1996.

Exterior detail, Wat Benjamabophit.

Dusit Zoo and Chitralada Palace

East of Ananta Samakom (former National Assembly building) is **Dusit Zoo** (open daily, 8am–6pm; entrance fee), also known as Khao Din – Mountain of Earth – for the small hill it holds. There are entrances both here and on Ratchawithi Road. Dusit Zoo is the city's main animal park and one of the most popular places in Bangkok for family outings. A lake with boats for hire is surrounded by cages containing the exotic wildlife of Asia: gibbons, Sumatran orangutans, an aviary, snakes and a host of other animals.

East of the zoo is **Chitralada Palace** , where the king and queen now reside. The palace was built in 1913 by King Vajiravudh (Rama VI) and is not open to the public, but keen observers might note some seemingly unroyal things in the grounds behind the high fence. The king has long had a deep interest in improving the agricultural well-being of his subjects, especially those in poorer areas of the country, and spends considerable personal time involved in agricultural research on the palace grounds, and at his own expense.

BELOW: Drum, at Benjamabophit.

Map on page 175

The marble temple

To the south of the Chulalongkorn statue is **Wat Benjamabophit ⑫** (Marble Temple; open daily; entrance fee), the last major temple built in Bangkok. Started by King Chulalongkorn in 1900, it was finished 10 years later. The *wat* was designed by Prince Naris, a half-brother of the king. A talented architect, Naris made a number of departures from the traditional style. The most obvious of these must be the enclosed courtyard; the Carrara marble from Italy, used to cover the main buildings, and the curved, yellow Chinese roof tiles. Also unique for the time are the *bot*'s stained-glass windows. The king was quite delighted with the result, writing: "I never flatter anyone, but I cannot help saying that you have captured my heart in accomplishing such beauty as this."

The *bot*'s principal Buddha image is a replica of the famous Phra Buddha Shinnarat of Phitsanulok (which is said to have wept tears of blood when Ayutthaya overran the northern center of Sukhothai in the 14th century). The base of the Buddha image contains the ashes of King Chulalongkorn. Behind the *bot* is a gallery holding 51 Buddha images from around Asia. The gallery also serves as a center of instruction in the many ways that the Buddha has been depicted throughout Asia.

Wat Benjamabophit (Marble Temple), a mix of Thai and 19th-century European design.

Through the rear entrance of the courtyard is a huge bodhi tree, approaching a century in age, said to be derived from a tree that came from Buddha's birthplace in India. Nearby is a pond of turtles, which are released there by people seeking to gain merit. The *wat* is most interesting in the early morning, when Buddhists gather before its gates to give food to monks and gain merit in their quest to reach nirvana. The Benjamabophit is also a popular gathering place for all Thais on the many Buddhist holidays throughout the year. ❑

BELOW: elephants at Bangkok Zoo.

WHITE ELEPHANTS

Among the most interesting animals in Dusit Zoo are the king's white elephants. By tradition, every white elephant found in Thailand belongs to the king. To newcomers, white elephants look nearly the same color as everyday gray ones. It is only by a complicated process involving an examination of skin color, hair and eyes by officials that the elephant's albino traits can be discovered.

Historically, throughout Southeast Asia, the white elephant has denoted regal power. Buddha's mother is said to have dreamed of a white elephant touching her side with his trunk, causing her to conceive. Buddha, in one of his previous incarnations, was expelled from his palace after giving a white elephant to a rival kingdom.

The number of white elephants a king owned signified his power; the more he had, the more powerful he was. Wars were fought over ownership of white elephants. One could not own a white elephant without providing all the care their exalted status demanded – special quarters and rare foods were necessary. If the king suspected that a minor prince was becoming too powerful, he would give him a white elephant. The prince would go bankrupt trying to feed and house it; hence, the term "white elephant" that denotes a gift or project too costly to maintain.

CHINATOWN

Map on page 182

While Thailand has never suffered from the ghetto atmosphere of many of its neighbors, the Chinese and Indian population in the capital have been proud to preserve reminders of their ancestry

Despite the seeming homogeneity of its population, Bangkok was built by a multitude of nationalities. Most have long since integrated into the city's social fabric. The Burmese traders and Khmers who dug Bangkok's canal systems, as well as immigrants from neighboring Laos, have completely assimilated into the Thai culture.

For generations, Chinese and Indians have represented a significant portion of Thailand's population. Many are as Thais, working and living side by side within the borders. Yet a section of Bangkok plays home to Chinese and Indian communities that have remained, in part, isolated.

Chinatown, or **Sampeng**, was settled by Chinese merchants in the 1780s, after vacating the spot where the Grand Palace now stands. In 1863, King Mongkut built Charoen Krung Road (New Road), the first paved street in Bangkok, and Chinatown soon began to expand northwards towards it. New Road runs over 6 km (4 miles), from the Royal Palace to a point where it drops into the river, just south of the Krung Thep Bridge.

Chinatown was then followed at Krung Kasem Canal by a Muslim district that, in turn, was followed by an area occupied by *farangs* (foreigners) where the Oriental Hotel now stands. Later, a third road, **Yaowarat**, was built between Charoen Krung and Sampeng, becoming the main road of Chinatown and the other name for the area.

Sampeng shopping

Sampeng has had a somewhat rowdy history. What began with mercantile pursuits soon degenerated into a raunchy entertainment area. By 1900, alleys led to opium dens and houses whose entrances were marked by *khom khiew* (green lanterns). A green-light district was like a Western red-light district, and while the lanterns have disappeared, the term *khom khiew* still signifies a brothel. Eventually, however, Sampeng changed into a sleepy lane of small shops selling goods imported from China.

Sampeng Lane ❶ (Soi Wanit 1) begins on Maha Chai Road and is bound at either end by Indian and Muslim shops. The western end, **Pahurat**, has a warren of tiny lanes filled with Indians and Sikhs selling textiles, spices and foods, metalware, and other products. A community which has carefully preserved its ethnic origins, Pahurat is the Indian counterpart of Chinatown. Many languages can be heard spoken on its streets, especially Hindi and Punjabi.

Serving as a focal point for the social life of the communities are its temples. At the southwest end of Chinatown, off Chak Phet Road, a Sikh temple called **Siri Guru Singh Sabha** can often be found occupied with hundreds of worshipers.

LEFT: young Chinatown resident.
BELOW: gold and red, the dominant colors of Chinatown.

The Old Siam Plaza is located opposite **Pahurat Market**. Established in 1993 to replace the decaying Ming Muang Market, the complex provides tourists visiting Rattanakosin Island with three floors of gift shopping. Gems, jewelry, decorative and ornamental items are on offer. Located in an historic district, designers of the new complex made use of an architectural style popular during the reign of King Rama V – a transitional period when Western influences were combined with Thai arts and culture. The top two floors of the structure were set aside as housing for residents of the old Ming Muang district.

On the same block, at the corner of Charoen Krung and Tri Phet roads, stands the **Sala Chalerm Krung Theatre** (tel: 222 1854). The theater was presented as a gift to the Siamese people from King Rama VII in 1933. One of the country's oldest movie theatres, it was the first to screen non-silent films and was also Thailand's first air-conditioned theater. In 1941, because of the scarcity of celluloid during World War II, the theater was converted into a performance venue for traditional Thai Khon plays. Famous as a gathering spot for Thai celebrities and movie stars, the theater continued to flourish over the years, and was renovated back to its original splendor in 1993. It continues to showcase the latest films and contemporary Thai drama, as well as housing traditional Thai dance-drama performances for tourists (*see page 125*).

Chinatown proper begins across the canal, with hundreds of shops selling inexpensive jewelry, tools, clothes, toys, shoes and novelties.

Temples and crocodiles

After crossing Chakrawat Road, turn right a short distance to the entrance of **Wat Chakrawat ❷** (open daily; entrance fee), an odd amalgam of buildings.

Chinatown's bustle can test the nerves of some visitors. If you don't want to walk the whole area, take taxis in between sights.

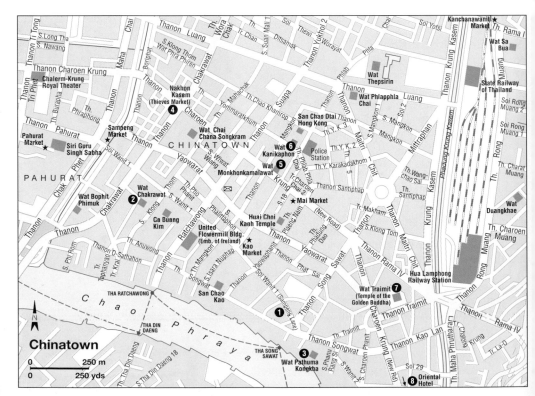

Chinatown

0   250 m
0   250 yds

Map
on page
182

Dating from the Ayutthaya period and thus predating Chinatown, it has a small grotto with a statue of a laughing monk. The myth claims that it is the likeness of a monk who was once so slim and handsome that he was constantly pestered by women. His devotion to Buddhism led him to produce a new appearance as a fat and stout man so that the women lost interest.

Thai *wats* normally serve as a humane society. Thais with a litter of puppies or kittens they cannot feed leave them at the *wat*, to be fed the leftovers from the monks' daily meals. This particular *wat*, however, is a departure from the norm, as the animals it houses are crocodiles. These crocodiles are the descendants, it's said, of a one-eyed crocodile named "Blind Old Guy." More than half a century ago a number of bathers in the canals found themselves on the beast's dinner menu. Finally captured, the *wat*'s abbot showed the killer mercy, giving him a home. The notorious reptile finally died in a battle with a younger crocodile.

Visitors can see the notorious "Blind Old Guy" for themselves – he is now stuffed and on display in the temple grounds.

Jewelers and thieves

Back on Sampeng, continue east and halfway down on the left is a handsome building that once served as the gold exchange. In the side alleys are quiet Chinese temples; farther down on the right are sweet-scented shops selling slabs of cinnamon and other spices. Here and there are small and dark wet markets that throb with life at dawn and are dead by mid-morning.

Near the end of Sampeng, notice that the shops bear Muslim names. The merchants here trade gems. Marking the eastern end of Sampeng is **Wat Pathuma Kongkha ❸**, also called Wat Sampeng, another temple from the Ayutthaya period. One of Bangkok's oldest temples, it was here that criminals of royal birth were executed for crimes against the state.

BELOW: wholesale market, Chinatown.

In places, Yaowarat Road looks much like a Hong Kong street with its forest of neon signs. It is best known for its gold dealers, and daily prices are scrawled on the windows of shops painted red for good luck. Mirrors and neon lights complete the decor. Prices are quoted in baht, an ancient unit of weight measurement which is equal to 15 grams (half an ounce).

Yaowarat is also an old entertainment area. Halfway down on the north side of the street is the famous "Seven Storey Mansion" that flourished well into the 1950s. It was designed so that those interested only in dining could do so on the ground floor. As the evening progressed, one would ascend the stairs, floor by floor, to more sybaritic delights; hedonists headed straight for the top floor.

Wat Monkhon (Neng Noi Yee Temple) contains objects of Chinese veneration.

Between Yaowarat and New roads, near the west end of Chinatown, is **Nakhon Kasem ❹** (Thieves' Market). A few decades ago, people who had been robbed would come here to recover their stolen goods. The market later developed into an antique dealer's area, but today, most of the antiques stalls have gone. You are more likely to find items of a less glamorous description and run-of-the-mill household appliances on sale. Nevertheless, if you search hard, it is still possible to find a few shops selling pottery and Buddha images.

New Road and Isara Nuphap

Near the eastern end of New Road is Chinatown's biggest Mahayana Buddhist temple, **Wat Monkhonkamalawat ❺** (Wat Monkhon or Neng Noi Yee Temple; open daily). From early in the morning it is aswirl with activity and incense smoke reminiscent of old China.

BELOW: terrace of the Oriental Hotel.

The most interesting lane is **Isara Nuphap**, which runs south from Phlab Phla Chai Road. It begins near a busy Mahayana Buddhist temple called Wat Hong Kong, and passes a Thai temple called **Wat Kanikaphon** (open daily), better known as Wat Mai Yai Fang after the brothel madam who built it to atone for her sins. Kanikaphon literally means "the profit from prostitution."

Map on page 182

Around the entrance to Isara Nuphap are shops selling miniature houses, Mercedes-Benz cars, household furniture and other items, all made of paper for the Chinese *kong tek* ceremony. The items are taken to the temple and burnt to send them to deceased relatives. Other shops sell the bright red-and-gold-trimmed shrines the Chinese install in homes to propitiate the spirits.

Hua Lamphong Railway Station, is a fine example of Thai Art Deco style. It was built in 1890 and modeled on one of the main-line terminals in Manchester, England. The first line went as far as Nakhon Ratchasima (Korat), and 30 years later, it was extended to Chiang Mai and Singapore. Nowadays, trains leave to most parts of the country. (The Eastern & Orient Express also terminates here.)

TIP

Isara Nuphap is a good spot for finding authentic Chinese food, with such Chinese specialties as bird's nest soup and shark's fin soup. Often expensive in other parts of the world, these delicacies are affordable here.

The Golden Buddha

Just east of the point where Yaowarat Road meets Charoen Krung Road is **Wat Traimit** (open daily; entrance fee) and the famous **Golden Buddha**. Found by accident in the 1950s at a riverside temple, when a construction company was extending its dock, the huge stucco figure was too heavy for the sling. It snapped and, to the horror of all, smashed to the ground, breaking one corner. A close examination showed a glint of yellow through the crack.

Further investigation revealed that stucco was only a thin coating and that inside was an image of solid gold weighing over 5 tons. Like many similar statues, it was probably made during the Ayutthayan period. To preserve it from Burmese invaders, it was covered in stucco to conceal its true composition, and rested undetected for centuries.

BELOW: Wat Traimit, Golden Buddha.

Luxury hotels

South of Wat Traimit, along New Road, mementos of the European *farang* (foreign) era are found in the many old buildings that line the river. Where Khlong Krung Kasem enters the Chao Phraya is the **River City Shopping Complex** and the Royal Orchid Sheraton Hotel. Just to the south of the boat pier, the Portuguese embassy and lush gardens hide behind tall walls, a reminder of a time when villas belonging to merchants and foreign embassies overlooked the river.

The **Oriental Hotel** is consistently rated as one of the world's finest. The old wing, where many luminaries have stayed, retains much of its old charm (guest rooms are now in a newer tower). Next to the hotel is a building once occupied by the Danish East Asiatic Company. Behind it is the tower of the **Catholic Assumption Cathedral**, a white-and-brown colonial-style building. English-language masses are held on Sundays. While the land along this part of the river is still full of hotels, much of the commercial activity is now on Silom Road. ❏

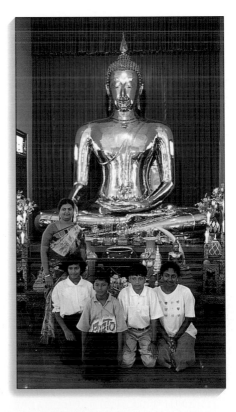

MODERN BANGKOK

A day spent wandering around the cluttered streets of contemporary Bangkok is not for the faint-hearted, but garden escapes are within easy reach of the city

Map on page 190

Travelers may find it tempting to stay in the old royal part of the city, Rattanakosin, with its many temples and traditional sights that are protected by canals from the outside. But there is another Bangkok beyond the canals, expanding and fussy and modern. Yet even within the modern Bangkok, there are gems that await to be seen.

On Khlong Maha Nag at the end of Soi Kasemsan II, across from the National Stadium on Rama I Road, stands **Jim Thompson's House ❶** (Rama I Road; open daily, 9am–4.30pm; tel: 216 7368; admission fee). This Thai-style house is, in truth, a collection of seven Thai houses joined together by the remarkable American, an intelligence officer who came to Thailand at the end of World War II and revived the Thai silk industry. In 1967, while on a visit to the Cameron Highlands in Malaysia, Thompson mysteriously disappeared; despite an extensive search, no trace has been found of him.

Besides his contribution to the silk business, Thompson is remembered for his fabulous collection of Asian art, and for the house in which he displayed it. Several teak houses were moved from Ayutthaya and reassembled at the edge of a canal. (Thai houses are built in panels attached to pillars by wooden pegs, so can be easily transported, if one wishes to do so.) The garden around the house is a luxuriant tropical mini-jungle.

Inside the house are 14 centuries' worth of Southeast Asian antiques. If you are looking to invest in antiques come here first and see the best. (*See Jim Thompson's House, page 196–197.*)

Shopping excess

The intersection of Rama I and Phaya Thai offers some of the city's best shops. On the southwest corner next to the **National Stadium ❷** is the eclectic **Mahboonkrong Shopping Center** (MBK; Phayathai Road; open daily, 10am–9pm) one of Bangkok's biggest complexes. Five floors of shops sell low-quality goods, but MBK offers a glimpse of what Thais actually buy, not just window-shop.

To the east across Phaya Thai and adjacent to Siam Center is the pricey **Discovery Center** (open daily, 10am–9pm) which sells up-market designer goods. Across the road is a sprawl of stores and streets known as **Siam Square ❸**. This is one of the oldest shopping areas in town.

This area encompasses movie theaters, bookstores, and a wealth of restaurants. Especially on the second-story level, close to Phaya Thai, are small shops and stalls selling fake designer clothing and goods. At the southern edge of the square, on the campus of Chulalongkorn University, are the premises of the British Council, which has an excellent library.

PRECEDING PAGES: view at dusk across the Chao Phraya. **LEFT:** Sukhumvit Road. **BELOW:** Silom Road, from Lumpini Park.

Just beyond on Rama I stands **Wat Pathum Wanaram** 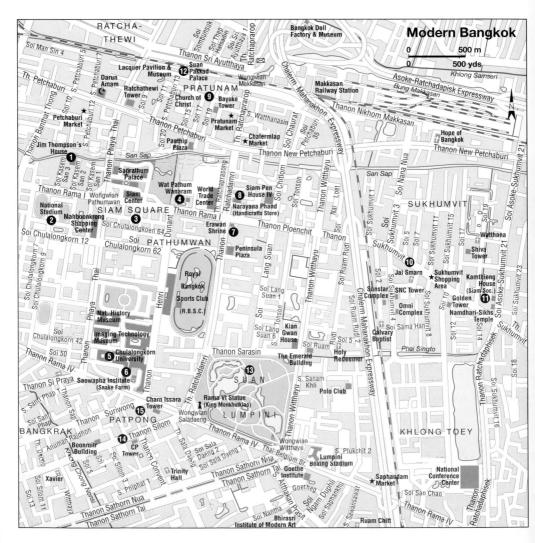 (open daily) called the Lotus Temple because of the great number of lotuses and water lilies blooming in the large pond behind it. The temple was built by King Mongkut in a large park that also held a palace, in which the king could escape the summer heat of the Grand Palace. The palace is gone, the trees have been cut and the ponds filled in to build the World Trade Center complex. The temple's *bot* contains attractive murals painted during the reign of Rama V (1868–1910). Just before it is a lovely stone stele bearing a bas-relief of the Buddha's face. If the style looks un-Thai, it is because the stele was carved by an Italian sculptor who resided at the *wat* a few years ago.

Wat Pathum Wanaram is the most popular temple in Bangkok among taxi drivers, who drive here to have their vehicles blessed against accidents.

To the south, along Henri Dunant Road (still called by its old name of Sanam Ma, or Race Course Road) are found two important old Bangkok institutions.

On the left, walking south from Siam Square, is the **Royal Bangkok Sports Club**, a private club with sports facilities, golf course, and horse racing on alternate Sundays during all but the rainiest months. The club is closed to nonmembers, but the race course is open to members of the public. Entrance to the race course is from Henri Dunant Road. Across the road stand the temple-like buildings of **Chulalongkorn University ❺**, the country's oldest and most prestigious institution of higher learning. The campus extends from Henri Dunant to Phaya Thai Road. Built in a mixture of Thai and Western styles, with spacious yellow-roofed pavilions, an open gallery and an assembly hall, the university was founded by King Vajiravudh (ruled 1911-25) and named after his father, King Chulalongkorn.

South of the university is the **Saowapha Institute ❻** (Snake Farm; open daily, 8.30am–4.30pm; tel: 252 01614; entrance fee). The entrance is on Rama IV Road directly opposite the Montien Hotel. Operated by the Thai Red Cross, its primary function is to produce antivenom serum to be used on snakebite victims (venom milking sessions take place at 10.30am and 2pm on weekdays, and at 10.30am on weekends). The Snake Farm, as it is better known, the second oldest of its kind in the world, produces serum from several types of snake, including king and Siamese cobras, and numerous vipers and other non-poisonous snakes, like pythons, are also exhibited. The institute is well-run, informative and well worth a visit.

At the end of Rama I is **Ratchaprasong intersection**, where the street intersects with Ratchadamri Road and briefly changes its name to Ploenchit Road before metamorphosing into Sukhumvit Road. The attraction here is the **Erawan Shrine ❼** or Saan Phra Phrom. The shrine is very popular among locals, who make offerings at a statue of the Hindu god, Brahma, to improve their fortunes or pass exams. Originally erected by the Erawan Hotel, now the Grand Hyatt Erawan, to counter a spate of bad luck, the shrine is redolent with incense smoke

Map
on page
190

Dancer at the Erawan Shrine.

BELOW: audience at the Snake Farm.

and jasmine. To repay the god for wishes granted, supplicants place floral garlands or wooden elephants at the god's feet, or hire a resident troupe to dance. Day or night, the shrine provides a fascinating spectacle, an enclave of peace amid the din of one of the city's busiest streets.

Across the street, to the north of Erawan Shrine, is the Gaysorn Plaza, yet another shopping center catering to the wealthy. To the west, the huge granite block called the **World Trade Center** (Ratchadamri Road; open daily, 10am–9pm) is yet another shopping center, modern and quite comprehensive, with restaurants, cinemas and an ice rink.

North, still on Ratchadamri and opposite the World Trade Center, is the government's handicrafts store, **Narayana Phand ❽** (open daily, 10am–9pm). It has an excellent selection of goods and is worth exploring, if for no other reason than to learn about the wide variety of Thai crafts.

Continue up Ratchadamri to Ratchadamri Arcade and Bangkok Bazaar. Both have the air of markets with numerous small shops crammed into a small space and vendors spilling off the sidewalks. One can often find some good handicraft bargains at small shops in Ratchadamri Arcade.

The pair serve as a link between the chic shops of Ratchaprasong and the bazaar atmosphere of the vast, sprawling area of **Pratunam ❾**, one block north, a favorite shopping place for many Thais. Pratunam means "Water Gate," referring to the lock at the bridge to prevent Khlong San Sap, to the east, from being flooded by the one to the west, which leads to the Chao Phraya River. Seafood street-side shops are available. The noodle shops of Pratunam market are popular late-night eateries after the bars and movie theaters close.

Bangkok's first computer shopping center, **Panthip Plaza** (open daily,

BELOW: traveling by tuk-tuk.

Map on page 190

10am–9pm), on New Petchburi Road, sits behind World Trade Center, a five-minute walk around the block. Unlike its orderly, Western-styled neighbor, Panthip adopts the air of a carnival especially on Sunday afternoons with all kinds of people on the look-out for computer-related bargains. This five-story bazaar also sells office furniture, CDs, food, radios and TVs, luggage, jewelry and toys – and this is just on the ground floor. On the upper levels are shops selling legal and (in some cases) illegal hard- and software.

Upper Petchburi Road to the east of Bangkok, off to Soi Asoke, was, before the financial crisis of 1997, a thriving business district where several large advertising and finance companies were based. After the crash, however, firms were shut down and many relocated to newer buildings along Sukhumvit Road.

TIP

Many smaller shops are closed on Mondays, and a few are open only on weekends. Friday is the best day to go shopping as most of the shops are open and less people are about than at the weekend.

Sukhumvit

As the main trunk road that links business districts in expanding Bangkok, Sukhumvit Road, known simply as **Sukhumvit ⑩**, is a prime shopping and entertainment area for locals and expats. From Asoke intersection to the east of Bangkok, the **Emporium Shopping Center** (open daily, 10am–9pm) on Sukhumvit 24 is a destination for the well-to-do. Further down the road is the **Major Cineplex Sukhumvit**, a modern-style stand-alone movie theater with shops inside. Off Sukhumvit Road on **Soi Thonglor** (Sukhumvit 55), is a collection of famous up-market restaurants, both Thai and international, which cater mainly for the wealthy of Bangkok.

The **Siam Society** (open Tues–Sun; 9am–5pm; admission fee) on Soi Asoke 131, east of downtown off Sukhumvit Road, is a royally-sponsored foundation established in 1904 to promote the study of Thai history, botany, zoology,

BELOW: market stall.

anthropology and linguistics. It publishes a scholarly journal containing articles by experts on those subjects, and also special books on specific subjects such as Thai orchids, Thai customs, and gardening. The reference library is an excellent resource for visitors with more than just a passing interest in Thailand.

Visitors interested in the culture of northern Thailand should visit the **Kamthieng House** ⓫ (open Tues–Sat; 9am–5pm; admission fee) in the Siam Society compound. This lovely old house, which is about a century and a half old, was the ancestral home of a prominent family in Chiang Mai. It was dismantled, brought to Bangkok and carefully reassembled in a garden composed mostly of traditional Thai plants. It has been converted to an ethnological museum devoted to folk art and implements of the north and is a good place to prepare yourself for a trip upcountry.

Opposite Soi Asoke, off Sukhumvit Road, is **Ratchadapisek Road**, the center of a new, fast-growing business district. The street is lined with new office buildings, 3-star hotels and lively bars, pubs and nightclubs. On the intersection of Ratchadapisek and Paholyothin is the Major Cineplex, which offers the world's largest movie screen and shows documentary films.

Garden escapes

There are private gardens that can be visited for a respite from the city's chaos. One of the prettiest is **Suan Pakkad** ⓬ (Cabbage Patch Palace; open Sun–Thur; 9am–4pm) at 352 Sri Ayutthaya Road (north of downtown, just east of the intersection with Phaya Thai Road).

BELOW: relaxing in Suan Lumpini.

The palace is also known as the Cabbage Patch Palace (*suan* means garden, *pakkad* means cabbage) because it was built on the site of a cabbage patch.

The splendid residence belonged to the late Princess Chumbhot, one of Thailand's leading gardeners and a prolific art collector. The beautifully-landscaped grounds contain numerous plants the princess brought from all over the world, as well as varieties found in the Thai jungle. The gardens are only one reason for visiting Suan Pakkad; another is its superb art collection (open Mon–Sat; 9am–4pm; entrance fee; guided tours available). Five old traditional Thai houses overlook gardens, ponds and lawns, around which pelicans strut imperiously. In the open-walled houses are displayed antique lacquer book cabinets, Buddha images, Khmer statues, old paintings, porcelain, musical instruments, the regalia of the late Prince Chumbhot, and other art objects.

At the back of the garden stands an exquisite little lacquer pavilion, which Prince Chumbhot discovered in a temple near Ayutthaya, brought to Bangkok, and had carefully restored. The pavilion's black and gold panels are considered masterpieces. Other buildings at Suan Pakkad contain collections of sea shells, mineral crystals, and pottery and bronze objects from the prehistoric burial ground at Ban Chiang, in northeast Thailand.

On the other end of Ratchadamri, at the intersection with Rama IV Road, is **Suan Lumpini** , Lumpini Park, central Bangkok's only park and the city's "green lung." Wander into the park as the sun is rising and see elderly Chinese practice tai chi chuan exercises, and later, watch the joggers pound along a 2.5-km (1½-mile) jogging circuit, an effort of either merit or folly, given the city's air pollution. Along the park's lakes, kiosks rent rowboats and paddleboats. Everything in the park stops at 6pm each night when the Thai national anthem is played and people stand still in a display of patriotism.

Map on page 190

TIP

Bangkok Metropolitan Administration sometimes organizes open-air concerts in Suan Lumpini during December.

Bangkrak and Silom

To the south of Suan Lumpini and just east of the Chao Phraya is the vibrant modern district of **Bangkrak**. At the western end is the Oriental Hotel, right on the bank of the Chao Phraya. From the Oriental, walk to the end of the *soi*, turn right and you'll soon be at the less exciting end of one of Bangkok's most exciting streets, **Silom Road** . There are some big eateries popular with tourists such as Silom Village, but much more appealing are the elegant restaurants patronized by locals tucked discreetly away in the lanes off Silom, especially on Pramuan Road.

The **Silom Night Market** is definitely worth a visit. It begins about half way down on the left-hand side of the street, crowding the narrow pavement with a colorful array of stalls on both sides. Here you must bargain fiercely for the fake watches, jeans, T-shirts, shirts and luggage on offer.

About half way along the night market, the stalls curve off to the left along to the noisy neon-lit street of **Patpong** ⓯. Patpong, which is actually two streets – Patpong I and Patpong II – has lost a lot of its atmosphere of unrelenting sleaze, but it is still exciting and sinful enough to intrigue most vistiors at least once. There are now more go-go bars on Suriwong Road, which runs parallel to Silom, and on Silom Soi 4, which runs parallel to Patpong and Patpong II. ❏

BELOW:
Patpong at night.

JIM THOMPSON'S THAI HOUSE

In a city increasingly dominated by Western architecture, visitors can experience Thailand's heritage and arts at the Jim Thompson House

Jim Thompson began his collection shortly after World War II, when the value of Thai antiques was still unknown. His assemblage includes precious Buddha images, porcelains, traditional paintings, and finely carved furniture and panels collected from old homes and temples throughout Thailand. He constructed a traditional Thai house for his collection from six different teakwood dwellings, the oldest dating back to the 1800s. Hued with the preservative red-brown paint characteristic of Thailand, the home features a dramatic, outward-sweeping roof covered with rare tiles designed and fired in the old capital of Ayutthaya. Curving gracefully in a *ngo* (peak), the wide roof allows the airy rooms to remain open all year long, sheltered from the downpours of the rainy season. The entire structure stands elevated a full story above the ground as a protection against flooding. Inside, restored antique sofas and chairs bathe in the light of electrified chandeliers, but even these are from Thai palaces of the 18th and 19th centuries.

Surrounding the entire house is a garden of indigenous foliage, providing a soothing contrast to the bustling city standing just outside Thompson's sanctuary.

▷ **BUDDHA STATUES**
One of the extensive collections of ancient sandstone Buddhas, some of which date back to the 17th century.

△ **THE GARDENS**
Although located in the heart of Bangkok, the gardens are resplendent with well-preserved indigenous shrubs and mature trees.

▷ **MASTER BEDROOM**
Decorated with antique paintings and colorful silk sheets and pillows, the bedroom reflects an impeccable taste.

◁ **ENTRANCE HALL**
The stunning entrance hall of the house and the stairs leads to the main living space on the second floor. The antique marble floor is from Rome.

▷ **LIVING ROOM**
Located in the center of the house, the living room is packed with practical antique pieces. The wood crafted table dates back to the Chulalongkorn's reign.

△ THE STUDY

The study, facing Khlong Saen Saeb, is decorated with a piece of an ancient sandstone Buddha statue and numerous paintings.

◁ MOUSE HOUSE

The antique Chinese miniature houses in this cabinet were homes to mice who had room to run and play and build their empires.

△ DINING ROOM

The antique chinaware in the dining room is priceless while the two wooden tables are dated to Chulalongkorn's reign.

▷ DHARMA BOOK CHEST

This priceless gilded lacquer book chest from Ayutthaya dates back to the 17th century.

△ ARTS AND CRAFTS

Alongside the antiques and artifacts is a huge collection of arts and crafts, some bought from local markets in Bangkok.

THE KING OF THAI SILK

One day in 1967 Jim Thompson went for a walk in the Malaysian jungles of the Cameron Highlands and never came back. After years of speculation the mystery of his disappearance is still unsolved. Born in Delaware, USA, Thompson fought in Europe and Asia during World War II. When the war ended, he served in Bangkok in the Office of Strategic Service (the forerunner of the CIA). He later returned to Bangkok and inspired by swatches of silk he had collected during his trips through Thailand, he decided to track down traditional silk weavers. Utilizing new techniques and colorings that raised the silk's quality to unrivaled standards, he set up the Thai Silk Company and his creations were exported around the world. Jim Thompson is one of the most celebrated *farang* (foreigners) in Thailand and his silks, still found in major shopping centers throughout Bangkok, remain a treasured part of Thailand's culture.

OUTSIDE BANGKOK

Heading out of the smog-ridden capital can give a taste of the beautiful landscape for which Thailand is renowned

Residents often say that the best thing about living in Bangkok is being able to leave it – a bit like hitting your head with a hammer: it's great when you stop. Of course, the city has much to offer, but when one does tire of its charms, there are a host of attractions within a few hours' drive. Now that major exit roads have been completed to the west, east, and north, and an eight-lane highway feeding the south is soon to be completed, what previously took hours, can now be done in minutes, easily allowing for leisurely day-trips.

Approximately 30 km (20 miles) west of Bangkok, the endearing attraction remains the Rose Garden. Features in the sprawling landscaped gardens include cultural shows, souvenir shops, and the chance to imagine what the country looked like years before pollution and urban degradation set in.

Further west, another old favorite on the tourist itinerary is Kanchanaburi, the legendary site of the bridge built across the River Kwai during World War II by prisoners of war held under atrocious conditions by the Japanese. While the destination has been overexposed, giving it an unsavory commercial feel, the area is home to a number of possibilities – river-rafting, trekking, or simply hanging out in isolated jungle retreats.

Turning north, Ayutthaya, dating from 1350, grandly displays its ruins. Day-trippers will have ample time to soak in the former capital's atmosphere before returning to its modern counterpart. Perhaps, however, the best attraction of Ayutthaya is getting there. Specifically, one can take a boat up the Chao Phraya River, absorbing scenes both on the river and on its surroundings that surely have not changed for centuries.

Switching to the more mundane, some 30 km (20 miles) southeast of Bangkok lies the prosaically named Samut Prakarn Crocodile Farm and Zoo. Unlike the trip to Ayutthaya, one barely leaves the ugly outskirts of Bangkok, which gives the farm the feel of an oasis in the midst of the urban jungle. More than 50,000 crocodiles bred at the farm are the main attraction, and their fearless handlers put on daily shows. A well-kept zoo, elephant shows and inexpensive restaurants provide a full day's attraction.

To the northeast of Bangkok, the main attraction is the province of Nakhon Nayok. It has long been a favorite spot for Thais seeking picturesque mountains, waterfalls, and a break from the heat of Bangkok. Central to the province is the Khao Yai National Park, the oldest and still one of the most attractive parks in the country. ❑

PRECEDING PAGES: road-side refreshments; temple in the Ancient City (Muang Boran) outdoor museum.
LEFT: flower sellers unpacking produce.

WEST OF BANGKOK

Map on page 206

The suburbs west of Bangkok and the area just beyond are packed with interesting things to do and see that can be fitted easily into a day-trip itinerary from the capital

Before setting out from Bangkok by road for a day trip, one should seriously consider one's schedule, as well as, the time of day. Nonetheless, outside of Bangkok there are numerous excursions well worth venturing into the suburbs, and beyond.

Rose Garden

Less than an hour's drive west from Bangkok, the **Suan Sam Phran ❶** (Rose Garden Country Resort; Petkasem Highway, Nakhon Pathom; tel: 295 32614; rose garden open daily, 8am–6pm; cultural village open daily, 10.30am–5pm; entrance fee) is the brainchild of a former lord mayor of the capital. The resort lies 30 km (20 miles) west of the capital on Route 4, en route to Nakhon Pathom. Its large area of well-landscaped gardens contains roses and orchids, and includes accommodations, cultural center, restaurants, tennis courts, artificial lake with paddle boats, children's playground and an excellent golf course.

Its premier attraction is a daily Thai cultural show held in the garden. In a large arena, beautifully-costumed Thai actors demonstrate folk dances, Thai boxing, a wedding ceremony and other rural entertainment. Outside, after this show, elephants put on their own performance, moving huge teak logs as they would in the forests of the north. The elephants then carry tourists around the compound for a small fee.

LEFT: Phra Pathom Chedi, Nakon Pathom.
BELOW: flower from the Rose Garden.

One demonstrated sport is *takraw (see page 121)*, which can be seen played in parks and temple courtyards throughout Thailand using a small rattan ball. In the basket form of the game, the ball is played back and forth, using feet, knees, elbows and heads – everything except hands – while trying to score goals. Besides *takraw*, other cultural performances include the fingernail dance, which originated in the north of Thailand and is usually performed as a gesture of greeting and welcome, and a Thai boxing show.

Phra Pathom Chedi

Just 50 km (30 miles) west of Bangkok, beyond the Rose Garden on Route 4, is the town of **Nakhon Pathom ❷**, known for the **Phra Pathom Chedi**. Measuring 130 meters (420 ft) in height, this colossal landmark is not only the the tallest Buddhist monument in the world but it is also the oldest in the country, dating from 300 BC.

The original Phra Pathom Chedi was small, built more than a thousand years ago by the Mon empire, whose culture flourished in Burma and Thailand. They established Nakhon Pathom as a religious center. In 1057, King Anawrahta of Burma besieged the town, leaving it in ruins for the next hundred years. It was not until King Mongkut visited the old *chedi*, and

was impressed by its significance as the oldest Buddhist monument in Thailand, that restoration of the temple began in 1853. A new *chedi* was built, taking 17 years to finish and covering the older one, originally built in the 4th century. Unfortunately, this collapsed in a rainstorm, and eventually the present structure was completed by King Chulalongkorn. Set in a huge square park, the massive *chedi* rests upon a circular terrace accented with trees associated with the Buddha's life. In November of each year, a huge fair in the temple grounds attracts crowds from far and near.

Keepers and elephant ready for a show at the Rose Garden.

In former times, a royal visit to Nakhon Pathom was more than a day's journey, so it is not surprising that a number of palaces and residences were built there. One of them, **Sanam Chan Palace**, has a fine sala, a meeting pavilion now used for government offices, and a building in a most unusual Thai interpretation of English Tudor architecture, used appropriately as a setting for Shakespearean drama. In front stands a statue of Yaleh, the pet dog of King Vajiravudh who commissioned the palace. The fierce dog, unpopular with the court, was poisoned by the king's attendants. Even as a statue, Yaleh looks insufferable. Most of the palace buildings are closed to the public apart from one which serves as a small museum and contains memorabilia of King Vajiravudh.

Samut Sakhon

A good way to approach the coastal port of **Samut Sakhon** ❸ (Ocean City) is by a branch railway connecting it with Thonburi, Bangkok's sister city. The line, called the Mae Khlong Railway, runs at a loss, but it is subsidized because of its usefulness to the population of the three provinces west of Bangkok. The 40-minute journey first passes through the suburbs, then through thriving

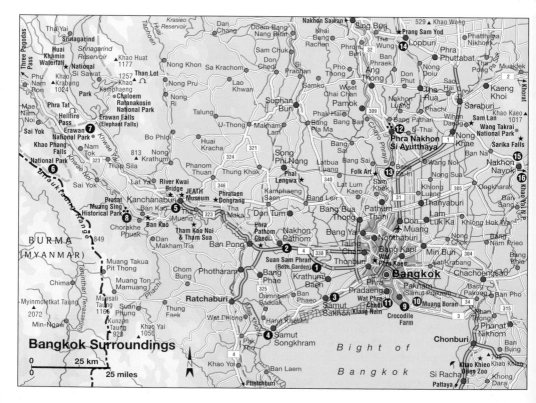

vegetable gardens, groves of coconut and areca palms, and rice fields. A busy fishing port, Samut Sakhon (also called Mahachai) lies at the meeting of the Tachin River, the Mahachai Canal and the Gulf of Thailand. The main landing stage on the river bank has a clock tower and a restaurant serving excellent seafood. Nearby, fishermen at the fish market unload fish, crabs, squids and prawns from their boats. At the fish market pier, it's possible to hire a boat for a round-trip to Samut Sakhon's principal temple, **Wat Chong Lom** (open daily), at the mouth of the Tachin River.

Most of the buildings are modern, except for an old *viharn* (assembly hall) immediately to the right of the temple's river landing. The *viharn* dates back about a century. The extensive grounds overlooking the water are charmingly laid out with shrubs and flowering trees. There is also a bronze statue of King Chulalongkorn commemorating his visit to the temple. His homburg hat does not in the least detract from his immense dignity.

Samut Songkhram

From Samut Sakhon, cross the river to the railway station on the opposite side. Here, board a second train for another 40-minute trip to **Samut Songkhram ❹**, on the banks of the Mae Khlong River. The journey goes through broad salt flats, with their picturesque windmills revolving slowly in the sea breezes. Samut Songkhram, also the name of Thailand's smallest province, is another pretty fishing town; wandering its wharf is an olfactory and a visual experience. Return to Bangkok along the same rail route or hire a long-tailed boat for a trip up the Mae Khlong River to Ratchaburi.

Alternatively, if you are traveling by car, turn off at Route 325 along the

Eighty kilometers (50 miles) southwest of Bangkok, near Samut Songkhram, is the town of Damnoen Saduak, famous for its dawn floating market. Buses leave from the southern bus terminal for Damnoen Saduak every half hour starting at 6am.

BELOW: harbor at Samut Songkhram.

Saluting the fallen at Kanchanaburi.

BELOW: crossing the modern bridge over the Kwai River.

Rama II Road (Route 35) heading south to Bangkok to the Ampawa District to the **Uttayan King Rama II Museum** (open daily Wed–Sun; 9am–6pm; entrance fee), situated at the birthplace of Rama II. This small museum houses displays of art and crafts from the early Rattanakosin periods and four reconstructed Thai-style houses illustrate how Thai people lived during the rule of King Rama II. In the well-maintained gardens around the museum are rare species of trees, some of which are mentioned in classical Thai literature. There is also a daily cultural show and Thai classical dances performed in the garden. A special exhibition is held every February to celebrate the birthday of Rama II.

Another option for car drivers is to drive back onto Rama II Road in the direction of Samut Songkhram and take the small road signposted to **Don Hoi Lot** at the mouth of the Mae Khlong River. Don Hoi Lot is in fact a bank of fossilized shells which has become a popular tourist attraction. It's a great place to enjoy fresh seafood and tube-like clams (*hoi lot* in Thai means straw clams). In the late afternoon when the tide is low, villagers search the river bank for clam burrows and put a little bit of lime at the entrance of the holes. The clams are caught when they come out from the ground to investigate the lime.

Kanchanaburi and the River Kwai

Established in the early 1800s, thus making it a young city by Thai standards, **Kanchanaburi** ❺ is about 120 km (75 miles) northwest of Bangkok, past Nakhon Pathom, and not far from the Thai border with Burma. It prospers from gem mining and a teak trade with Burma. The world's smallest species of bat, about the size of a bumblebee, was discovered near an odd-looking railway bridge crossing the Mae Khlong River, also known as the Kwai Yai, a few kilo-

meters outside of Kanchanaburi. The bridge is contoured with a series of ellip-
tical spans, with an awkwardly rectangular center. This is the so-called "**Bridge
on the River Kwai**." In fact, it's not. The bridge that spanned the mightier
Kwai River and inspired the novel and film was farther north. Of course, the
original bridge no longer exists.

Seeking to shorten supply lines between Japan and Burma in preparation for
an eventual attack on British India, the Japanese began work on a railway
between Thailand and Burma in 1942. For a large part of its 400-plus kilometers (260 miles), the railway followed the river valley; although the logistics of
doing so were often nightmarish, following the valley allowed construction of
the railway simultaneously in different areas. In the end, there were nearly
15 km (9 miles) of bridges completed. The Japanese forced 250,000 Asian
laborers and 61,000 Allied prisoners of war to construct 260 km (160 miles) of
rail on the Thai side, leading to the Three Pagodas Pass on the border. It is estimated that 100,000 Asian laborers and 16,000 Allied prisoners lost their lives
from beatings, starvation, disease and exhaustion.

In Kanchanaburi, graves mark 6,982 of those Allied soldiers. There are two
cemeteries in Kanchanaburi. The larger is on the main road nearly opposite the
railway station; the second, Chonkai, is across the river on the banks of the
Kwai Noi. Both hold the remains of Dutch, Australian, British, Danish, New
Zealander and other Allied prisoners of war; American war dead were removed
to Arlington Cemetery, in Washington, D.C.

An appreciation of the enormous obstacles the prisoners faced is provided by
the **JEATH Museum** (Wisuttharangsi Road; open daily, 8.30am–4.30pm;
entrance fee), near the end of Lak Muang Road. (The museum's name derives

In November there is a
week-long fair that
celebrates the Allied
attack on the bridge
on the River Kwai. It
features a very
popular light and
sound show and
reservations should be
made well in advance.

BELOW: the
JEATH museum.

Map on page 206

from the first initial of those nationalities involved in the construction.) Established in 1977 by the monks of **Wat Chaichumpol** (Wat Chanasongkhram) next door, the museum is constructed like the bamboo huts in which the war prisoners lived. Utensils, paintings, writings and other objects donated by prisoners who survived reveal some of the horror of their hell-like existence.

Located beside the bridge is another museum, the newer and rather tacky **World War II Museum** (open daily, 9am–4.30pm; entrance fee) containing an odd mixture of exhibits which include displays of prehistoric Thai village life and a collection of Thai stamps and currency.

Although the current memorial bridge is mistaken for the one made famous in print and film, it is worthwhile visiting from an historical point of view. It can be reached by boat or rickshaw from Kanchanaburi. The bridge has lost some of its mystery and awe with commercialization, but walking across it is a sobering experience. (Niches between the spans provide an escape in case a train passes by.) A steam locomotive used shortly after the war is displayed beside the tiny Kanchanaburi station platform, along with an ingenious Japanese supply truck that could run on both roads and rails. Floating restaurants and hotels line the banks of the attractive river.

Today, most of the old railway tracks have been removed, except for a section that runs peacefully from Kanchanaburi to the terminus at Nam Tok, a 50-km (30-mile) journey taking about one-and-a-half hours across one of the shakiest bridges in the world; the wooden pillars and sleepers creak and groan as the train moves slowly across them. The Asian Highway now runs from Kanchanaburi to the Burmese border at the Three Pagodas Pass (an old trade link between western Thailand and southern Burma), a distance of 250 km (150 miles).

BELOW: popular mode of transport. **RIGHT:** local seller of dried fish.

Around Kanchanaburi

About 20 km (12 miles) further up Highway 323, and also reachable by boat from Nam Tok, is the the **Sai Yok National Park ❻** (open daily; entrance fee), which contains the beautiful Sai Yok and Sai Yok Noi waterfalls. The **Erawan National Park ❼** (open daily; entrance fee), 70 km (40 miles) north of Kanchanaburi, features the **Erawan Falls**, which is one of the most popular waterfalls in Thailand.

Close by are the **Khao Phang Falls**, where the water sluices down a series of limestone steps. Nearly the entire length of the river is now dappled with attractive resorts perched on bamboo rafts.

Long before it assumed its strategic role in the last war, Kanchanaburi had been a battlefield for warring Siamese and Burmese, and old battlements still remain. North of Ban Keo, about 43 km (27 miles) from Kanchanaburi, just before Wang Po station, are the 13th-century Khmer ruins of **Muang Sing** (Lion City) contained in one of the country's most interesting archaeological sites, the **Prasat Muang Sing Historical Park ❽** (Sai Yok District, Kanchanaburi; open Wed–Sun; 8.30am–4.30pm; entrance fee).

Apart from the Khmer town ruins and the principal shrine of Prasat Muang Sing, there is also a museum which houses some art objects and sculptures found when the site was renovated. ❑

Map
on page
206

SOUTHEAST OF BANGKOK

*A short journey south from the center of Bangkok is the Samut Prakarn
Province, which thrives on theme parks that benefit from
Thailand's abundant culture and wildlife*

Samut Prakarn Province, near the river-mouth town of Paknam (Samut
Prakarn), is 30 km (20 miles) and about half an hour's drive southeast of
Bangkok. Although not on every tourist's itinerary, a trip out of the city to
this small area is well worthwhile if you can spare the time.

Breeding crocodiles

The **Crocodile Farm** ❾ (open daily, 7am–6pm; tel: 387 0020; entrance fee)
is located on the old Sukhumvit Highway (Route 3). Described as "a happy
marriage between wildlife conservation and commercial enterprise," there can
be no denying that some of the crocodiles are eventually skinned for handbags for wealthy ladies. But seeing the reptiles in natural surroundings is a
fascinating experience.

Started in the 1960s with an initial investment of about 10,000 baht (less than
US$300), the owner now has three farms (two in the northeast) worth 100 mil-
lion baht (US$2.8 million). At present, the Samut Prakarn farm has about 50,000
freshwater and saltwater local crocodiles (making it the largest crocodile farm
in the world), as well as some South American caimans and Nile River crocodiles. They are hatched in incubation cells and raised in tanks. The young must
be protected by netting from mosquitoes, which can
blind them by biting their eyes.

BELOW:
Crocodile Farm.

One of the highlights of a visit to the farm are the
eight shows a day (from 9–11am and 1–4pm) in
which handlers enter a pond teeming with crocodiles
to wrestle them, including placing their heads in the
beasts' mouths. While this sounds dangerous, the
lethargic, cold-blooded reptiles are more likely to bite
because their nap has been interrupted, rather than
through innate viciousness. After the crocodiles are
skinned, their meat is sold to restaurants in Samut
Prakarn and Bangkok, while artifacts made from their
skin are on sale at the farm's shops.

The farm also has a well-maintained zoo featuring
tigers, chimpanzees, ostriches, camels and elephants,
and an amusement park with rides, including a miniature train. The irony of the Crocodile Farm –which
touts itself as the biggest of its kind in the world – is
that the owners have succeeded in preserving the reptile; nearly all wild Asian species have been hunted to
extinction.

Ancient City

A few kilometers from the Crocodile Farm, is the
Muang Boran ❿ (Ancient City; open daily, 8am–
5pm; entrance fee) which bills itself as the world's
largest outdoor museum. The brainchild of a Bangkok
millionaire with a passion for Thai art and history, it

took around three years to construct. In what used to be 80 hectares (200 acres) of rice fields, designers sketched an area roughly the shape of Thailand and placed the individual attractions as close to their real sites as possible. There are replicas – some full-size, most one-third the size of the originals – of famous monuments and temples from all parts of the kingdom. Some are reconstructions of buildings that no longer exist, such as the Grand Palace and Royal Chapel of Ayutthaya, others are copies of buildings such as the temple of Khao Phra Viharn on the Thai-Cambodian border. Experts from the National Museum worked as consultants to ensure historical accuracy of the reproductions.

At present, there are more than 60 monuments, covering 15 centuries of Thai history. There is a lot to see here and you may like to spend a whole day looking around. Also, the monuments are spread over a large area; it may be most convenient to drive between them. However, the grounds are beautifully landscaped with small waterfalls, creeks, ponds, rock gardens and lush greenery, and deer graze freely among the interesting sculptures representing figures from Thai literature and Hindu mythology.

Paknam

Paknam is a bustling fishing town with an interesting market along its docks, not to mention seafood restaurants famed around the country for their fresh produce. Cross the river by ferry to **Wat Phra Chedi Klang Nam** ⑪ (open daily; entrance free), which, contrary to its name ("*chedi* in the middle of the river") is now on solid land, the result of the river shifting its course. Thai kings used to stop at this temple en route to state visits abroad, praying for success in their journeys or thanks on their return. ❏

TIP

In addition to the monuments, the Ancient City also has a model Thai village, in which artisans work on handicrafts such as lacquerware, ceramics, and paper umbrellas.

BELOW:
Ancient City.

AYUTTHAYA: NORTH OF BANGKOK

Maps:
Area 206
City 216

Ayutthaya's full name in Thai is "Phra Nakhon Si Ayuthaya" (Sacred City of Ayodhya), reflecting the fact that Ayutthaya was for centuries the undisputed capital of the kingdom

Were one ignorant of the importance and history of **Ayutthaya** , one would nonetheless be impressed by the beauty and grandeur of this city built by 33 Ayutthayan kings over 400 years. From the ruins, it is easy to appreciate the genius of the kings who built it. Located 85 km (55 miles) north of Bangkok, Ayutthaya was laid out at the junction of three rivers: Chao Phraya, Pa Sak, and Lopburi. Engineers had only to cut a canal across the loop of the Chao Phraya to create an island. Canals were also constructed as streets; palaces and temples were erected alongside.

Foundations of Ayutthaya

Ayutthaya was founded around 1350 by a prince of U-Thong. Thirty years later, the kingdom of Sukhothai was under Ayutthaya rule, which then spread to Angkor in the east, and to Pegu, in Burma, to the west. It was one of the richest cities in Asia by the 1600s – exporting rice, animal skins, ivory – and with a population of one million, greater than that of contemporary London. Merchants came from Europe, the Middle East and elsewhere in Asia to trade in its markets. Europeans wrote awed accounts of the fabulous wealth of the courts and of the 2,000 temple spires clad in gilded gold.

LEFT: *chedi* of Wat Phra Ram, Ayutthaya.
BELOW: ornate ceiling of a *wat*.

Thirty-three kings left their mark on the old capital before Burmese invaders despoiled it in 1767. Yet, very impressive remnants of Ayutthaya's rich architectural and cultural achievements can still be seen. As fast as it rose to greatness, it collapsed, suffering a destruction so complete that it was never rebuilt. Burmese armies had been pounding on its doors for centuries before occupying it for a period in the 16th century. Siamese kings then expelled them and reasserted independence. In 1767, however, the Burmese triumphed again. In a rampage, they burned and looted, destroying most of the city's monuments, and enslaving, killing, or scattering the population.

Within a year, Ayutthaya was nearly a ghost town, its population reduced to fewer than 10,000 inhabitants. Even after the Burmese garrison was defeated, Ayutthaya was beyond repair, a fabled city left to crumble into dust. Today, the ruins stand on the western half of the island, with the modern city of Ayutthaya concentrated on the eastern side. The city ruins are open daily between 8am–4.30pm; and small entrance fee usually is charged.

Start close to the junction of the Nam Pa Sak and Chao Phraya rivers, passing by the imposing **Wat Phanan Choeng** . Records suggest that the *wat*

was established 26 years prior to Ayutthaya's foundation in 1350. The temple houses a huge seated Buddha, so tightly crowded against the roof that he appears to be holding it up. Wat Phanan Choeng was a favorite with Chinese traders, who prayed there before setting out on long voyages; it still has an unmistakably Chinese atmosphere.

Ayutthaya was at one time surrounded by stout walls, only portions of which remain. One of the best-preserved sections is at **Phom Phet**, across the river from Wat Phanan Choeng. Upstream from Wat Phanan Choeng, the restored **Wat Buddhaisawan** **Ⓑ** (Phutthaisawan) stands serenely on the riverbank. Seldom visited, it is quiet, and the landing is an excellent place to enjoy the river's tranquility in the evenings. Farther upstream, the restored Cathedral of St Joseph is a Catholic reminder of the large European population that lived in the city at its prime.

Where the river bends to the north is one of Ayutthaya's most romantic ruins, **Wat Chai Wattanaram** **Ⓒ**, erected in 1630. Perched high on a pedestal in front of the ruins, a Buddha keeps solitary watch. The stately *prang* with its surrounding *chedi* and rows of headless Buddhas make a fine contrast to the restored **Queen Suriyothai Chedi** **Ⓓ** on the city side of river. Dressed as a man, the valiant Ayutthaya queen rode into battle, her elephant beside that of her husband. When she saw him attacked by a Burmese prince, she moved between them with her elephant and received a lance blow intended for her husband.

Chan Kasem Palace **Ⓔ**, known as the Palace of the Front, was originally constructed outside the city walls, close to the junction of the rivers and the new canal. King Naresuen built it as a defensive bastion while he was engaged in wars against his northern rivals from Chiang Mai. In 1767, the Burmese

Wat Phra Sri Sanphet, one of the numerous temples to see.

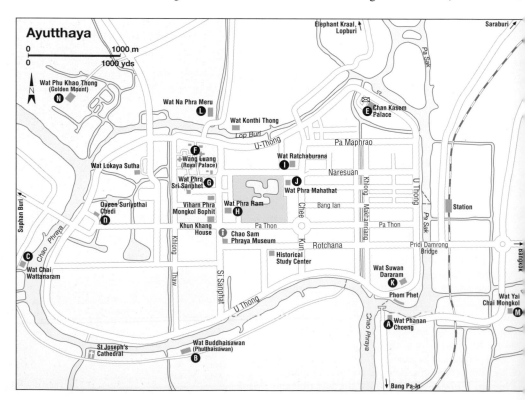

destroyed the palace, but King Mongkut later resurrected it in the 19th century as a royal summer retreat for escaping the lowland heat. Now housing a small museum (open daily, 9am–4pm; entrance fee), the palace looks out on the noisiest part of the modern town.

Map on page 216

The Royal Palace

The old royal palace, **Wang Luang ⑤** (Royal Palace), was of substantial size, if the foundations for the stables of 100 elephants are any indication. It was later razed by the Burmese. The bricks were removed to Bangkok to build its defensive walls, so only remnants of the foundations survive to mark the site. Close by stand the three *chedi* of **Wat Phra Sri Sanphet ⑥**, a royal temple built in 1491 that honors three 15th-century kings. The identical restored *chedi* stand in regal contrast to the surrounding ruins.

For two centuries after Ayutthaya's fall, a huge bronze Buddha sat unsheltered near Wat Phra Sri Sanphet. Its flame of knowledge and one of his arms had been broken when the roof, set on fire by the Burmese, collapsed. Based on the original, a new building, the **Viharn Phra Mongkol Bophit**, was built in 1956 around the restored statue.

Across the road to the east, **Wat Phra Ram ⑦** is one of Ayutthaya's oldest temples. Founded in 1369 by the son of Ayutthaya's founder, its buildings dating from the 1400s have been restored twice. Elephant gates punctuate the old walls, and the central terrace is dominated by a crumbling *prang* to which clings a gallery of stucco *naga*, *garuda*, and Buddha statues. The reflection of Wat Phra Ram's *prang* shimmers in the pool that surrounds the complex. Once a marshy swamp, the pool was dug to provide landfill for the temple's foundations.

BELOW: reclining Buddha, outside Ayutthaya.

Two of Ayutthaya's finest temples stand side by side across the lake from Wat Phra Ram. Built in 1424 by the seventh king of Ayutthaya as a memorial to his brothers, the well-known **Wat Ratchaburana** ❶ dominates its surroundings. Excavations during its restoration in 1958 revealed a crypt containing gold jewelry, Buddha images and other art objects, among them a charming, intricately-decorated elephant – all probably the property of the interned brothers. These treasures are now kept in the **Chao Sam Phraya Museum** (open daily, 9am–4pm; entrance fee), to the south. In addition, what may be Thailand's finest ancient paintings cover the walls of the crypt.

Opposite Chao Sam Phraya Museum stands the **Ayutthaya Historical Study Center** (Rotchana Road; open Wed–Sun; 9am–4.30pm; entrance fee). Funded by Japanese government, the modern building houses hi-tech exhibits which guide visitors through centuries of city development, trade, administration and social changes over the 400 years of the Ayutthaya period.

On the corner of Chee Kun and Nareauan roads is **Wat Phra Mahathat** ❶, one of the most beautiful temple complexes in Ayutthaya, and one of its oldest, dating from the 1380s. Its glory is its huge *prang*, which originally stood 46 meters (150 ft) high. The *prang* later collapsed, but it was rebuilt 4 meters (13 ft) higher than before. Stone Buddha faces, each a meter in height, stand silently around the ruins. Together with the restored *chedi* that ring the *prang*, these combine to make this one of the most impressive sites in Ayutthaya. Next door, the government has built a model of how the royal city may have once looked. **Wat Suwan Dararam** ❶, built near the close of the Ayutthaya period, has been beautifully restored. The foundations of the *bot* dip in the center, in emulation of the graceful deck line of a boat. This typical Ayutthayan decoration

BELOW: the restored Wat Phra Ram.

is meant to suggest a boat that carries pious Buddhists to salvation. Delicately carved columns support the roof, and the interior walls are decorated with brilliantly-colored frescoes. Still used as a temple, the *wat* is magical in the early evening as the monks chant their prayers.

Map on page 216

Crossing the River

Across the river from the old palace stands another restored temple, **Wat Na Phra Meru** . Here, a large stone Buddha is seated in the "European fashion" on a throne, a sharp contrast to the yoga position of most seated Buddhas. Found in the ruins of Wat Mahathat, the statue is believed to be one of five that originally sat in a recently-unearthed Dvaravati-period complex in Nakhon Pathom. The *bot* contains an Ayutthaya-style seated Buddha on the altar. Across a bridge from Wat Na Phra Meru are the ruins of Wat Konthi Thong.

To the east is **Wat Yai Chai Mongkol** ⓜ, originally established in the mid-1300s. In single-handed combat on elephant-back, King Naresuan slew the crown prince of Burma in 1592. The immense *chedi*, built to match the Phu Khao Thong Pagoda just north of Ayutthaya, celebrates the victory.

Just north of Ayutthaya, the **Wat Phu Khao Thong** ⓝ, better known as the **Golden Mount**, stands with its 80-meter-high (260-ft) *chedi* alone amidst the rice fields, its upper terraces commanding a panoramic view of the countryside. While the *wat* dates from 1387, the *chedi* was built by the Burmese after their earlier and less destructive conquest in 1569. It was later remodeled by the Siamese in their own style. In 1957, to mark 2,500 years of Buddhism, a 2,500-gram (5.5-lb) gold ball was mounted on top of the *chedi*. In the opposite direction from the Golden Mount, the road runs to the only **elephant kraal** left in

IN THE EVENT OF UNFAIR TRADING PLEASE NOTIFY ATP
AYUTTHAYA TOURIST POLICE
(ATP)

The tourist police can be found opposite Chao Sam Museum on Si Sanphet Road (open daily 8.30am–4.30pm; tel: 246077 or 246076)

BELOW: canal-side homes.

Thailand. This 16th-century kraal is a reminder of the days when elephants were not only caught and trained to work in the jungles, but were also an essential requisite for a strong army. The last elephant roundup was in 1903. Standing at the edge of the restored stockade with its huge teak columns, one can imagine the thunder of the mighty beasts.

Bang Pa-In , a charming collection of palaces and pavilions once used as a royal summer retreat, lies a short distance downriver from the ruins of Ayutthaya. The rulers of Ayutthaya used Bang Pa-in as long ago as the 17th century, but the buildings one sees today date from the late 19th- and early 20th-century reigns of Rama V and Rama VI, who used to come up from Bangkok. The attractive palace, a mixture of Italian and Victorian styles built by Rama V, is closed to the public, but visitors can tour an ornate Chinese-style palace in which the king stayed during visits. A Thai-style pavilion called the Aisawan Tippaya Asna, in the middle of the adjacent lake as one enters the grounds, is regarded as one of the finest examples of Thai architecture.

Lopburi

The former summer capital of Siam, **Lopburi** lies 150 km (100 miles) north of Bangkok, a four-hour drive through the fertile rice bowl of Thailand. Just 10 km (6 miles) north of Ayutthaya, the hills of the Korat Plateau appear on the horizon, the first break in the flatness of the central plains. It was not until the mid-1600s that Ayutthaya became a bustling international city with upward of three dozen nationalities represented. Some French architects even ventured to Lopburi, where King Narai retreated each summer to escape Ayutthaya's heat. The grounds of the **Lopburi Palace** (also called King Narai's Palace, or **Narai**

BELOW:
elephant roundup
at Ayutthaya's
kraal, 1895.

Ratchaniwet), built between 1665 and 1677, are enclosed by massive walls, which still dominate the center of the modern town. The palace grounds have three sections enclosing its official, ceremonial and residential buildings. The outer grounds contained the facilities for utilities and maintenance. Moving inward, the middle section enclosed the Dusit Maha Prasat Hall, Chantra Paisan Pavilion, and Phiman Mongkut Pavilion. The inner courtyard was that of the king, where his residence, Suttha Sawan Pavilion, nestled amid gardens and ponds. Of King Narai's buildings, the only one that has substantially survived is the **Dusit Maha Prasat Hall**. This was built for the audience granted by the king in 1685 to the ambassador of Louis XIV. It is recorded that the walls of the front structure were paneled with mirrors given by the French king. Holes for the mirrors can still be seen.

Near the Dusit Maha Prasat Hall is the **Phiman Mongkut Pavilion**, a three-story mansion in the colonial style, built in the mid-19th century by King Mongkut. The immensely thick walls and high ceilings show how the summer heat was averted before air-conditioning arrived. The mansion, small but full of character, displays a mixture of bronze statues, Chinese and Sukhothai porcelain, coins, Buddhist fans, and shadow play puppets. Some of the pieces, particularly the Ayutthaya bronze heads and Bencharong porcelain, are superb. Another surviving building of the Narai period is the Chantra Paisan Pavilion, also in the palace grounds. It was the first structure built by King Narai, and later restored by King Mongkut. The remains of a grand palace in Lopburi, said to have belonged to Constantine Phaulkon, rival those of the royal palace. Located just north of Narai's residence, the buildings show European influences, with straight-sided walls and decorations over Western-style windows. ❑

Map on page 206

TIP

Thais call Lopburi the City of Monkeys, after the monkey warrior Hanuman's legendary reign over the city in reward for helping King Rama defeat of the demon king in the tales of the *Ramayana*.

BELOW: Phaulkon's palace, Lopburi.

NORTHEAST OF BANGKOK

The area to the northeast of the capital offers rare glimpses of native rainforest, as well as the opportunity to canoe on waterfall-fed rivers and spot various indigenous animals

Map on page 206

The most scenic route to the northeast province is Route 305, which branches off Route 1 (Friendship Highway) just north of Rangsit, 30 km (20 miles) north of Bangkok. This wide road runs northeast along a lovely canal, passing rice paddy fields and small rivers to reach the provincial capital of Nakhon Nayok.

Nakhon Nayok and Salika Falls

The eastern province of **Nakhon Nayok** ⓰ is just 140 km (90 miles) from the capital, and has long been overshadowed by the more famous tourist destinations in Thailand – so much so that it is often referred to as "Nakhon Nowhere." In fact, nothing could be further from the truth. Thai visitors have recognized its abundant attractions – its natural forests, craggy gorges and tumbling waterfalls, and its temperate climate and tranquil setting which offer a rare respite from the simmering heat and chaos of the city.

LEFT: Hew Narok waterfall in Khao Yai National Park. **BELOW:** Sambar deer stag, Khao Yai National Park.

Other than a glimpse of a typical rural center, however Nakhon Nayok as a town does not have much to offer. From the town center, Route 33 heads northwest and then, within just a few kilometers, a second road leads off to the right toward two waterfalls, one of which is **Salika Falls**.

Near the parking lot are several pleasant outdoor restaurants and stalls selling fresh fruits and drinks. The waterfall itself is impressive around the end of the rainy season, from September to November. But remember to wear sturdy shoes; the stone paths are notoriously slippery.

Wang Takrai Park

En route to the nearby Wang Takrai Park is the **Temple of Chao Pau Khun Dan** (open daily; entrance free), named after one of King Naresuan's advisors whose spirit is believed to protect the area.

Prince Chumbhot (of Suan Pakkad Palace in Bangkok) established the 80-hectare (195-acre) **Wang Takrai Park** (open daily; entrance fee) in the 1950s; a statue of him stands on the opposite bank of the small river flowing through the park. His wife, Princess Chumbhot, planted many varieties of flowers and trees, including some imported species.

Cultivated gardens sit among tall trees, which line both banks of the main stream flowing through the 2-km (1-mile) area of the park. For those wishing to stay overnight in the area, attractive bungalows are available for rent.

If you have time before returning to Bangkok have dinner at the park restaurant. Just outside the park entrance, the road on the left crosses a river and continues 5 km (3 miles) to **Nang Rong Falls**, an

inviting three-tiered cascade situated in a steep valley. Canoeing day-trips along the river can be arranged during the wet season. Any of the guest bungalows in the area will have information.

Khao Yai National Park

Khao Yai National Park ⓰ (open daily; entrance fee) is the nearest hill resort to Bangkok. It lies 200 km (125 miles) north of the capital, and covers 2,000 sq. km (770 sq. miles). Established in 1962, it is the oldest national park in Thailand, and the area around Khao Yai had been a notorious forest refuge for gangsters. Because of its proximity to Bangkok, its visitors are approaching 1 million each year.

This cool retreat boasts bungalows, motels, restaurants, an 18-hole golf course, and many nature trails and roads. It takes about three hours to drive to **Khao Yai** (Big Mountain) from Bangkok, via one of two routes.

The long route leads up Route 1. Just before entering Sara Buri, about 110 km (70 miles) from the capital, a right turn onto the Friendship Highway (Route 1) eventually ends up at the foot of the park. The road climbs and twists among the hills for 15 km (9 miles) until it reaches **Nong Khing Village**. Here you can dine at the Khao Yai Restaurant and check out the accommodations.

The second route requires driving to Nakhon Nayok via the roads described above. Just beyond Nakhon Nayok, a road leads to the left for about 50 km (30 miles) along a twisting road to the park headquarters.

Accommodation in the park can be booked through the tourist office in Bangkok (*see Travel Tips, page 264*). If camping, notify the park officials at the headquarters of your whereabouts and make sure you bring adequate mosquito

TIP

Although Khao Yai's waterfalls are best in the wet season, the area is prone to flash-floods, making swimming dangerous. In the early 1990s several visitors died following a deluge on what had been a balmy afternoon moments before.

BELOW:
banyan trees.

nets and insect repellent. Dormitory-style accommodation is also available and camping out in one of the observation towers may also be a possibility. The State Railways of Thailand also offer a day-trip every Saturday at reasonable rates, starting from Hua Lamphong Railway Station in central Bangkok (tel: 225 0300 for further details).

Wildlife and waterfalls

Khao Yai's highest peaks lie in the east along a landform known as the Korat Plateau. **Khao Laem** (Shadow Mountain) is 1,350 meters (4,430 ft) high and **Khao Kaeo** (Green Mountain), 1,020 meters (3,350 ft). Evergreen and decid-uous trees, palms and bamboo provide ample greenery throughout the park; unlike much of Thailand, patches of indigenous rainforest can still be seen here. Monkeys, gibbons and langurs are the wildlife most commonly seen. Wild, but not considered dangerous, are the bears, guars, boars and deer that roam the huge, protected reserve, and other large mammals including leopards and other large cats have been sighted. Khao Yai is also home to approximately 200 ele-phants and a few dozen tigers, but they are rarely seen. In addition, over 300 species of migrant birds have been identified. After dark, the park conducts "hunts" in large trucks, shining spotlights on night-feeding animals such as deer. At night, winter temperatures may drop to below 15°C (60°F) so make sure you have warm clothes handy. More than 50 km (30 miles) of marked trails criss-cross the park, most of them originally forged and still used by elephants. In several clearings, there are observation towers to watch animals feed.

Other attractions in the park include the Hew Narok and Hew Sawat water-falls, which can easily be reached from the park headquarters. ❑

Map on page 206

Elephant crossing road sign, Khao Yai National Park.

BELOW: happy campers at Khao Yai National Park.

UPCOUNTRY

*Take time out from the city to discover Thailand's sprawling
ruins, dense rainforest and spectacular beaches*

Regardless of which compass heading one follows in escaping the Bangkok area, one is often said to be going "upcountry," even if traveling south. Finding someplace beyond the magnetic pull of Bangkok is exceedingly simple, as diversity and contrast characterize both Thailand's people and its geography. Within an area of 514,000 sq. km (198,450 sq. miles) – roughly the size of France – set in the center of the political jigsaw puzzle of Southeast Asia are tropical rain forests, broad rice plains and forest-clad hills – and those ever-seductive beaches and warm waters in the south.

In the Central Plains to the north of Bangkok, several major rivers flow through the fertile land. Most notable of these is the Chao Phraya, which winds down from the north to nurture the rice before slicing through the center of Metropolitan Bangkok and emptying into the Gulf of Thailand.

The course of the Chao Phraya is that of Thailand's history: the Angkor-style towers of Lopburi, where the Khmers once ruled; the spectacular history of Sukhothai, perhaps the finest era in the nation's long history; the ruins of Ayutthaya farther south and just north of Bangkok; and then Bangkok itself.

Farther to the north still, Chiang Mai nestles at the foot of the highlands, and has become one of Thailand's most popular visitor destinations. Travelers seek both the natural ambience of the northern regions and the diversity of the region's hilltribes.

South along the Gulf of Thailand coast, Pattaya offers expansive beaches, lively nightlife, and superb waters just a few hours from downtown Bangkok. Once the resort gem of Asia, Pattaya has slid into the shadow of Ko Samui and Phuket. But it is undergoing an overhaul in both image and facilities, and may one day regain its dominant resort standing.

Phuket, of course, has become synonomous with both beach laziness and resort nightlife. The island has managed to establish an appeal for just about any type of traveler, whether moneyed aristocrat or frugal backpacker. Neighboring areas such as Ko Phi Phi and Krabi are increasingly pulling visitors from Phuket, although one sometimes wonders if, like Bangkok's traffic, anyone has given the consequences any thought.

On the other side of the isthmus from Phuket is Ko Samui, once the enclave of budget travelers seeking the end of the earth and now, for better or worse, seducing the first-class traveler, while the trendsetting young crowd have moved on to Ko Pha Ngan, internationally famous for its monthly full-moon rave parties. ❏

PRECEDING PAGES: limestone islands near Phuket.
LEFT: the idyllic waters of Ko Phi Phi.

SUKHOTHAI

The importance of the many temples of Sukhothai have turned the city into a historical site; nearby are national parks that illustrate the beauty of the Thai countryside

Maps
City: 232
Area: 233

The route to the ancient city of **Sukhothai** ❶ (Dawn of Happiness) passes through "new" Sukhothai, a modern town of concrete shops, 427 km (267 miles) north of Bangkok. A further 10 km (7 miles) on, the road enters the limits of old Sukhothai, through the **Kamphaenghak** Ⓐ (Broken Wall Gate); the authorities chose to run the road directly through the ruins, rather than around them.

Near the gate is the **Ramkamhaeng National Museum** Ⓑ (open daily, 8.30am–4pm; entrance fee), which has an extensive collection of sculpture, ceramics and other art objects found in the area.

The Sukhothai Kingdom began in 1240, when King Intradit drove away the Khmers. It grew to include most of modern-day Thailand and parts of the Malay Peninsula and Burma, and was synonymous with some of the finest artistic endeavors in Thai history, including many exquisite Buddha images. Unfortunately the golden age was short-lived – just two centuries and nine reigns long. The upstart Ayutthaya absorbed Sukhothai in 1438. The most notable Sukhothai king was King Ramkamhaeng, who, among other accomplishments, developed the Thai script, introduced Theravada Buddhism and solidified links with China.

LEFT: Wat Mahathat.
BELOW: standing Buddha at Wat Saphan Hin.

The remains of ancient Sukhothai's massive walls reveal that the inner city was protected by three rows of earthen ramparts and two moats. The north and south walls are each 2,000-meters (6,500-ft) long, while the east and west are 1,600-meters (5,200-ft) long. They are divided by four gates. The city was begun by Khmers, who left behind three buildings and the beginnings of a water system, similar to that of Angkor Wat in Cambodia.

After the Angkorian Empire began shrinking, the Khmers abandoned the ancient Sukhothai and the Thais moved in, building their own structures. They eschewed the intricate Khmer irrigation system, installing a much less complex one of their own. It is suggested that water, or the lack of it, in part contributed to the city's demise. It is possible that the city was originally served by the Yom River, which later shifted course and deprived Sukhothai of a dependable source of water.

Palaces and temples

The **Sukhothai Historical Park** (open daily, 6am–6pm; tel: 055 611110; entrance fee) is located near Wat Phra Phai Luang about 12 km (7½ miles) from the modern town. Buses run between the new town and the park entrance daily; bicycles can be hired at the park and are a good way of getting about.

Within the walls of Sukhothai are the ruins of the royal palace and some twenty *wats* and monuments; the greatest of which is **Wat Mahathat** Ⓒ (open

BELOW: seated Buddha at Wat Si Chum.

daily), with a customary main *chedi* in a lotus-bud shape. At the base of the *chedi* stand Buddhist disciples in adoration, and on a pedestal are seated Buddha images. It is not known who started this shrine but it is presumed to have been the first king of Sukhothai. Wat Mahathat owes its present form, however, to a remodeling completed by King Lo Thai, in about 1345.

Wat Sri Sawai ⑩ (open daily), southwest of Wat Mahathat, was originally a Hindu shrine that contained an image of Shiva. Triple towers remain, built in a modified Khmer style; the stucco decoration, added to the towers in the 15th century, shows mythical birds and divinities.

Wat Sra Sri ⑪ (open daily), on the way to the southern gate of the city, has a Sri Lankan-style *chedi*. The ordination hall (*bot*) lies on an island to the east of the spire. The ruins of the main shrine consist of six rows of columns, which lead to a restored, seated Buddha image. **Wat Chana Songkhram** (open daily) and **Wat Trakuan** (open daily), located north of Wat Mahathat, also have fine Sri Lankan-style *chedi*, of which only the lower parts survive. Wat Trakuan also has many bronze images of the Chiang Saen period.

Leaving the walled city by the northern **San Luang** (Royal Shrine Gate), after 1 km (half a mile), one arrives at the important shrine of **Wat Phra Phai Luang** ⑫ (open daily). It originally consisted of three laterite towers covered with stucco, probably built in the late 12th century. This shrine might have been the original center of Sukhothai, since Wat Mahathat is of a later period. A seated stone Buddha image, dated to 1191 and the reign of the Khmer King Jayavarman VII, was found here and is now in the grounds of the Ramkamhaeng Museum. During restoration in the 1960s, a large stucco image of Buddha in the central tower collapsed, disclosing many smaller images inside. Some date

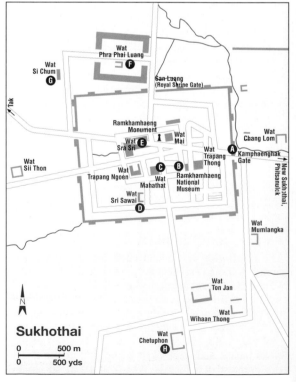

Sukhothai

these to the second half of the 13th century. Beyond Wat Phra Phai Luang is **Wat Si Chum G** (open daily), which has one of the largest seated Buddha images in the kingdom.

Map on page 232

The *mondop* (enclosing shrine) was built in the second half of the 14th century, but the image itself, called Phra Achana ("The Venerable") is believed to be the one mentioned in King Ramkamhaeng's inscription. There is a stairway within the walls of the *mondop* that leads to the roof (larger persons should not attempt to ascend the narrow passage). The ceiling of the stairway is made up of more than 50 carved slate slabs illustrating scenes from Buddhist folklore, to turn the climbing of the stairs into a symbolic ascent to Buddhahood.

There is a story that troops gathered here before an ancient battle and were inspired by an ethereal voice that seemed to come from the Buddha itself. Some suggest it was a ploy by a general who hid one of his men on the stairway and instructed him to speak through one of the windows concealed by the body of the image; the effect was magical, however, and the soldiers routed the enemy.

The produce market in Old Sukhothai.

South Sukhothai

South of the walled city is another group of shrines and monasteries. One of the most interesting is **Wat Chetuphon H** (open daily), where the protecting wall of the *viharn* is made of slate slabs imitating wood. The gates are also formed of huge plates of slate mined in the nearby hills. On a small scale, they resemble the megaliths of England's Stonehenge. The moat bridges that surround the temple are also made of stone slabs. On the central tower of the *wat* are Buddha images in the standing, reclining, walking and sitting postures. The walking Buddha here is regarded as one of the country's finest.

BELOW:
Wat Chetuphon.

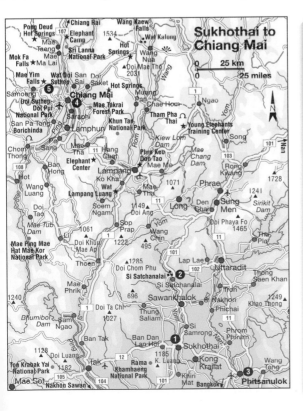

Map on page 233

TIP

Buddhist Ordination Ceremonies, with a spectacular parade of novice monks riding elephants, take place in Si Satchanalai every April 7–8 and should not be missed.

BELOW: Wat Chang Lom in Si Satchanalai.
RIGHT: temple attendant at Wat Mahathat.

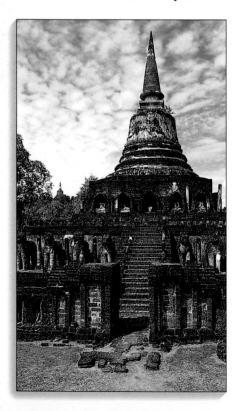

Si Satchanalai

About 50 km (35 miles) north of the modern town of Sukhothai, along a concrete highway, lies the old city of **Si Satchanalai ❷**, on the banks of the Yom River. Founded in the mid-13th century, it served as the seat of the viceroys of Sukhothai and was always mentioned as the twin city of the capital. Whereas restoration, removal of trees, and the installation of lawns have removed some of the grandeur of Sukhothai, Si Satchanalai's setting gives it an aura few other ancient sites have. It is a pleasure to wander through the wooded complex, rounding a corner and being surprised by a new *wat* or monument.

The first and most important monument is **Wat Chang Lom** (open daily; entrance fee). There can be little doubt that this is the "Elephant-girdled Shrine" described in King Ramkamhaeng's stone inscription. The great king records that he started to build it in 1285 to house some holy relics of the Lord Buddha, and that it was finished six years later. It is the only surviving stupa that can be attributed with certainty to King Ramkamhaeng. Built of laterite and stucco, it is a large bell-shaped Sri Lankan-style spire standing on a two-story, square basement. The upper tier contains niches for Buddha images, now mostly empty, while the lower level contains 39 elephant caryatids.

Si Satchanalai is also associated with the famed Sawankhalok ceramics, which were among Thailand's first export products. The brown bowls and their distinctive double-fish design were sent to China aboard junks; remains of them have been found off the coast of Pattaya. It is still possible to buy genuine antique Sawankhalok ceramics in the area; most, however, are copies.

For a first-hand look at some of the excavated wares, visit the **Celadon Kiln Site Study and Conservation Center** (open daily; tel: 055 679211; entrance fee). The center is approximately 5 km (3 miles) to the north of the Si Satchanalai Historical Park.

Outside the city, the **Si Satchanalai National Park** (open daily, 8am–6pm; tel: 055 619214; entrance fee) offers high undulating mountains covered with tropical jungle, and several waterfalls, hot springs, and caves. Accommodation is also available.

Phitsanulok

Some 50 km (30 miles) southeast from Sukhothai, **Phitsanulok ❸** now has only a few mementoes of the past; a fire in the 1960s razed most of the old town except **Wat Phra Sri Ratana Mahathat** (open daily; entrance free), the principal shrine in Phitsanulok. The new city is a rather dull collection of concrete shop houses. However, nothing can detract from its superb location along the Nan River, with its quays shaded by flowering trees and its houseboats moored beside the steep banks. A daytime market that turns into night-time food stalls offers as good a spot as any to watch the world go by. It is located off Boromtrailokanart Road, near the clocktower in the center of town.

Phitsanulok serves as a central location for excursions into the countryside, with the **Namtok Chatrakhan National Park** (open daily; tel: 02 579 5734; entrance fee) and **Tung Salaengluang National Park** (open daily; tel: 01 978 0943; entrance fee), two good examples within a 100-km (60-mile) radius. ❏

CHIANG MAI

Thailand's northern city may have inherited some of the mass tourism of Bangkok, but it remains a traditional city, proud of its ancient history and cultural importance

Time and progress have wrought transformations on the once-remote "Rose of the North," Chiang Mai. However, despite new traffic jams, high-rise condominiums, mushrooming of industry and an influx of tourism, Chiang Mai remains an atmospheric and fascinating city.

Despite its increasingly rapid urbanization, 700-year-old **Chiang Mai** ❹ remains prized as a pleasant escape from the sticky humidity of Bangkok. Situated 305 meters (1,000 ft) above sea level in a broad valley divided by the picturesque 560-km-long (350-mile) **Ping River**, and nestled in the protecting embrace of a ring of mountains, the city reigned for seven centuries as the capital of the Lan Na Kingdom. The city's northern remoteness kept the region outside the rule of Bangkok well into the 20th century.

In its splendid isolation, Chiang Mai developed a culture quite removed from that of the Central Plains, with wooden temples of exquisite beauty and a host of unique crafts, including lacquerware, silverware, woodcarving, ceramics and umbrella-making. Its people pride themselves on a language and culture of their own that is both unique and intriguing.

Its dozen hilltribes only add to its luster as an exotic far-flung realm. Although hospitality of both the hilltribes and the northern Thais is being strained by the sheer numbers of visitors, they remain a gracious and friendly people adding a charm to Chiang Mai to be envied by many cities to the south.

In spite of being the second city in Thailand, with tourists and entrepreneurs alike eager to flee the high prices, chaos and pollution of Bangkok, 700 km (400 miles) to the south, Chiang Mai is still a tourist destination and a city that does not appear to have lost a sense of its own heritage.

Modern Chiang Mai

Although many visitors spend only a few days in Chiang Mai, once they are here there is much to see. Shopping is plentiful, diverse and relatively cheap. Governmental organizations are beginning to safeguard forests, turning them into nature reserves and parks. Industry and commerce have been less affected by the recent economic downturn and are booming to bring new wealth to its residents; and a new awareness of its own cultural heritage is bringing campaigns of preserving traditions and crafts.

Despite its size, modern Chiang Mai – anchored by the old city, which is defined by a moat and wall built in the 19th century – is an easy city to navigate. The town is dominated by the green **Doi Suthep**, a modest mountain 15 km (10 miles) to the northwest, looming protectively over the city. On its crown is a *wat*, which appears with crystalline clarity most days.

LEFT:
Wat Chedi Luang.
BELOW:
nipping about
in Chiang Mai.

Near the moat, a minibus fills with hardy trekkers setting off for Fang, 150 km (90 miles) to the north, and for jungle-trekking. Reflected in the water is a caravan of saffron-robed Buddhist monks on their morning alms walk. Padding silently on bare feet, they pause briefly before houses and shops, people putting rice and curries into their bowls.

The tourist area centers around **Ta Phae Gate**, with a number of hotels, shops and guesthouses. A new form of tourism is attracting many tourists to attend cooking classes, traditional massage courses, Thai kick-boxing schools and meditation groups. **Huai Kaeo Road** which leads to Doi Suthep, is also becoming a hub with new hotels, shopping malls, business centers and pubs.

The old city

The city's history began with **Wat Chiang Man Ⓐ** (Chiang Mai; open daily; entrance fee), translated as "foundation of the city." It was the first temple to be built by King Mengrai, who resided here during the construction of the city in 1296. Located in the northeast part of the old city, it is the oldest of Chiang Mai's 300-plus *wats*. Two ancient, venerated Buddha images are kept in the abbot's quarters and can be seen on request. *Phra Sae Tang Tamani* is a small 10-cm-high (4-in) crystal Buddha image taken by Mengrai to Chiang Mai from Lamphun, where it had reputedly resided for 600 years.

Apart from a short sojourn to Ayutthaya, the image has remained in Chiang Mai ever since. During Songkran (April 13–15) it is ceremonially paraded through the streets. The second image, a stone *Phra Sila Buddha* in bas-relief, is believed to have originated in India around the 8th century AD. Both statues are said to possess the power to bring rain to protect the city from fire.

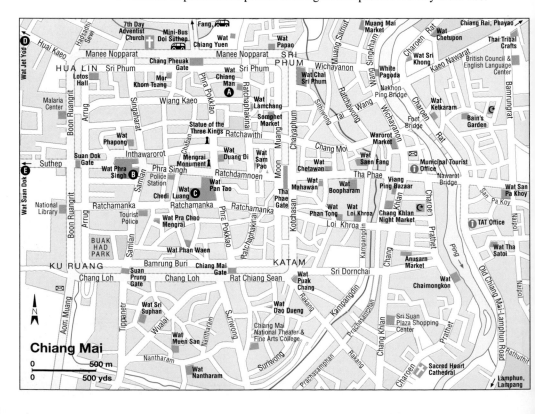

Chiang Mai

0   500 m
0   500 yds

Map on page 238

The only other important structure in Wat Chiang Man is *Chang Lom*, a 15th-century square *chedi* buttressed by rows of stucco elephants. Imperiously occupying the head of one of the city's principal streets is **Wat Phra Singh B** (open daily), Chiang Mai's largest temple. Founded in 1345, its thick walls shut out the urban bustle. Calamity is associated with **Wat Chedi Luang C** (open daily), built in 1401 to the east of Wat Phra Singh. A century and a half later, a violent earthquake shook its then 90-meter-high (295-ft) pagoda, reducing its height to 42 meters (140 ft). It was never rebuilt, although there have been attempts at restoration. But even in ruins, the colossal monument is impressive. For 84 years the Emerald Buddha was housed here before being moved to Vientiane. King Mengrai was reportedly killed nearby by a bolt of lightning. Close to the *wat*'s entrance stands an ancient, tall gum tree, whose longevity is tied to that of the city. When it falls, says a legend, so will the city. The *lak muang* (city boundary stone) in which the spirit of the city is said to reside, is near its base.

Located north of the city walls, **Wat Jet Yod D** (open daily) was completed by King Trailokaraja in 1455. As its name "Seven Spires" suggests, it is a replica of the Mahabodhi Temple in India's Bodhgaya, where Buddha gained enlightenment while spending seven weeks in its gardens. The beautiful stucco angels that decorate its walls are said to bear faces of Trailokaraja's own family. The Burmese severely damaged the temple during their invasion of 1566.

One of the most impressive city temple complexes is **Wat Suan Dok E** (open daily) to the west of the western gate. At its northwest corner are white-washed *chedi* containing the ashes of Chiang Mai's royal family; the huge central *chedi* is said to hold no fewer than eight relics of Buddha. **Wat Chetawan** (open daily), near the east gate, has three tiled *chedi* and mythical animals.

The calm interior of Golden Buddha, Wat Phra Singh.

BELOW: grounds of Wat Chiang Man.

Beyond the old city

A road leaves the old city at its northwest corner, passing the north's most famous educational institution, **Chiang Mai University**, officially opened in 1965 on a 200-hectare (600-acre) campus. Nearby, in Ratchamankla Park, is the **Tribal Research Center** (open Mon–Fri, 9am–4pm; tel: 053 210872; entrance free), a small ethnographical museum where one can compare the costumes and implements of several Thai hilltribes. A bit farther from the university is an arboretum with many species of northern Thai trees. Next to it is the **Chiang Mai Zoo** (open daily, 9am–5pm; entrance fee), started as a private collection by an American missionary in 1978. Given the extensive poaching in recent decades, it may contain more wild animals than the hills.

A steep series of hairpin curves rises 12 km (8 miles) up the flanks of Doi Suthep to Chiang Mai's best-known temple, **Wat Doi Suthep** ➎ (open daily). The site was selected in the mid-1300s by an elephant that was turned loose with a Buddha relic strapped to its back; the temple was built at the point at which it stopped and would go no further. From the parking area of Wat Doi Suthep the road ascends to **Phuping Palace**. When the royal family is absent the well-tended palace gardens are open to the public from Friday to Sunday and on offical holidays.

Hilltribes

There are still hundreds of hilltribe villages in Chiang Mai and north Thailand that remain untouched by tourism, where people live as they have lived for centuries. However, due to their fascinating lifestyle, there are some villages that have succumbed to crass commercialization. From the Phuping Palace entrance on Doi Suthep, the road continues through pine forests to the Meo hilltribe

The Hmong tribe village of Doi Pui offers visitors without the time to go deeper into the northern hills an example of hill-tribe life.

BELOW:
Wat Suan Dok.

village of **Doi Pui**. The village has been on the tourist track for some time, but recent improvements have brought benefits – perhaps – to its inhabitants, including a paved street hemmed by souvenir stands; with a bit of perseverance, it is possible to wander by the houses to see how the people live. The tribespeople have learned that visitors come bearing gifts, and a camera automatically triggers a hand extended for a donation.

Also in the village are the **Opium Museum** (open daily; entrance fee) which documents how opium is grown and processed, and the **Hilltribe Museum** (open daily; entrance fee) displaying implements used by the Hmong tribespeople in daily life.

Tourist attractions and festivals

Apart from temples and shopping, Chiang Mai has much to offer: elephant camps; orchid farms; snake farms; spectacular drives through mountains and rice valleys; and waterfalls accessible by car or mountain bike. The **National Museum** (open Wed–Sun 9am–4pm; entrance fee) houses an impressive display of antiques and artifacts .

The best time to visit Chiang Mai is in late November to early February, when it is abloom with a variety of beautiful flowers. Numerous resorts in nearby Mae Sa Valley carpet the hillsides with flower gardens, and each February the **Chiang Mai Flower Festival** fills the streets with floral parades. The **Songkran Festival** in April is when Chiang Mai turns into a center of arts and stages the world's biggest water fight. **Loy Krathong** during the full moon of November is also a time of festivities with hundreds of lanterns and fireworks illuminating thousands of floats on the Ping River. ❑

Map on page 233

TIP

The banks of the Ping River are lined with, lively restaurants and pubs. Fine Thai food or traditional Kantoke Lanna cuisine accompanied by Lanna dancing can be found all over the city. Nimmanhaemin Road is famous for its busy pubs and Huay Keaw Road for its discos.

BELOW:
Songkran Festival, Chiang Mai.

SOUTH TO PATTAYA

The coast southeast of Bangkok along the Gulf of Thailand offers travellers powdery beaches and turquoise seas, national parks and tropical island resorts

Map
on page
244

The main route along the Eastern Gulf Coast is Sukhumvit Highway, which becomes Route 3 outside of Bangkok. Route 3 officially originates at Bangkok's busy Ratchadamri intersection, at the Erawan Shrine. Eventually it leads to the Cambodian border.

Chonburi ❶, a sprawling and industrious town of about a quarter million merchants, traders and craftsmen, is but a lunch break or rest stop for most visitors on the way to Pattaya. However, Chonburi has its fair share of attractions. Just outside of town is **Wat Buddhabat Sam Yot** (open daily), Buddha's Footprint Mountain of Three Summits. Built amid green trees by an Ayutthayan king and renovated during the reign of King Chulalongkorn, this hilltop monastery was once used to conduct the water oath of allegiance, when princes and governors drank the waters of fealty, pledging loyalty to the throne.

Near the center of Chonburi, a colossal gold-mosaic image of Buddha dominates **Wat Dhamma Nimitr** (open daily). The largest image in the Eastern Gulf region, and the only one in the country depicting the Buddha in a boat, the 40-meter-high (135-ft) statue recalls the story of the Buddha's journey to the cholera-ridden town of Pai Salee. On the same hill is the local Chinese Buddhist Society, with the burial shrines of prominent Society members.

Most of Thailand's oyster population breeds off the Chonburi coast, and farther south along the gulf. But the coastal town is better known for its production of animal feed made from tapioca, which is grown in the region. During the 1970s and early 1980s, the area around Chonburi enjoyed a minor boom as a tapioca center. Within a few years, this crop, formerly cultivated only for local use, became the country's number-one foreign exchange earner.

South of Chonburi

On the road past Ang Sila, the beach at **Bang Saen** comes alive each weekend as hordes of Thai middle-class tourists descend in buses. A profusion of beach umbrellas, inner tubes and wrinkled watermelon rinds quickly cover the sandy beach, the surf filled with bobbing heads. At the Bang Saen Reservoir Bird Refuge (open daily; entrance fee), with permission it is possible to sit in a blind and observe waterfowl.

Up the hill behind the reserve is the **Khao Khieo Open Zoo** (open daily; entrance fee). Operated by Bangkok's Dusit Zoo, it presents animals in their natural setting; in one section, visitors can wander among deer, elephants and other wild animals. On the hill above are some simple, but comfortable, bungalows (contact Dusit Zoo for reservations tel: 281 2000). **Si Racha** ❷, south of Chonburi, descends from the hills and extends into the sea on tentacle-

LEFT: boat heading towards Ko Larn.
BELOW: unloading supplies after a downpour.

like piers. Its famous hot sauce – *nam prik si racha* – can be enjoyed at waterfront restaurants, where delicious and fresh shrimp, crab, oyster, mussel or abalone are dipped into the thick, tangy red liquid. An offshore rock supports a picturesque *wat* with Thai and Chinese elements. The footprint of the Buddha, cast in bronze, graces the *wat*, as do pictures of the goddess of mercy, Kuan Yin, and the Monkey God.

Thai Riviera

A few kilometers south of Si Racha is the beach resort of **Pattaya** ❸ the longest reigning premier resort in Thailand. Few areas in Asia have undergone such a precipitous rise to fame and plummet in popularity. This huge resort was once a quiet beach known only to a handful – just a few clusters of bungalows, a rough clubhouse for a group of sailing enthusiasts, some good seafood restaurants and a small fishing village that gave the place its name. But it had all the ingredients for success: a graceful, 4-km-long (2½-mile) crescent of golden sand lapped by gentle waves, warm tropical water, balmy breezes, tranquility.

By the 1970s, others were beginning to discover its charms. A new road cut travel time to two hours, bringing the resort within easy reach of Bangkok. Big hotels began to rise along the beach.

By the 1980s, Europeans flocked to its beaches, and those of Jomtien, the neighboring beach 4 km (2½ miles) south. In the capitals of Asia, a beach vacation anywhere but in Pattaya was unheard of. It fell on shady times, but Pattaya is attempting to change its reputation from a party town to a family resort. Indeed, with 20,000 hotel rooms and nearly 3 million visitors annually, Pattaya may soon again be a world-class beach resort. Pattaya's two busiest main

TIP

The *Pattaya Mail* newspaper is a good local source of information about things to do, nightlife, eating out and excursions.

BELOW:
Pattaya resort.

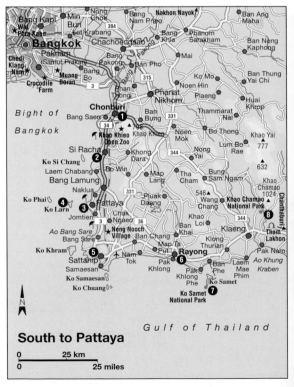

South to Pattaya

Gulf of Thailand

roads run parallel to the 4-km-long (2½-mile) bay. The northern portion of Beach Road is dominated by first-class hotels, restaurants and open-air bars. Second Road also has many hotels and restaurants interspersed with bars, discotheques, shows and other night spots. Numerous *soi* connecting the Beach Road and Second Road hold small hotels, restaurants and a number of bars.

Pattaya's hill separates the main resort area from an area of luxury hotels and private beaches. Farther south is the resort of **Jomtien**, with beaches only marginally better than Pattaya's. Here are bungalow complexes, some fine hotels and a host of good seafood and other restaurants. Pattaya and Jomtien are good locations for water sports lovers, with equipment for windsurfing, sailing, snorkeling and diving available for rent, along with jetskis, water scooters and waterskiing equipment. The brave may try parasailing, strapped into a parachute harness and towed aloft by a speedboat.

Off shore, **Ko Larn ❹** – identified in brochures as Coral Island but whose name translates as Bald Island – used to be known for its coral reefs. These have long since been destroyed by fishermen using dynamite to stun fish. Yet glass-bottomed boats still ferry visitors from the trawlers to the shore, their passengers peering in vain at the dead gray coral in the hope of seeing something alive and moving.

Ko Larn has the wide, soft sand beaches that Pattaya lacks and it is a wonderful place to spend a leisurely day. The shore is filled with good seafood restaurants, and there are water sports facilities for those who want to stir from their beach chairs. The island also has a golf course.

Year by year, visitors have been exploring farther and farther south of Pattaya, discovering new resort areas with perhaps less noise and crowds. One popular

Map on page 244

Local boats can take you to and from Ko Larn.

BELOW: mopeds for hire.

resist is **Nong Nooch Village**, a complex of bungalows situated in parkland around a lake, offering a wide variety of activities, including an elephant show, an orchid nursery and a cactus garden.

South of Pattaya

Overlooking a scenic bay sprinkled with small islands, the small fishing town of **Sattahip ❺**, about 20 km (13 miles) south of Pattaya, blossomed overnight to become an attractive, busy deep-water port. It now acts as a headquarters for the Thai navy. In the heart of town, a large and modern temple rests on turquoise pedestals, while in the commercial center, a boisterous market teems with fish, fruit and vegetables. Sattahip offers little more to do than stroll past the shops or sit in an open-front coffee shop sipping an *oliang* (the great local version of sweet iced coffee that came from French Cambodia). Enjoy a spicy curry near the market, or browse over teak elephants in the shops.

Situated 220 km (140 miles) from Bangkok is Thailand's newest industrial area, **Rayong ❻**. Apart from its industry, Rayong is famed for its *nam plaa* (fish sauce) the source of salt in Thai diets. *Nam plaa* is made from a small silver fish that abounds in the Gulf; it is decomposed for about seven months to produce a ruddy liquid, which is filtered and then bottled. Mixed with chili, it becomes *nam plaa prik*. The resorts in Rayong are on a strip of beach to the southeast of Rayong.

Idyllic isle no more

BELOW: the elephant show at Nong Nooch Village.

This scenic fishing port is sheltered on the west by a rocky outcrop, and by the 6-km-long (4-mile) island of **Ko Samet ❼** to the south. The island is remembered by students of Thai literature as the place where Sunthorn Phu, a

flamboyantly romantic court poet, retired to compose some of his works. Born in nearby Klaeng, Sunthorn called the island Ko Kaeo Phisadan, or "island with sand like crushed crystal."

Sunthorn's assessment was as practical as it was poetic; the island and the beaches of the mainland produce some of the finest sand in the world, a fact appreciated by glass makers. From a quiet poetic retreat, the island has gained popularity as a superb resort, but not without controversy. Cheap bungalow complexes are quickly being razed to build small hotels, and while the loss of budget lodging is to be regretted, the increasing garbage will not.

Most of the resort and bungalow development is, in fact, illegal. The island is part of a national park, and development along the coast has progressed despite the law. The government has virtually closed down the island several times, banning overnight stays. Locals claim it is their right to do what they want with the island. There is no question, however, that the island has lost its pristine appeal.

Further south on Route 3, the **Khao Chamao National Park** ❽ (open daily; entrance fee) has a waterfall with eight levels. Ascent is relatively easy with the aid of special bridges and walkways. Nearby are the **Khao Wong Caves**, about 60 in all, many of which are inhabited by Buddhist monks. One cave has been turned into a shrine with a replica of the Buddha's footprints. Villagers claim photographs shot from the mystic jagged peaks in the park invariably turn out blank when processed. Nothing in the gray-streaked outcrop suggests magical power; it dominates a valley of red dust and farmlands.

In Tam Plak, a hollow near the *wat*, water drips on the brow of a stalagmite image of Lord Buddha. Worshippers visit the cave to pray and light candles. ❏

Map on page 244

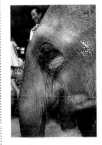

Elephants are no longer used for logging in Thailand but many are still domesticated and trained for transport.

BELOW: enjoying the water.

THE SOUTHERN ISLANDS

Countless islands are scattered along the narrow strip of land leading to Malaysia. Larger islands like Ko Samui and Phuket are developed for tourism; few of the many other islands are visited

Map on page 250

For decades, **Phuket**  was known to only a few. The long road south from Bangkok to reach it, the lack of a bridge across the causeway, bad roads on the island itself and a seeming disinterest in developing it for recreation meant that it languished in isolation – but a rich one with its tin deposits, rubber and coconuts – for decades.

In the 1970s, it began appearing on the maps of budget backpackers. Word spread, and eventually its airport was expanded to handle jets from Europe, Australia and elsewhere in Asia. Phuket's wealth, traditionally drawn from tin and rubber, comes today almost exclusively from tourism.

Urban Phuket

Unlike many provincial towns, **Phuket Town** has an identity of its own. The style is set by the beautiful colonial-style houses built by tin and rubber barons at the end of the 19th century, following a disastrous fire that destroyed the downtown area. Tours of these beautiful old buildings are available from several local agents. Three stories high, the rowhouses were built by middle-income Chinese to house their extended families. The ground floor normally serves as a shop and reception hall; the upper floors are the living quarters. The charm of Phuket's old buildings is complemented by the many Chinese shrines that accent the town with bright splashes of color. Of note is the brightly painted temple of **Jui Tui** and its smaller companion, Put Jaw, next door, which sit just past the market on the Ranong Road. The temple is the starting point for the five-day Phuket Vegetarian Festival each October.

Phuket's glory, however, lies in its many beautiful beaches, and it has a wealth of them. All are located on the western side of the island; the eastern shore is primarily of rocky shoals.

The most developed beach is **Patong**, due west of the town of Phuket and north of Karon. In the early 1970s, Patong was little more than a huge banana plantation wedged between the mountains and a wide crescent of sand. It has, however, made up for lost time, and with a vengeance. The banana plantation has been replaced by hotels, supermarkets, arcades, entertainment centers and a range of tourist amenities. Unlike most other Phuket beaches, Patong has a wide range of water sports facilities, including scuba diving, windsurfing, waterskiing, parasailing, jetskis, sailing and boogie boards. Dive shops offer trips into the bay or west to the Similan Islands National Marine Reserve, considered one of the best diving areas in Asia, with crystal-clear water and a multitude of marine life. One can also snorkel at Kata Noi, two beaches to the south, or at Phi Phi island, four hours

LEFT:
Ko Samui beach.
BELOW: limestone, or *karst*, pillars are common sights.

TIP

Phuket's most
important festival is
the Vegetarian Festival
which takes place in
late September or
October. Along with
the religious
celebrations, there are
firecrackers, dancing
and the occasional act
of self-mortification.

BELOW:
the picturesque
bay of Kata Noi.

east of Phuket. Patong has many restaurants specializing in Thai seafood. The prize item on the menu is the giant Phuket Lobster, weighing up to 3 kg (6 lb) and enough to feed two hungry diners.

The long **Bang Thao Beach** is dominated by the immense Laguna Phuket Resort, housing five resorts within a combined 1,300 guest rooms. Nai Yang beach, just south of the airport is now under the jurisdiction of **Sirinat National Park**. There are a few bungalows for rent in the national park and an offshore reef allows all-year round swimming in the shallow bay.

Beyond Nai Yang is Phuket's longest beach, **Mai Khao**. The 9-km-long (6-mile) beach is as yet undeveloped, despite attempts by entrepreneurs wishing to cover it in resorts. The thwarting concern is environmental. Here, every night from December to February, giant sea turtles still lay their eggs in deep holes they laboriously dig in the sand with their powerful flippers.

South of Patong is Relax Bay, with its single hotel, Le Meridien Phuket. Beyond is **Karon Beach**, and past a small ridge running a finger into the sea, Kata Beach. Karon has several large- and medium-sized hotels, but is otherwise occupied by a myriad of bungalows. Not as developed as Patong, Karon and Kata both have clean, wide beaches and water sport facilities. Karon even has enough wave action for surfing.

The picturesque bay of **Kata** is the site of Asia's second Club Med, a tribute to its beauty. There are other bungalow complexes, as well as some good restaurants, including The Boathouse, a small boutique bungalow retreat anchored by a renowned restaurant offering the island's best wine list. Water sports facilities are limited to windsurf boards, jetskis and sailboats. The coastal road continues along a ridge to **Nai Harn**, providing spectacular views for several

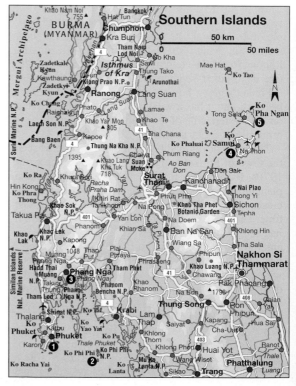

Map on page 250

kilometers along the coast. At the southwestern edge of Phuket, Nai Harn is one of the island's prettiest beaches. Nestled between two tall hills, fronted by a calm sea and backed by a lagoon, it is an idyllic setting. Its only resort is Mandarin Oriental's Phuket Yacht Club, boasting rooms with truly a view. Nai Harn is renowned for its sunsets.

South along the coast from the town of Phuket is **Rawai**. The town offers many good seafood snacks including local clams which are collected when the tide is low. Rawai also holds one of the island's two *chao lay*, or sea gypsy, villages. The sea gypsies were once nomadic fishing families, roaming from island to island. They are skilled fishermen both above and below the water. From a young age, they used to dive to great depths in search of giant lobsters, staying below for up to three minutes. However, recent environmental and tourism concerns have robbed the sea gypsies of their traditional fishing grounds, and now they live primarily on public assistance and handouts from tourists.

Phuket is the departure point for journeys to Ko Phi Phi, a few hours east by boat, and Phang Nga Bay to the north.

The shrub-covered limestone crag of Ko Phi Phi Ley.

Ko Phi Phi and Phang Nga

Turquoise waves caress a beach so dazzlingly white, it is almost painful to the eye. Colorful fishing boats seem suspended in midair, so crystalline is the water. With palm-fringed beaches and lofty limestone mountains as a backdrop, **Ko Phi Phi ❷** rivals Phuket as one of the most beautiful islands in Asia. Phi Phi lies equidistant, about 3 km (nearly 2 miles), from both Phuket and Krabi. It comprises two islands: the smaller **Phi Phi Ley**, a craggy limestone monolith similar to the other barren peaks of Phang Nga Bay, and **Phi Phi Don**, a national

BELOW: arriving at Ko Phi Phi.

park with an epicentre of anarchic tourism development. Ironically it is the unprotected Phi Phi Ley which remains envrinomentally pristine. The small population of Phi Phi Don, which once lived in quaint little fishing villages, has in the last decade sold the entire island to developers, and now the beaches are lined with tacky resorts and bungalow complexes. The pristine white sand is covered with lounging tourists, and the surf is often fouled with their garbage.

The only advantage in visiting Phi Phi lies offshore. While the reefs of Phuket were destroyed by tin mining before World War I, the reefs that surround Ko Phi Phi are still thriving. For the interested diver or snorkeler who prefers swimming from the beach rather than off a boat, Phi Phi provides days' worth of stunning underwater beauty. It is questionable, though, how long the reefs will survive.

The nearby Phi Phi Ley is renowned as a site for swallows who build their nests on the ceilings of rocky caverns. Men climb up precarious ladders to collect the swallows' nests, which are sold as delicacies to Chinese gourmets. Tours may be booked to view this gathering, although travelers should be aware that no demonstration is made in any cave that still hosts swallows.

One of the wonders of the world is **Phang Nga Bay ❸** – a collection of enormous limestone mountains that rise straight out of the sea. The boat winds among these on its way to the outer islands, leaving the traveler's imagination to drift and imagine animals and mythical beasts that the contorted shapes suggest. Just before the mouth of Phang Nga River, the boat approaches the base of Khao Kien mountain, where a cavern contains primitive paintings depicting human and animal forms. To the right lies a large rock island called Ko Pannyi, where an entire Muslim fishing village stands on stilts over the water. On what seems a collision course with a huge limestone outcrop, the boat slips into a

BELOW:
one of the caves
in Phang Nga Bay.

barely discernible, overgrown entrance of **Tham Lod cave**. For more than 50 meters (164 ft), the boat slides under giant stalactites. Rocks protruding from the water appear to have been sliced by a sword-wielding god.

In **Tham Nak cave**, a twisted stalagmite at the entrance resembles a *naga* serpent, giving this cave its name. Green stalactites burst from the ceiling like a frozen waterfall. The whole mountain-island seems, from the outside, to drip with streaked limestone.

Ko Talu receives its name from *talu*, meaning to pass from one side to the other – in this case, not over the mountain, but under it. The boat squeezes through a cave filled with stalactites. **Ko Khao Ping Gun** is perhaps the most spectacular of Phang Nga's islands. Behind the beach, the mountain seems to have split in two, the halves leaning against each other. Locals say they are two lovers. A small staircase leads to a cavern above the water; limestone formations look like large mounds of spilled glue. Well, maybe. This area was the setting for part of the 1974 James Bond movie, *The Man with the Golden Gun*. A small beach overlooks another island, **Ko Tapoo**, or Nail Island, which looks like a thorny spike driven into the sea.

Ko Samui

In the last few years, the **Ko Samui ❹** archipelago of over 80 islands has captured the imagination of travelers seeking perhaps the definitive tropical island. The 250-sq. km (100-sq. miles) island, Thailand's third-largest and about the same size as Penang, has a unique ambience that is very different from that of Phuket. Nowadays, about 3 million tourists descend upon Ko Samui every year. There are luxury hotels, fancy restaurants, a modern airport, easy transport,

 Map on page 250

After a hard day's sunbathing take a stroll along a Ko Samui beach at dusk.

BELOW: Bo Phut, on Ko Samui.

TIP

In Ko Samui's interior
are several waterfalls,
descending from the
heights of Khao Phulu,
the island's highest
point at 635 meters
(2,080 ft).

and the full panoply of water sports and other diversions. Despite that, the 250 sq. km (100 sq. miles) of the island retain much natural beauty. The interior is still the preserve of coconut farmers and dense forested hills. Unlike high-rise Phuket, buildings are prohibited from surpassing the height of palm trees on Samui. Hire a motorbike or hop on a circulating *songtao* – pick-up trucks with benches in back—and follow the paved, well-fringed rolling road that rings the island to discover more.

The charm of Samui is in its idyllic yet understated beaches, hills, forest waterfalls, and rocky coves that support a relatively unchanged way of life.

Around the island's dozen or so minor beaches, there is an informal mix of affordable and affluent resorts, often side-by-side. Accommodation in Samui now ranges from elegantly-deluxe to rustic-hammock.

The water is warm but not quite as clear as Phuket and Phi Phi. In Samui, there is adequate sunshine for a beach holiday in all months except October and November, when rain prevails.

Visitors will find a crowded selection of landscaped resorts and a vibrant nightlife scene centred around **Chaweng Beach**, on the island's east side. Ever-popular Chaweng has the biggest choice of accommodation, mostly in the mid-range. Gently-curving bays with fine white sand and crystal-clear water follow each other in succession over a distance of 6 km (4 miles).

South of Chaweng is **Lamai Beach**, with its small plots of family-owned land. The sand and beaches are not quite as good as at Chaweng. In the center of the bay, almost directly on the beach, is an entertainment strip filled with discos, pubs and a few less salubrious beer bars. At both ends of the lovely bay are a number of moderately-priced hotels. Almost the entire northern coast of Ko

BELOW:
beach snack seller.

Samui is occupied by three lovely bays. On a cliff to the northeast sits the island's true landmark, a huge Buddha statue. **Bangrak Beach**, which ends by the cliff, was subsequently rechristened Big Buddha Beach. **Choeng Mon**, on the island's northeastern spur, has decent sand and is within quick access of Chaweng's facilities.

Most of Samui's sacred sites are in the southeast part of the island: the jade Buddha image at **Wat Sumret**; the Buddha footprint; the Coral Buddha image. Perhaps the most interesting, if not curious, place to visit is **Wat Khunaraam**, not so much for the *wat* as for the so-called mummified monk. A revered teacher of meditation during his life, the monk meditated his way into the next world here in 1973; he left his body in such a dehydrated condition that decomposition did not occur. The body now sits in a glass coffin.

Ko Pha Ngan

If Ko Samui is the land of package tours and brief vacations, its neighbour 15 km (9 miles) to the north, **Ko Pha Ngan ❺** is a refuge for backpackers on leisurely world tours and Europeans whiling away winter-long holidays. Smaller, rustic and rugged, and with horrible roads, Pha Ngan lacks Samui's spectacular beaches, but has plenty of secluded, craggy bays sheltering small sandy jewels adorned with coral, which makes the island excellent for snorkeling. **Hat Rin** is best known for its monthly full moon parties, the biggest of which take place in December and January.

As of last count, more than a dozen of these bays host a bungalow resort or two (or 40, in the case of Hat Rin), where US$5 will get you a sturdy roof, a cold-water bath and electricity at least until midnight.   ❏

The impressive Namuang waterfalls, at the center of Ko Samui.

BELOW: small fishing boat in still waters.

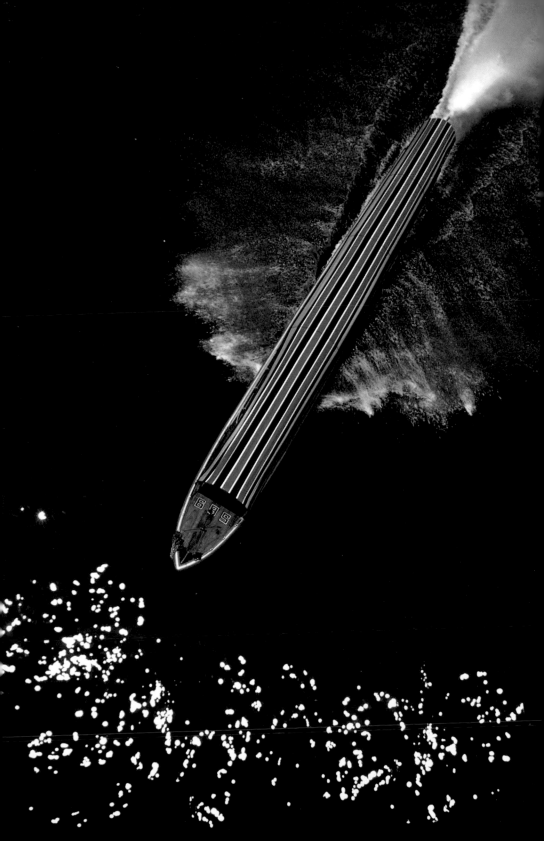

TRAVEL TIPS

Insight Guides portray destinations in depth, providing the complete picture and the top photography

Insight Pocket Guides focus on the best choices for places to see and things to do and include large fold-out maps

Insight Compact Guides' portability makes them the perfect books to carry with you for on-the-spot reference

Three types of guide for all types of travel

INSIGHT GUIDES Different people need different kinds of information. Some want *background information* to help them prepare for the trip. Others seek *personal recommendations* from someone who knows the destination well. And others look for *compactly presented data* for on-the-spot reference. With three carefully designed series, Insight Guides offer readers the perfect choice. Insight Guides will turn your visit into an experience.

The world's largest collection of visual travel guides

CONTENTS

Getting Acquainted

The Place

Area: The city covers a total area of 1,565 sq. km (602 sq. miles) of delta land, of which no natural area is more than 2 meters (7 ft) above any other.

Situation: Bangkok is situated at 14 degrees north latitude. It is a city divided into halves by a river, the Chao Phraya, which separates central Bangkok and Thonburi.

Population: About 10 million.

Language: Thai.

Religion: Most people (95 percent) are Theravada Buddhists. The 2 percent of the population who are Confucianist are mainly in the Chinatown area of Bangkok.

Time Zone: Thailand Standard Time is 7 hours ahead of Greenwich Mean Time.

Currency: The Thai Baht.

Weights and Measures: Thailand uses the metric system.

Electricity: Electrical outlets are rated at 220 volts, 50 cycles and accept flat-pronged or round-pronged plugs.

International Dialing Code: Country code: 66; Bangkok: 02.

Climate

There are three seasons in Thailand: hot, rainy and cool. But to the tourist winging in from anywhere north or south of the 30th parallel, Thailand has only one temperature: hot. To make things worse, the temperature drops only a few degrees during the night and is accompanied 24 hours by humidity above 70 percent. Only air-conditioning makes Bangkok and other major towns tolerable during the hot season. The countryside is somewhat cooler, but, surprisingly, the northern regions can be hotter in March and April than in Bangkok.

Adding together the yearly daytime highs and the night-time lows for major world cities, the World Meteorological Organization has declared Bangkok to be the world's hottest city. When the monsoon rains fall, the country swelters.

Temperatures

The following temperature ranges give a reliable guide to the degree of heat to be expected in Bangkok:

● Hot season (March to mid-June): 27°–35°C (80°–95°F)
● Rainy season (June to October): 24°–32°C (75°–90°F)
● Cool season (November to February): 18°–32°C (65°–90°F), but with less humidity.

The People

Bangkok's population is around 10 million, although a semi-permanent migrant population has, in recent years, swelled that number. The city functions as the epicenter of the country's political, business and religious life, a city some 35 times larger than Thailand's second – and third-largest cities of Chiang Mai and Korat.

Economy

Nearly 70 percent of Thailand's population are farmers who till alluvial land so rich that Thailand is a world leader in the export of tapioca (No. 1), rice (No. 2), rubber (No. 2), canned pineapple (No. 3), and a top-ranked exporter of sugar, maize and tin. Increasingly, Thailand is turning to manufacturing, especially in clothing, machinery, and electronics.

Government

The structure of the government is defined by the 1932 constitution. Despite the many revisions, the constitution has remained true to the spirit of the original aim of placing power in the hands of the people, although the exercising of it has favored certain groups over others, especially the military, which has often abused its power.

Modeled loosely on the British system, the Thai government consists of three branches: legislative, executive and judiciary, each acting independently of the others in a system of checks and balances. According to the current constitution which was enacted in 1997, the legislative branch is composed of a senate and a house of representatives. The senate is made up of 200 leading members of society, including business people, educators and a high percentage of high-ranking military officers. They must be over 40 years of age and must not be members of any political party. Members are selected by the prime minister and approved by the king. The house of representatives comprises 500 members of which 100 come from a "party list" and 400 are elected by popular vote from each of the 76 provinces of Thailand.

The executive branch is represented by a prime minister, who must be an elected member of parliament. He is selected by a single party or coalition of parties, and rules through a cabinet of ministers, the exact number dependent on his own needs. They, in turn, implement their programs through the very powerful civil service.

The judiciary consists of a supreme court, an appellate court, and a pyramid of provincial and lower courts. It acts independently to interpret points of law and counsels the other two branches on the appropriateness of actions.

The Monarchy

Thailand is a constitutional monarchy headed by His Majesty, King Bhumibol. The power of the royalty has decreased considerably since the period before the 1932 revolution. However, the present king can, by the force of his personality and moral authority, influence the direction of important decisions merely by a word or two.

Although he no longer rules as the absolute monarch of previous centuries did, he is still regarded as one of the three pillars of society – monarchy, religion and the nation. This concept is represented in the five-banded national flag: the outer red bands symbolizing the nation; the inner white bands the purity of the Buddhist religion; and the thick blue band at the center representing the monarchy.

The decades he has spent working with farmers to improve their lands and yields has influenced others to follow his example in serving the people. Her Majesty, Queen Sirikit, and other members of the royal family have also been active in promoting the interests of Thais in the lower economic strata. Thus, the photographs of the king and queen hang in nearly every home, shop and office, placed there, not out of blind devotion, but out of genuine respect for the royal family.

Planning the Trip

Getting There

BY AIR

Bangkok is a gateway between East and West and a transportation hub for Southeast Asia. Served by more than 50 regularly-scheduled airlines, Thailand has four international airports: Chiang Mai, Phuket, Hat Yai and Bangkok. The flying time from the UK is about 12 hours, from the west coast of America, about 21 hours. Flights from Australia and New Zealand take about 9 hours.

Thai Airways serves more than 50 cities on four continents. Its domestic arm operates a network of daily flights to 21 of Thailand's major towns aboard a fleet of 737s and Airbuses.

Airline Offices

Bangkok Airways
Queen Sirikit National Convention Center, New Ratchadaphisek Road.
Tel: 229 3456/3434.
British Airways
Unit 2, 14th Floor,
Abdulrahim Place,
990 Rama IV Road.
Tel: 636 1700
Airport: 535 2220.
Canadian Airlines
6th Floor, Maneeya Building,
518/2 Ploenchit Road.
Tel: 251 4521
Airport: 535 2227/8.
Cathay Pacific
898 Ploenchit Tower, 11th Floor,
Ploenchit Road.
Tel: 263 0606
Airport: 535 2155.
Delta Airlines
Panjapat Bldg, 6th Floor,
1 Suriwongse Road.

Tel: 237 6838
Airport: 535 2991.
Qantas
Abdulrahim Building,
Rama IV Road.
Tel: 636 1747
Airport: 535 2149.
Singapore Airlines and Silk Air
12th floor, Silom Center Building,
2 Silom Road.
Tel: 236 0440/0303/0222/5294
Airport: 523 2260.
Thai Airways
head office:
89 Vibhavadi Rangsit Road
Tel: 545 1000;
Silom office:
485 Silom Road
Tel: 233 3810;
Rajawong office:
45 Anuwong Road
Tel: 224 9602/3;
Asia Hotel office:
296 Phyathai Road
Tel: 215 0787/8
Airport: 535 2846/7.
TWA
12th floor Charn Issara Tower,
942/147 Rama IV Road.
Tel: 267 2100/19.

BY RAIL

Trains operated by the State Railways of Thailand are clean, cheap and reliable, albeit a little slow. There are only two railroad entry points into Thailand, both from Malaysia on the southern Thai border. The trip north to Bangkok serves as a scenic introduction to Thailand.

The Malay Mail leaves Kuala Lumpur every day at 7.30am and 8.15am, 3pm, 8.30pm and 10pm, arriving 7 to 9 hours later at Butterworth, the port opposite Malaysia's Penang Island at 1.35pm, 5.50pm, 9.10pm, 5.30am and 6.40am respectively. A daily train leaves Butterworth at 1.40pm, crossing the border into Thailand and arriving in Bangkok at 9.30 the next morning. There are second-class cars with seats which are made into upper and lower sleeping berths at night. There are also air-conditioned first-class sleepers and dining cars serving Thai food. Prices from Butterworth to Bangkok are US$50 or less, depending upon class of service. Trains leave Bangkok's Hualampong Station daily at 3.15pm for the return journey to Malaysia.

If you like to travel in style and prefer not to fly, the **Eastern & Oriental Express** (Tel: 251 4862) is Asia's most exclusive travel experience. Traveling several times a month between Singapore, Kuala Lumpur and Bangkok, the 22-carriage train, with its distinctive green-and-cream livery, passes through spectacular scenery. It's very expensive, but classically elegant.

Immigration Office

Visa extensions on Soi Suan Phlu (off Sathorn Tai Road). Tel: 287 3101. Open Monday to Friday 8.30am–4pm.

BY ROAD

Malaysia provides the main road access into Thailand, with crossings near Betong and Sungai Kolok. It is possible to cross to and from Laos from Nong Khai by using the Friendship Bridge across the Mekong River. Visitors need visas. Drivers will find that most Thai roads are modern and well maintained. The Malaysian border closes at 6pm but that may one day be extended.

Visas and Passports

Travelers should check visa regulations at a Thai embassy or consulate before starting their journey. All foreign nationals entering Thailand must have valid passports. At the airport, nationals from most countries will be granted a free **transit visa** valid up to 15 days, provided that they have a fully-paid ticket out of Thailand. A 30-day transit visa may also be issued to some visitors.

Tourist visas, obtained from the Thai embassy prior to arrival, allow

for a 60-day stay from the date of entry into the kingdom. People who are waiting for a work permit to be issued can apply for a **non-immigrant visa** which is good for 90 days. A letter of guarantee is needed from the Thai company you intend to work for and this visa can be obtained from a Thai embassy or consulate at home.

Visitors wishing to leave Thailand and return before their visas have expired can apply for a **re-entry permit** prior to their departure at immigration offices in Bangkok, Chiang Mai, Pattaya, Phuket and Hat Yai. An exit visa, however, is not required.

If planning a longer stay, a transit visa valid for 30 days or a tourist visa valid for 60 days must be obtained from a Thai embassy or consulate abroad by filing an application, supplying three passport-sized photographs and paying a fee. Visas can be extended before the visa's expiration date.

Passport Division
(Ministry of Foreign Affairs)
123 Chaengwattana Road
Pakkred, Nonthaburi.
General telephone: 981 7170/99.
Public Relations: ext. 2001/3.
Passport Section: 981 7276/7.
Visa and Travel Documents: 575 1062/4.

Passport offices (Suburbs)
Imperial Bangna,
Bangna Road.
Tel: 744 0893/7
Fax: 744 0891.
Central Plaza Pinklao,
Raj Chonnani Road.
Tel: 884 8829/30
Fax: 884 8823.

Passport offices (Provincial)
Chiang Mai,
Kad Suan Kaew.
Tel: (053) 894 405/10.
Khon Kaen,
Thai Red Cross Building,
Na Muang Road.
Tel: (043) 242 707.
Hat Yai,
37/65 Sri Puwanat Road.
Tel: (074) 235 724.

Customs

The Thai government prohibits the import of drugs, dangerous chemicals, pornography, firearms and ammunition. Attempting to smuggle heroin or other hard drugs may be punishable by death. Scores of foreigners are serving long prison terms for this offence.

Foreign tourists may freely bring in foreign banknotes or other types of foreign exchange. For travelers leaving Thailand, the maximum amount permitted to be taken out in Thai currency without prior authorization is 50,000 baht.

Foreign guests are allowed to import without tax, one camera with five rolls of film, 200 cigarettes, and one litre of wine or spirits.

Customs Department
(Ministry of Finance)
Sunthornkasa Road
General telephone: (old building) 240 2617/8, 240 0431/40; (new building) 269 7051/100.
Public Relations and Information: 249 9017/3298.
Tariff Classification Standard Division: 671 7550 ext. 9388, 9405
Director General of Customs Department: 249 0442.
Export Inspection Department: 671 7892, 672 7150.
Technical and Foreign Bureau: 240 2617, 249 4016.
Investigation and Suppression Bureau: 249 4205.

Health and Insurance
Vaccinations
Visitors entering the kingdom are no longer required to show evidence of vaccination for smallpox or cholera. But before you leave home, check that tetanus boosters are up-to-date. Immunization against cholera is a good idea if traveling extensively in rural areas. Malaria and dengue fever persist in the rural areas but not in Bangkok. When in the hills, especially in the monsoon season, apply mosquito repellent on exposed skin when the sun begins to set.

Heat exhaustion

Most first-time visitors experience a degree of heat exhaustion and dehydration that can be avoided by drinking lots of bottled water and slightly increasing the amount of salt in the diet. Sunblock is essential.

Sexually Transmitted Diseases

AIDS and other sexually transmitted diseases are not confined to "high risk" sections of the population in Thailand and visitors are at serious risk from casual sex if they do not use condoms.

Drinking Water

Do not drink tap water. Visitors are advised to drink bottled water or soft drinks. Both are produced under strict supervision, as is the ice used in large hotels and restaurants.

Insurance

It is essential to take out travel insurance before traveling to Bangkok. Your policy should include repatriation by air if necessary (see Medical Treatment page 266).

Money Matters

Currency

The baht is the principal Thai monetary unit. It is divided into 100 units called satangs.

Banknote denominations include 1,000 (gray), 500 (purple), 100 (red), 50 (blue), 20 (green), and 10 (brown).

There is a 10-baht coin (brass center with silver rim), a 5-baht coin (silver with copper side), a 1-baht coin (silver), and two small coins of 50 and 25 satang (both are brass-colored).

Banking Hours

Banking hours are 9.30am–3.30pm, Monday to Friday, but nearly every bank maintains money-changing kiosks. These kiosks may be found in Bangkok as well as Thailand's other major cities. Hotels generally give poor exchange-rates in comparison with banks.

Credit Cards

American Express, Diner's Club, MasterCard and Visa are widely accepted throughout Bangkok. In upcountry destinations, it is better to check that plastic is accepted, and not to count on using cards. Credit cards can be used to draw emergency cash at most banks.

Notification of loss of credit cards can be made at the following offices in Bangkok:

American Express
388 Phaholyothin Road.
Tel: 273 0033.
Open 8.30am–5.30pm, Monday to Friday.

Diner's Club
191 Silom Road.
Tel: 234 5715.
Open 8.30am–5pm Monday to Friday.

Visa and **MasterCard**
Thai Farmers Bank,
400 Phaholyothin Road.
Tel: 273 1199.
Open 8.30am–3pm, Monday to Friday.

Credit Card Warning

Credit card fraud is a major problem in Thailand. Don't leave your credit card in safe-deposit boxes. When making a purchase, make sure that you obtain the carbons, rip them up and throw them away elsewhere.

Traveler's Checks

Thailand has a sophisticated banking system with representation by the major banks of most foreign countries. Money can be imported in cash or traveler's checks and converted into baht. It is also possible to arrange telex bank drafts from one's hometown bank. There is no minimum requirement on the amount of money that must be converted. Both cash and traveler's checks can be changed in hundreds of bank branches throughout the city; rates are more favorable for traveler's checks than for cash.

Overseas Banks

Bank of America
2/2 Wireless Road.

Tel: 251 6333.
Bank of Tokyo
Thaniya Bldg, 62 Silom Road.
Tel: 236 0119/9103.
Banque Nationale de Paris
990 Abdulahim Bldg 29th Floor,
Rama IV Road.
Tel: 636 1900.
Chase Manhattan Bank
North Sathorn Road.
Tel: 235 7978.
Citibank
82 Sathorn Nua Road.
Tel: 232 2696.
Credit Lyonnais Bangkok
Silom complex Bldg 15th Floor,
191 Silom Road.
Tel: 231 3926.
Deutsche Bank
208 Wireless Road.
Tel: 256 7052.
Hongkong Bank
64 Silom Road.
Tel: 267 2960.
Standard Chartered Bank
990 Rama IV Road.
Tel: 636 1000.

What to Bring

Clothing

Clothes should be light and loose; fabrics made from natural blends that breathe are preferable to synthetics. Open shoes (sandals during the height of the rainy season, when some Bangkok streets get flooded) and sleeveless dresses for women, short-sleeved shirts for men, are appropriate.

Suits are worn for business and in

Temple Dress Code

Shorts are taboo for women and for men wanting to enter some of the important temples. Women wearing sleeveless dresses and short skirts may also be barred from certain temples. Improperly dressed and unkempt visitors will be turned away from large temples like the Wat Phra Kaeo (Temple of the Emerald Buddha) and from the Grand Palace. Dress properly in deference to the religion and to Thai sensitivities.

many large hotels but, in general, Thailand does not have the formal dress code of Hong Kong or Tokyo. Casual but neat and clean clothes are suitable for most occasions. Some formality is needed for business appointments. Sunglasses, hats and sunscreens are essential items to protect eyes and sensitive skin from the tropical sun.

Tourist Offices Overseas

Planning a trip to Thailand can be made easier if you contact a travel agent or an office of the Tourism Authority of Thailand (TAT). These offices offer promotional brochures, maps and videotapes of the country's many attractions.

Asia Pacific
Australia:
Level 2, 75 Pitt Street,
Sydney NSW 2000.
Tel: (02) 247 7549
Fax: (02) 251 2465
E-mail: info@thailand.net.au
Hong Kong:
Room 401, Fairmont House,
8 Cotton Tree Drive, Central.
Tel: (852) 868 0732/0854
Fax: (852) 868 4585
E-mail: tathkg@hk.super.net
Malaysia:
Suite 22.01, Level 22,
Menara Lion,
165, Jalan Ampang,
50450 Kuala Lumpur.
Tel: (093) 262 3480
Fax: (093) 262 3486
E-mail: sawatdi@po.jaring.my
Singapore:
c/o Royal Thai Embassy,
370 Orchard Road,
Singapore. 238870.
Tel: (65) 235 7694/7901/0637
Fax: 733 5653
E-mail: tatsin@inbox5.singnet.com.jp

Europe
France:
90 Avenue des Champs-Élysées,
75008 Paris.
Tel: (01) 45 62 86 56
Fax: (01) 45 63 78 88
E-mail: tatpar@wanadoo.fr
Italy:

Ente Nazionale per il Turismo Tailandese, Via Barberini, 68, 4th floor, 00187, Rome, Italy.
Tel: (06) 487 3479, 475 5471
Fax: (06) 487 3500
E-mail: tat.rome@iol.it
UK:
49 Albemarle St,
London WIX 3FE.
Tel: (171) 499 7670/9
Fax: (171) 629 5519
E-mail: info@tat-uk.demon.co.uk
Germany:
Thailandisches Fremdenverkehrsamt Bethmannstr. 58 D-60311 Frankfurt/M. Germany.
Tel: (069) 138 1390
Fax: (069) 281 468
E-mail: tatfra@t-online.de

USA
New York:
5 World Trade Center, Suite 3443,
New York,
NY 10048.
Tel: (212) 432 0433/0435
Fax: (212) 912 0920.
E-mail: tatny@aol.com
Los Angeles:
611 North Larchmont Blvd,
1st floor, Los Angeles, CA 90004.
Tel: (323) 461 9814
Fax: (323) 461 9834.
E-mail: tatla@ix.netcom.com

Public Holidays

● **January** New Year's Day (1)
● **February or March** (full moon) Magha Bucha Day, Chinese New Year, is not an official public holiday, but many businesses are closed for several days.
● **April** Chakri Day (6) **Songkran** (Thai New Year) (13–15)
● **May** Labor Day (1), Coronation Day (5), Plowing Ceremony (variable), Visakha Puja (full moon)
● **July** Asalha Bucha Day (full moon), Khao Pansa (Beginning of Buddhist Lent – variable)
● **August** Queen's Birthday (12)
● **October** Chulalongkorn Day (23)
● **December** King's Birthday (5), Constitution Day (10), New Year's Eve (31)

Practical Tips

Media

PRINT

Thailand has two long-standing English-language dailies, *The Bangkok Post* and *The Nation*. If you are familiar with newspapers in any of the neighboring countries, you will be pleasantly surprised by the free-wheeling coverage. Many big hotels will supply one or both of these papers at no charge. There is also a smaller English newspaper called *Business Day*, partially owned by the Singapore *Straits Times*.

Foreign Press
The International Herald Tribune and the *Asian Wall Street Journal* are sold in Bangkok, although at relatively few newsstands. It's most fruitful to look in hotel shops and outlets of Asia Books, DK and Bookazine. In Bangkok, such vendors often also sell the *Financial Times* and Belgian, French, German, Italian, Japanese and Spanish dailies.

Magazines and Periodicals
At any one time, probably about a dozen English-language magazines are being published in Thailand. In addition to basic survival advice, the listings include recommended restaurants and music venues. The English-language "business" magazines, mostly monthly, have a broad interpretation of the term. The slickest is *Manager*.

The most curious of the English-language periodicals are called "hi-so" by Thais and "suck-up" rags by expats. Among them are *Living in Thailand*, *Thailand Tatler* and sporadic glossy hotel productions.

New Insight Maps

Maps in Insight Guides are tailored to complement the text. But when you're on the road you sometimes need the big picture that only a large-scale map can provide. This new range of durable Insight Fleximaps has been designed to meet just that need.

Detailed, clear cartography
makes the comprehensive route and city maps easy to follow, highlights all the major tourist sites and provides valuable motoring information plus a full index.

Informative and easy to use
with additional text and photographs covering a destination's top 10 essential sites, plus useful addresses, facts about the destination and handy tips on getting around.

Laminated finish
allows you to mark your route on the map using a non-permanent marker pen, and wipe it off. It makes the maps more durable and easier to fold than traditional maps.

The first titles
cover many popular destinations. They include Algarve, Amsterdam, Bangkok, California, Cyprus, Dominican Republic, Florence, Hong Kong, Ireland, London, Mallorca, Paris, Prague, Rome, San Francisco, Sydney, Thailand, Tuscany, USA Southwest, Venice, and Vienna.

☯ INSIGHT GUIDES
The world's largest collection of visual travel guides

Each issue consists of photos and profiles of Thai millionaires and many jewelry ads. Every interviewee, whether a drop-out from New Secretarial Institute or the proud progeny of an ex-director, is treated with the same swooning flattery. No slightly unpleasant fact about Thailand ever intrudes. Foreigners find these rags hilarious or appalling, but they do convey much about how the Thai elite still wish to be regarded.

RADIO

AM radio is devoted entirely to Thai-language programs. FM frequencies include several English language stations with the latest pop hits. Some frequencies have bilingual DJs and play a mixture of Thai and English songs in the same program. Radio Thailand offers 4 hours of English-language broadcasts each day at 97 MHz. Of value to visitors is an English-language program of travel tips broadcast regularly throughout the day. The Tourism Authority of Thailand also offers useful tips to tourists on 105.5 MHz. every hour.

TELEVISION

Bangkok has six Thai language television channels. The latest of these, ITV or Independent Television, specializes in news and documentaries. The rest mainly air soaps, songs and game shows with a sprinkling of news. In addition, there is UBC, a cable television network which provides subscribers with a choice of 17 international channels. All major hotels and many smaller ones also have satellite dishes that bring news and entertainment from all over into your room.

Postal Services

The Thai postal service is not very reliable. The odds for domestic mail can be improved by registering or sending items EMS. EMS costs 15

Thai Greetings

The common greeting and farewell in Thailand is *Sawasdee*, spoken while raising the hands in a prayer-like gesture, the fingertips touching the nose, and bowing the head slightly.

baht for a business-sized letter. EMS is supposed to guarantee that a letter reaches a domestic destination in two days.

If you wish to send valuable parcels, bulky documents or irreplaceable film overseas, turn to DHL, Federal Express, TNT Skypak, UPS or other private international courier services. Never send or attempt to receive credit cards or blank checks through the Thai postal service. Ask your international correspondents to use boring stamps or a postal meter; a plausible theory holds that Thai postal staff pilfer foreign mail in order to obtain the colorful stamps.

The **General Post Office** in Bangkok is located on the riverside between Suriwongse and Siphya roads on Charoen Krung Road (New Road). It is open from 7.30am to 4.30pm, Monday to Friday; and from 9am to noon on Saturdays, Sundays and holidays. The **Banglampoo** post office, close to Khao San Road, is open Saturday mornings from 9am to noon. Offices elsewhere in Bangkok and throughout the country usually open around 8am and close at 4 or 4.30pm on weekdays. The GPO and many larger offices sell packing boxes and materials.

Mini post offices, little more than windows, actually pop up in Bangkok in unexpected places, such as office buildings and hotels. A red sign in English will confirm suspicions; outdoors, there may be no indication of a post office within. These outlets offer basic mail services and accept small packages, but, unlike full-scale post offices, have no telecommunications services. Mail boxes have one or two slots. In the latter case, one is for destination Bangkok and the

other is for everywhere else in the world. In Bangkok, although not elsewhere, the slots are usually marked in English.

Branch post offices are located throughout the city and many of these stay open until 6pm. Kiosks along some of the city's busier streets sell stamps and aerograms and ship small parcels. Hotel reception counters will send letters for their guests at no extra charge.

Post and Telegraph Department
Chaengwattana Road
International Service Division:
tel: 271 3515.
International Post Section:
tel: 279 6196.
International Telecommunications Section: tel: 271 3512.

Useful Numbers

Directory Assistance: (in English) 13
Tourist Police: 1155, 285 5501

Telecommunications

Thailand's telephone system is being rapidly modernized. There are a great number of telephone booths from which local and domestic long-distance calls can be made. Many areas that tourists frequent also have card-operated phones for international calls. Business travelers can rent mobile phones at the airport.

Top-notch hotels usually allow international callers to directly connect with operators in other countries. Smaller hotels, however, will require the caller to go through a local operator. Be warned that the majority of hotels levy a sometimes hefty service charge on inter-national calls. Remember that call rates are higher than in the West (at least a third more than in the United States). Calling collect (reversing charges) is therefore advisable.

A good alternative is going to the main post office. In the grounds of the Bangkok GPO, on Charoen Krung Road (New Road) near The Oriental hotel, is an annex with the country's most advanced telecommunications equipment. It is open 24 hours a day and you can make direct international calls. International fax rates are the best here. Ask to use the self-service fax machines.

International credit-card operating phone booths (most of which are painted yellow) are increasingly common and are found primarily in major shopping and tourist areas. There is no longer a serious shortage of telephone lines in Bangkok. Some three million telephone lines have been added but the modernization has meant that many telephone numbers have changed. If you have a problem getting through, call 13 to verify the number. The operators speak English.

Telephone Lines

Thailand is rehabilitating and overhauling its communications system, but this does not mean that the network is in perfect working order yet; the lines have a habit of getting jammed, like the traffic, especially after a heavy rain. Most hotels have telephones, telegrams, telexes and fax facilities.

Business Hours

Government offices
Open from 8.30am–4.30pm, Monday to Friday.

Businesses
Business hours are from 8am–5.30pm, Monday to Friday. Some businesses are open half days from 8.30am to noon on Saturdays.

Banks
Banks in Bangkok are open from 9.30am–3.30pm, five days per week, but they operate money-changing kiosks throughout the city which are open until 8 o'clock in the evening, seven days a week.

Department stores
Most department stores are open 10.30am–9pm seven days a week.

Shops
Ordinary shops open at 8.30am or 9am and close between 6pm and 8pm, depending on the location and type of business.

Pharmacies
Some pharmacies in the major cities remain open all night.

Small restaurants
Small open-air coffee shops and restaurants open at 7am and close at 8.30pm, though some stay open past midnight.

Large restaurants
Large **restaurants** generally close at 11pm. Most **coffee shops** close at midnight; some stay open 24 hours.

Tourist Offices

Listed below are some of the main Tourism Authorities of Thailand (TAT) offices:

Ayutthaya
108/22 Moo 4 Tambon Pratuchai.
Tel: (035) 246 06/7,
fax: (035) 246 078.

Bangkok
202 Le Concorde Plaza
Ratchadaphisek Road, Huay Kwang, Bangkok 10310.
Tel: 694-1222, fax: 694-1325.

Chiang Mai
105/1 Chiang Mai-Lamphun Road.
Tel: (053) 248 604, 248 607, 241

Tourist Offices in Bangkok

The **Tourism Authority of Thailand (TAT)** is the Thai government's official tourism promotion organization.
TAT head office: 202 Le Concorde Plaza on Rachadapisek Road. Tel: 694-1222, fax: 694 1324. Tourist Assistance: tel: 694 1222 ext. 1084-9. Provides essential tourist information,
The Tourist Service Center: 4 Ratchadamnern Nok Avenue. Tel: 1155, 281-5051. Has a wealth of brochures on various

466, fax: (053) 248 605.
Chiang Rai
448/16 Singha Klai Road.
Tel: (053) 717 433, 744 674/5,
fax: (053) 717 434.
Chon Buri
382/1 Chai Had Road.
Tel: (038) 427 667, 428 750,
fax: (038) 429 113.
Pattaya
382/1 Chaihat Road, Pattaya City.
Tel: (038) 428 750, 427 667,
fax: (038) 429 113.
Petchaburi
500/51 Phetkasem Road.
Tel: (032) 471 005/6,
fax: (032) 471 502.
Phuket
73-75 Phuket Road.
Tel: (076) 212 213, 211 036;
fax: (076) 213 582.

Embassies and Consulates

Australia
37 Sathorn Tai Road.
Tel: 287 2680, fax: 287 2029.
Visas: 8.15am–12.15pm.
Canada
138 Boonmitr Bldg, 11th & 12th floors, Silom Road.
Tel: 237 4125, fax: 236 6463.
Visas: 8–11am.
France
35 Soi 36 (Soi Rong Phasi Kao), Charoen Krung Road.
Tel: 234 0950–6, fax: 236 7973.
Visas: 8.30am–noon issued by Consular Section, 29 Sathorn Tai Road. Tel: 213 2181/4.

attractions, and personnel to answer questions.
TAT website:
http://www.tourismthailand.org, www.amazingthailand.th, and www.exoticthailand.com.

Inquiries can also be sent to specific departments such as the Information Section, Tourist Service Center, and local offices. Check e-mail addresses in their websites and click "E-mail adresses".

Germany
9 Sathorn Tai Road.
Tel: 213 2331/6, 213 2413-4,
fax: 287 1776.
Visas: 8.30–11.30am.
Italy
399 Nang Linchee Road, Tung
Mahamek.
Tel: 285 4090-3, fax: 285 4793.
Visas: 9.30–11.30am.
Japan
1674/4 New Petchaburi Road.
Tel: 252 6151/9, fax: 253 4153.
Visas: 8.30am–noon at Asoke
Tower, Sukhumvit 21.
Tel: 259 0234/7.
United Kingdom
1031 Ploenchit Road.
Tel: 253 0191/9, fax: 254 9578.
Visas: 8–11am, (Friday: 8am–noon)
United States
120-122 Wireless Road.
Tel: 205 4000, fax: 254 2990, 205
4131. Visas: 7.30–10am.

Business Travelers

Most hotels have business centers
with communications and
secretarial services in several
languages. Elsewhere in Bangkok, it
is possible to lease small offices
with clerical staff.

Government Offices
Board of Investment (BOI)
(Office of Prime Minister)
555 Vibhavadi Rangsit Road.
Tel: 537 8111
Fax: 537 8177.

The BOI is authorized to grant tax
holidays and other incentives to
promote certain industries.
However, it is fruitless to phone,
write or fax this agency. Potential
investors must visit in person or
check information from the website:
www.boi.go.th.

Ministry of Commerce
**Department of Commercial
Registration**
4 Sanamchai, Pranakorn District.
Tel: 438 5957/6005
Fax: 225 8493.
Commercial Registration: tel: 622
0585-90.
Public Relations: tel: 225 8411-9.

Travelers with Disabilities

The facilities for the disabled are underdeveloped. Sidewalks are uneven,
studded with obstructions and there are no ramps. Few buildings in
Bangkok have wheelchair ramps.

Department of Export
Promotion of Thailand
Ratchadaphisek-Ladprao Road
General telephone: 512 0093-104.
Exhibition Division: tel: 513 1908-18.
Foreign Marketing Division: tel: 511
5066 77, 513 1909-18.
Information Division: tel: 513 1907.
Trade Information Division:
tel: 511 5066-77, 511 4263.

Business Organizations
American Chamber of Commerce,
140 Wireless Road.
Tel: 251 1605, 251 9266.
Open 8.30am–noon, 1–4.30pm
Monday to Friday.
British Chamber of Commerce
54 Soi 21 Sukhumvit Road.
Tel: 260 7288, 234 1169.
Open 8am–noon, 1–4.30pm
Monday to Friday.
British Council
Soi 9 Siam Square, Rama I Road.
Tel: 652 5480-9, 252 6136, 252
6111.
Open 8.30am–4pm Monday to
Friday.
Franco-Thai Chamber of Commerce
104 Wireless Road.
Tel: 251 9385.
Open 8.30am–noon, 2–5pm
Monday to Friday.
German-Thai Chamber
699 Klongboonma Bldg, Silom Road.
Tel: 266 4924/5, 235 3510-3.
Open 8am–4pm Monday to Friday.
Goethe Institute
18/1 Soi Ngamduplee,
Rama IV Road.
Tel: 287 0942-4.
Open 8am–4pm Monday to Friday;
and from 8am–noon on Saturday.
Japanese Chamber of Commerce,
15th Fl, Amarin Tower,
500 Ploenchit Road.
Tel: 256 9170-3.
Open 9am–5pm Monday to Friday;
and 9am–noon Saturday. (The
Chamber is closed on the first
Saturday of each month.)

Thai Law Firms
These Bangkok law firms employ
foreign, native English-speaking
lawyers and/or Thai lawyers who
speak and write very fluent English.
Baker and McKenzie
92/54-7 N. Sathorn Road.
Tel: 636 2000, fax: 636 2111.
A franchise of the mega-
multinational US firm.
Domnern, Somgiat and Boonma
719 Siphya Road, Bangrak 10500.
Tel: 639 1955, fax: 639 1956/7.
Specializes in international property
law.
Internet Law Consultants
191 Silom Complex, 22F, Silom
Road, Bangrak 10500.
Tel: 231 3391-4, fax: 231 3395.
Tilleke and Gibbins
64/1 Soi Tonson, Ploenchit Road
10330. Tel: 254 2640-58, fax: 254
4302/4. US-affiliated.

Gay Travelers

Gays quickly discover that Thailand
is one of the most tolerant countries
in the world. In Bangkok, most gay
bars are on Patpong 3 or the upper
end of Silom Road, especially Silom
Soi 2. Transvestites and transvestite
shows are common in Bangkok, as
well as in Phuket and Pattaya. There
are also quite a number of small
eateries all around the city where
the clientele is almost totally gay.
Utopia (116/1 Soi 23, Sukhumvit
Road; tel: 259 9619; website:
www.utopia–asia.com) is Bangkok's
center for gays and lesbians. It's a
good place to make contacts and to
find out what's going on.

Religious Services

Interdenominational
International Church of Bangkok,
67 Soi 19, Sukhumvit Road.
Tel: 260 8187. Services: 8am.
International Christian Assembly,
196 Soi Yasoop 1, Ekamai Road.

Important Numbers

Police emergency number: 191
**Tourist Service Center and
Tourist Police:** tel: 1155, 281
5051 (on Rachadamnoen Nok
Road)
Tourist Police Division:
tel: 678 6800-9, 678 6852 (on
1st floor of TPI Tower Chan Road)
Khaosan Tourist Centre: tel: 282
2323 ext. 117 (on Khaosan
Road, in front of Chanasongkram
Police Station).

Tel: 391 4387.
Services: 10.30am, 6pm.
Catholic
Holy Redeemer Church, 123/19 Soi
Ruam Rudi, Wireless Road.
Tel: 256 6305. Sunday Mass:
8.30am, 9.45am, 11am, 5.30pm.
St Louis Church, 215/2 South
Sathorn Road. Tel: 211 0220.
Mass: 6am, 8am, 10am, 5.30pm.
Hindu
Thamsapha Association
50 Soi Wat Prok, New Road.
Tel: 211 3840.
Services: 7am–10pm.
Jewish
Even Chen Synagogue (Sephardic),
The Bossotel, 55/12-14 Charoen
Krung Road, (near Shangri-La
Hotel). Tel: 234 9409. Services:
9.30am on Saturday.
Muslim
Sha-Roh-Tal Islam Mosque

133 Soi I Sukhapiban Road. Tel: 328
8950. Services: 12.30–2pm.
Sikh
Wat Sirikurusing Saha,
565 Chuckrapetch Road. Tel: 221
1011. Services: 6am, 5pm.

Medical Treatment

Hospitals

Bamrungrad and Samitivej hospitals
bear the closest resemblance to
Western hospitals, but so do their
fees. For those with comprehensive
medical insurance, these are the
places to go. Otherwise, the other
hospitals listed below have
reasonable standards, accept
credit cards and employ English-
speaking staff.

Thai physicians are often too
eager to order tests that employ
'high techonology' and they tend to
over-prescribe both antibiotics and
painkillers. Use your prerogative as
a foreigner and find out precisely
what is being prescribed. If you are
in pain, insist that you do not need
painkillers. Every physician and
genuine pharmacist will have a
pharmaceutical reference book in
English. Many drugs banned in
Western countries are quite
common in Thailand. Most of these
hospitals also have dental clinics
that provide emergency services.
Note that for both medical and
dental services, Bangkok Adventist
hospital provides only for

emergencies on Friday afternoon
and Saturday, but operates full
services on Sunday and the rest of
the week.

Bangkok Adventist Hospital
430 Phitsanuloke Road
Tel: 281 1422, 282 1100.
Bangkok Christian Hospital
124 Silom Road. Tel: 233 6981/9.
Bangkok General Hospital
2 Soi Soonvijai, New Petchaburi Road
Tel: 318 0066.
BNH Hospital
9/1 Convent Rd, Silom
Tel. 632 0550, 632 0560.

Dental Clinics

In Bangkok, one clinic with a
long-standing reputation is the
Dental Polyclinic, at 211-3 New
Petchburi Road, tel: 314 5070.
The Dental Hospital, 88/88 Soi
49, Sukhumvit Road, tel: 260
5000/15 looks more like a hotel
than a dental hospital and has
the latest imported dental
equipment.

Bamrungrad Hospital
33 Soi 3, Sukhumvit Road
Tel: 253 0250/69.
Deja General Hospital
346 Sri Ayutthaya. Tel: 246 0137.
St. Louis Hospital
215 Sathorn Thai Road
Tel: 212 0033.

Pharmacies

In theory, pharmaceuticals are
subject to three levels of control.
In practice, just about everything is
sold just about everywhere.

With a bit of caution, Thailand is
a great place to stock up. A staffer
in a white coat is not necessarily a
pharmacist and outside of
Bangkok, it is unlikely that she or
he is. A genuine pharmacist will
speak a little English and will have
a pharmaceutical reference book
in English.

More so than physicians, these
pharmacists or clerks often
recklessly recommend powerful

drugs, including drugs banned in
Western countries, for minor
ailments. They also always initially
offer the highest dosage of a drug.
Ask for a smaller one (*lek kwaa*).
It's always possible to purchase
one tablet, one capsule or one
bandage.

The quality of drugs is
acceptable, although one should
check expiration dates and be
aware that exposure to heat may
mean that a drug expires even
earlier. For this reason, it may be
wise to buy drugs in an air-
conditioned venue, such as a

supermarket or large pharmacy.
Brand-name Western drugs,
usually British or German, are
much cheaper than at home. Even
cheaper are the thousands of
drugs (no one knows how many)
manufactured by about 100 Thai
firms. Their speciality is "off-
patent" drugs, that is, copies of
old Western drugs whose patents
have expired.

Although they are most easily
found in Chinatown, Chinese
herbal medicine shops exist all
over Bangkok. Often they sell both
Western and Chinese medications.

Samitivej Hospital
133 Soi 49, Sukhumvit Road
Tel: 392 0010.
Siam General Hospital
15/10 Soi Chokchai 4, Lardprao
Tel: 514 2157/9.
Sukhumvit Hospital
1411 Sukhumvit Road
Tel: 391 0011.
Thonburi Hospital
34/1 Issarapab Road
Tel: 411 0401, 412 0020.

Medical Clinics

For minor problems, the **British Dispensary**, located at 109 Sukhumvit Road (between Soi 3 and 5). Tel: 252 8056. Has British doctors on its staff. Most international hotels also have an on-premises clinic, or a physician on call.

Other Services

Counseling: Community Services of Bangkok, 15/1 Sukhumvit Soi 3. Tel: 258-4998. This nonprofit organization offers classes and services for foreigners living in Bangkok. Counseling services are provided by Western-trained professionals. While English is the usual language, the friendly volunteer staffers can probably recommend professionals who speak other languages. They also have contacts with self-help and support groups.
HIV: Snake Farm, 1871 Rama IV Road. Provides anonymous testing and counseling. This is also a good place to get inoculations, including the popular Japanese encephalitis series.
Alcoholics Anonymous, Holy Redeemer Church, 123 Soi Ruam Rudi 5, off Ploenchit Road. Tel: 256 6305 or 235 6157.
The Samaritans of Bangkok. Tel: 249 9977/7530. Anonymous counseling service, in English, 24 hours daily.

Security and Crime

Bangkok is a relatively safe city in terms of muggings and physical attack. The worst risk to travelers is from scams and con artists (see

Crime Risks

● Touts posing as Boy Scouts soliciting donations on Bangkok's sidewalks. The real Boy Scouts obtain funds from other sources.
● Touts on Patpong offering upstairs live sex shows. Once inside, one is handed an exorbitant bill and threatened if he or she protests.
   Pay, take the receipt, and go immediately to the Tourist Police to gain restitution, which may or

crime risks box). If you do run into trouble in Bangkok, there are Tourist Police assigned specially to assist travelers.
Tourist Police:
Tourist Service Center
TAT headquarters
4 Rachadamnern Nok Avenue.
Tel: 281 5051.
Most members of the force speak English.
   Tourist police booths can also be found in many tourist areas including Lumpini Park (near the intersection of Rama IV and Silom Roads) and Patpong (at Silom Road intersection).

Etiquette

Thais are remarkably tolerant and forgiving of foreigners' foibles, but there are a few things that will rouse them to anger.

The Royal Family

Thais regard the royal family with a reverence unmatched in other countries; they react strongly if they consider any member of royalty has been insulted.

Chatting with Thais

Thais converse readily with any stranger who shows the least sign of willingness. Struggle to speak a few words of Thai and they respond even more eagerly.
   Be prepared, however, for questions considered rude in Western societies such as: How

may not be forthcoming.
● Persons offering free or very cheap boat rides into the canals. Once you are well into the canal, you are given the choice of paying a high fee or being stranded.
● Persons offering to take you to a gem factory for a "special deal." The gems bought on these occasions are usually flawed and there is no way to get your money back.

Ill-considered remarks or refusing to stand for the royal anthem before the start of a movie will earn some very hard stares.

Buddhism

A similar degree of respect is accorded the second pillar of society, Buddhism. Disrespect towards Buddha images, temples or monks is not taken lightly. Monks observe vows of chastity that prohibit their being touched by women, even their mother.
   When in the vicinity of a monk, a woman should try to stay clear to avoid accidentally brushing against him.
   When visiting a temple, it is acceptable for both sexes to wear long pants but not shorts. Scruffy dressers are frequently turned away from major temples.

Terms of Address

Thais are addressed by their first rather than their last names. The name is usually preceded by the word *khun*, a term of honor. Thus Silpachai Krishnamra would be addressed as Khun Silpachai.

old are you? How much money do you earn? How much does that watch (camera, etc.) cost? Thais regard these questions as part of ordinary conversation and will not understand a reluctance to answer them.

Head and Feet

From the Hindu religion has come the belief that the head is the fount of wisdom and the feet are unclean. For this reason, it is insulting to touch another person on the head, point one's feet at or step over another person. Kicking in anger is worse than spitting. In formal situations, when wishing to pass someone who is seated on the floor, bow slightly while walking and point an arm down to indicate the path to be taken. It is also believed that spirits dwell in the raised doorsills of temples and traditional Thai houses, and that when one steps on them, the spirits become angry and curse the building with bad luck.

Dress

Thais believe in personal cleanliness. Even the poorest among them bathe daily and dress cleanly and neatly. They frown on those who do not share these concerns.

Public Behavior

Twenty years ago, Thai couples showed no intimacy in public. That has changed due to Western influence on the young, but intimacy rarely extends beyond holding hands. As in many traditional societies, displaying open affection in public is a sign of bad manners.

Tipping

Tipping is not a custom in Thailand, although it is becoming more prevalent. A service charge of 10 percent is generally included in restaurant bills and is divided among the staff. A bit extra for the waitress is appreciated. Do not tip non-metered taxi or tuk-tuk drivers unless the traffic has been particularly bad and he has been especially patient; 10 baht would suffice for a long journey over 60 baht. Hotel room boys and porters are becoming used to being tipped but will not hover with hand extended.

Getting Around

On Arrival

The journey from Bangkok International Airport into the central city can take from 45 minutes to four hours, depending on traffic conditions. The worst period is between 4 and 9pm.

Negotiating an exit from the airport is daunting. If you are on a business trip, you will quickly understand why it is the norm for Bangkok hosts to deploy a personal greeter and escort. Emerging in the arrival hall, you may be harangued by touts both inside and outside the barriers. Never volunteer your name or destination to these people. If you already have a reservation at a big hotel, a hotel representative will be waving your name on a sign and be ready to take you via air-conditioned mini-bus to the hotel.

Taxis

All taxis officially serving the airport are air-conditioned and metered. At a counter in the arrival hall and close to the exit, a clerk hands out a numbered slip.

If you are going to a difficult destination (such as a private home), ask the clerk to write it in Thai. You give the slip to a taxi driver right outside the door. If the taxi already has a passenger, refuse to get in. Make sure the driver turns on the meter. You have to pay an additional 50 baht to the driver and the charges for the expressway if you wish to use it. Now the fun begins.

Another option is to take a taxi that hasn't paid the airport concession fee. Go upstairs to the departure area, where taxis are dropping passengers on their way to flights. These drivers are not supposed to pick up new fares, but they are on the lookout and will take a long time to pull away from the curb. Again check the meter is running and only pay the metered fare.

Another alternative is to take the pedestrian overpass in front of the airport. When you reach the other side of the highway, there are usually a half-dozen air-conditioned metered taxis waiting. In both these "alternative" taxis, the drivers will also try to wangle an extra 100 baht or so. But they seem to be less persistent, perhaps because they aren't attempting to recoup the concession fees as the official cabs are.

Unmetered taxis

You may come across two types of unmetered taxis. For an experienced haggler, it's okay to take one of the nearly extinct non-metered marked taxis, but don't take an unmarked "black cab."

Buses

Buses into the city stop in front of the airport. The number 29, in both the air-conditioned and regular varieties, ends up at Hualampong train station. The air-con number 10 goes to Victory Monument. Many new air-con routes have been added; the clerks at the Tourist Authority desk in the arrival hall may be able to assist you. Since it's unlikely that a bus will go directly to your final destination, Victory Monument is a good target. From there, you can catch another bus or a taxi.

Air-con buses stop running around 10pm. All buses are intended for basic commuting and are not designed to take bulky luggage. Even if you have a small pack, it's not advisable to mount a bus between 4 and 8pm. During this rush period buses may be packed to the gills. Thais won't say anything to you, but they will disapprove.

Airport Bus Service

The most comfortable way to get into town is the Airport Bus service. With guaranteed seats and adequate space for bulky luggage, the airport buses get downtown in about 30 minutes. Starting from the International terminal 1, the bus stops at terminal 2 and the domestic terminal. Buses leave every 15 minutes between 5am and 11pm and the fare is 70 baht. There are three routes: A1: to Silom; A2: to Sanamluang; and A3: to Thonglor.

Getting Home

It is always a good idea to have a destination written in Thai or Roman capital letters. Your memory may be good, but your pronunciation probably isn't. Thais often don't know the names of small roads and lanes, even if they live close by. They will respond better to the name of a landmark, temple, big hotel or big market.

Train

Another fast and cheap way into the city is to take the train. The station is across the street from the airport. In about half an hour and for 5 baht, you can be at the main Hualampong station, not far from Chinatown. There are trains at least every hour during the daytime; ask at the Tourist Authority counter. Some visitors decide to skip Bangkok altogether and take the train in the other direction; Ayutthaya is a good start. One drawback: if you have heavy luggage, humping it over the pedestrian bridge and onto the train may not be easy. Another is that you should not count on an air-conditioned car or even a seat.

Upcountry Destinations

Arriving on an overseas flight, many people immediately transfer by small bus to the domestic terminal in the same airport and thus avoid battling Bangkok altogether. The privately-owned Bangkok Airlines

provides service to Ko Samui, Phuket, Hua Hin, Trang, Mae Hong Son, U Taphao and Loei.

Airport Helicopter Service

You can skip over some of Bangkok's justly notorious traffic by taking a helicopter 'taxi' between the international airport and the Shangri-La Hotel. A one-way trip in either direction costs around 14,000 baht (approx US$389) for three passengers. Additional passengers pay 3,500 baht each but the number of passengers must not exceed eight. Flights can be made only between 6am and 6pm, depending on the weather, so it's impossible to fly over the heaviest traffic evening gridlock. Bookings should be made at least 24 hours in advance.

If you are staying at the Shangri-La, you can request the helicopter at the same time that you book a room. Even if you are not staying at the hotel, you can still use the service by booking through the concierge via the hotel's general number (tel: 236 7777). Some nearby riverside hotels are also accustomed to arranging the service. Or you can contact the helicopter company itself, Sichang Flying Service, at tel: 535 5672/4914.

Returning to the Airport

For the return trip to the airport, the **Authorized Transportation Service** has in-town offices at 485 Silom Road (Tel: 235 4365/4366). Most major hotels have air-conditioned limousines. Metered taxis will be less expensive if there are no traffic jams on the way. An alternative is the Airport Bus Service though it may take a little longer than a taxi. The river express shuttle is also worthy of consideration; you can be at the airport check-in counter in an hour and traffic is not an issue.

Domestic Travel

BY AIR

THAI operates a domestic network serving nearly two dozen towns,

Left Luggage

There are two left luggage facilities at Bangkok International Airport. One is on the 1st floor at the northern end of the arrival hall after passing through customs. The second is in the departure hall on the 3rd floor near the currency exchange counter. The fee is 20 baht per bag per day.

offering seven daily services to some of them, such as Chiang Mai and Phuket. Bangkok Airways operates daily services from Bangkok to Ko Samui and between Samui and several provincial towns.

Bangkok Airways is Thailand's first privately-owned domestic airline and provides a highly efficient, first-class service to most of the major resort destinations in Thailand, as well as Phnom Penh in Cambodia.

If you are planning a trip to the tropical island of Ko Samui from Bangkok, you will save much traveling time if you go by air, as the same journey by road and boat may take up to 14 hours.

Cross-country Buses

Air-conditioned bus service is available to most destinations in Thailand. VIP coaches with extra leg room are the best for overnight journeys to Phuket and Chiang Mai. Air-conditioned coaches also leave half-hourly from the eastern bus terminal on Sukhumvit Road (opposite Soi 63) for Pattaya and other points beyond. For the very adventurous, there are fan-cooled buses filled with passengers and tons of luggage that are used by poorer Thais for their journeys across the country.

To reach a small town from a large one, there are smaller buses or baht buses – pick-up trucks with a passenger compartment on the back.

BY TRAIN

The State Railways of Thailand operates three principal routes from Hualampong Railway Station. The northern route passes through Ayutthaya, Phitsanuloke, Lampang and terminates at Chiang Mai. The northeastern route passes through Ayutthaya, Sara Buri, Nakhon Ratchasima, Khon Kaen, Udon Thani and terminates at Nong Khai. The southern route crosses the Rama 6 bridge and calls at Nakhon Pathom, Petchburi, Hua Hin and Chumphon. It branches at Hat Yai, one branch running southwest through Betong and on down the western coast of Malaysia to Singapore. The southeastern branch goes via Pattani and Yala to the Thai border opposite the Malaysian town of Kota Bharu.

In addition, there is a line from Makkasan to Aranyaprathet on the Cambodian border. Another leaves Bangkok Noi Railway Station for Kanchanaburi and other destinations beyond along the old Death Railway. There is also a short route leaving Wongwian Yai station in Thonburi that travels west along the rim of the Gulf of Thailand to Samut Sakhon and then to Samut Songkram.

Express and rapid services on the main lines offer first-class air-conditioned or second-class fan-cooled cars with sleeping cabins or berths and dining cars. There are also special air-conditioned express day coaches that travel to key towns along the main lines. 20-day rail passes are available. In Bangkok, details from:

Hualampong Station
Rama 4 Road. Tel: 233 0341-8.
Bangkok Noi Station
Tel: 411 3102.

Public City Transport

Taxis
The introduction of metered taxis a few years ago has virtually wiped out non-metered taxis. It seems that Thais don't like to bargain either. There's no need to settle for a non-metered taxi; a metered taxi will soon show up. All are air-conditioned. Drivers don't speak much English, but they know the locations of all major hotels.

Foreigners frequently mangle Thai pronunciation, so it's a good idea to have a destination printed on a piece of paper. Thai drivers can usually understand street addresses printed in capital Roman letters, but few can read maps. Try to get someone to write the destination in Thai.

Taxi drivers will ask for expressway tolls, but they are not supposed to exact extra fees for luggage or additional passengers. Nonetheless, it's good form to add a little in such cases.

Tuk-tuks
If the English fluency of taxi drivers is limited, that of tuk-tuk drivers is even less. Tuk-tuk are the brightly-colored three-wheeled taxis whose name comes from the noise their two-cycle engines make.

Since the introduction of metered taxis, there's little reason why foreigners continue to take tuk-tuks, unless they wish to say they have tried one. Except for the most experienced hagglers, few tourists will be able to bargain a tuk-tuk fare that is lower than that of a metered taxi.

Some tuk-tuk drivers loitering around hotels will offer as 10-baht fare "anywhere". The hitch is that you must stop at a tourist shop where the driver will get gas coupons in exchange for bringing you in. If you don't mind pretending to examine jewelry for 10 minutes, this isn't a bad deal.

Motorcycle Taxis
The side roads leading off the major roads are called *soi*. Motorcycle taxi stands are clustered at the most hazardous spots near *soi* intersections with main roads and the exits of shopping centers (in theory, motorcycle taxis are illegal, but are likely to be legalized in the near future). You don't have to search for them. These are the young men in fluorescent jackets who pester you with shouts of "Moto-sigh! Moto-sigh!"

It is, of course, extremely dangerous to climb on the back of one of these things, but the drivers are experts at weaving through Bangkok's heavy traffic and may cut travel time in half. Only hire a driver who provides a passenger helmet. Motorcycle drivers must be bargained with. Because they know you are desperate, don't count on a figure that is any lower than a taxi fare.

Buses and Mini-buses
Public buses come in four varieties: microbus, Euro II bus, air-conditioned and non-air-conditioned "ordinary."

The pink-and-gray **microbuses** constitute the city's premium service. Air-conditioned and equipped with squalling music videos, they don't accept more passengers once all 20 or so seats are filled. The fare is 20 baht and no change is given. The problem is that these bus routes are not listed on any map and even Thais find the routes baffling.

The orange **Euro II** buses run on the same routes as the blue air-conditioned buses but are a bit more comfortable and cost more. The fare begins at 8 baht and increases with distance.

Fares on the blue **air-conditioned buses** start at 6 baht and increase with distance. The **ordinary buses** are either red and (dirty) white or blue and (dirty) white. A subset are the privately-run green **mini-buses** which have the same numbers as ordinary buses and follow the same routes. The drivers of these ramshackle buses are quite reckless. The usual fare on ordinary buses is 3 baht, 50 satang, but it goes up to 5 baht after 10pm. On both the air-conditioned and ordinary buses, a conductor provides change and a small receipt. Hold onto the receipt; an inspector may come aboard.

In theory, the routes of both air-conditioned and ordinary buses appear on standard bus maps. Note

Bus Stations

For bus and coach journeys to destinations outside Bangkok, the major terminals are:
Eastern: Opposite Soi 63 (Ekamai), Sukhumvit Road. Tel: 391 8907.
Northern and Northeastern: Moh Chit II, Chatuchak, Khampaengphet Road. Tel: 936 3666/ 537 8055. Information: 936 2841/8, 936 2996; Northern Route: 936 2841/8 ext. 311; Northeastern Route: 936 2841/8 ext. 601.
Southern: Boromrat Chonnani Rd. Tel: 434 7192, 435 1200.

that despite the same numbers, air-con buses seldom follow the same routes as ordinary ones. In practice, routes change and many air-con routes have been added in recent years. No map is up-to-date.

Also, sometimes routes are truncated or buses may take "short-cuts" via the expressway. These deviations are indicated in Thai on a removable sign close to the door. If a conductor on an air-con bus persistently asks your destination, he is probably trying to find out whether you are aware that you are on an expressway bus.

The conductors on air-con buses may understand a little English, or at least will be used to the way that foreigners distort the pronunciation of roads and places; expect less on the ordinary buses. A few passengers on microbuses and air-con buses may speak some English.

Try to avoid taking buses during the peak periods, that is, roughly from 7–9am and 4–9pm. At the best of times, it's difficult to predict whether a bus will stop to pick up passengers. During peak periods, the odds decline. Both air-con and ordinary buses are packed, with passengers hanging from the doors. Female Westerners sometimes faint (in which case, Thai women are very helpful). Don't even consider forcing a Western child under the age of 6 onto one of these buses.

Boats
White express boats with red trim run regular routes at 20–30 minute intervals up and down the Chao Phraya River, going all the way to Nonthaburi, 10 km (6 miles) north of the city. There are five routes, and these are indicated by different colored flags. All routes start from Nonthaburi and end at either Wat Rachasingara near Krungthep Bridge or the Ratburana area. The service begins at 6am and ceases at 6.30pm. Fares are less than 10 baht for short distances.

Ferries, often red, cross the river at dozens of points and cost just 2 baht per journey. They begin operating at 6am and stop at midnight.

A basic mode of city transport are the **longboats** plying the canal. They start at Wat Saket or Tha Phanfa (Phanfa pier), near Democracy Monument, and run along New Petchaburi Road and beyond. Glance at the map and you'll deduce that the stops include Jim Thompson's House, the World Trade Center and Asoke Lane. Fares start at 5 baht. Make sure you tell the boatman where you wish to alight; the boat won't necessarily stop otherwise. These canal "taxis" run only during daylight, roughly between 6am and 6.15pm.

The trip provides an interesting view of the backside of Bangkok, but the canal water is inky black and smells like a sewer. Many people would prefer to pay this price rather than endure road traffic.

Private City Transport
Limousines
Most major hotels operate air-conditioned limousine services. Although the prices are at least twice those of ordinary taxis, they offer the convenience of English-speaking drivers and door-to-door service.

Rental Cars
Unless you are planning to drive "upcountry" there is no reason why you should want to drive in Bangkok. Should you want to hire a car in Bangkok to take upcountry Thailand has a good road system with over 50,000 km (31,000 miles) of paved highways and more are being built every year. Road signs are in both Thai and English and you should have no difficulty following a map. An international driver's license is required.

Driving on a narrow but busy road can be a terrifying experience with right-of-way determined by size. It is not unusual for a bus to overtake a truck despite the fact that the oncoming lane is filled with vehicles. Add to that, many of the long-distance drivers consume pep pills and have the throttle to the floor because they are getting paid for beating schedules. One is strongly advised to avoid driving at night for this reason. When dusk comes, pull in at a hotel and get an early start the next morning.

Upcountry, agencies can be found in major towns like Chiang Mai and Phuket. These also rent four-wheel-drive jeeps and mini-vans. Ask for first-class insurance.

Car Rental Agencies

Avis, 2/12 Wireless Road. Tel: 255 5300/4; and International Airport Bldg 2. Tel: 535 4031/2 and 535 3004/5.
Budget, 19/23 RCA Building A, Petchburi Road. Tel: 203 0250. Hertz, Soi 71, Sukhumvit Road. Tel: 711 0574/8.
Grand Car Rent, 233-5 Soi Asoke. Tel: 248 2991/2 943 5600/4.
Khlong Toey Car Rent, 1921 Rama IV Road. Tel: 251 9856, 252 0807 and 250 1141.
Petchburee Car Rent, Petchburi Building, 1st floor, Petchburi Road. Tel: 319 7255.
It is possible to rent vans for day trips in Bangkok or beyond from private companies. The fees probably won't be more than 1,500 baht (approx US$41) per day. The drivers will speak some English. Try J&J Car Rent, tel: 531 2262.

Where to Stay

Choosing Accommodations

The hotel accommodations in all the major tourist destinations in Thailand is equal to the very best anywhere in the world. The facilities in the first-class hotels may have as many as 10 or more different restaurants serving Western and Asian cuisine, coffee shops, swimming pools, exercise rooms, business centers, banqueting halls, shopping arcades, and cable and satellite television. The service is second to none. Indeed, most of the moderately-priced hotels rival what in Europe would be considered a first-class hotel. Even the budget and inexpensive hotels will invariably have a swimming pool and more than one food outlet.

If on a limited budget, there are numerous guesthouses offering clean, economical accommodation. Once of primary interest only to backpackers because of their sparse facilities, many have now been upgraded to include fans, air-conditioning and bathrooms in the rooms rather than down the hall. As such, they afford a viable alternative to more up-market travelers. Prices range from 100 to 500 baht. Generally possessing no more than a dozen rooms, they are more like pensions than hotels and appeal to travelers who like personalized service, friendly staff and a more relaxed pace. Their numbers are legion and to list them all would fill several books. In Bangkok they are to be found along Khao San Road, in the Banglamphoo area and Soi Ngam Duphli, off Rama IV Road in the Sathorn area. Guesthouses are given a separate listing category in this section.

Location

Where you decide to stay in Bangkok determines how much time you will spend traveling to and from other places, so it's important to consider what you want to do in the city first, and then base yourself in that area.

Hotel Listings

The hotels in this section are listed by price and in alphabetical order. Prices are for one night in a double room in the high season:
Expensive 4,000 baht plus
Moderate 2,500–4,000 baht
Inexpensive 1,000–3.000 baht
Budget less than 1,000

Expensive
Amari Airport
333 Choet Wutthakat Road
Tel: 566 1020/1, 566 2060/9
Fax: 566 1941
Closest hotel to international airport and therefore popular with travelers arriving late and departing early. Connected to airport with footbridge and shuttle bus.
Amari Boulevard
Soi 7, Sukhumvit Road
Tel: 255 2930, 255 2940
Fax: 255 2950
Small but luxurious. An oasis in a raucous tourist area filled with street markets, noodle shops and bars.
Amari Watergate
847 Petchaburi Road
Tel: 653 9000/19
Fax: 653 9044
New highrise hotel in old market area. The roaring expressway in front of it can be a problem for guests.
The Arnoma Hotel
99 Ratchadamri Road
Tel: 255 3410
Fax: 255 3456/8
Good location for business visitors and tourists. Good restaurants and service.
Bel-Aire Princess
16 Soi 5 Sukhumvit Road
Tel: 253 4300/30
Fax: 255 8850

One of the small "boutique" hotels offering personalized service. Close to many of the big business organizations.
Central Grand Plaza Bangkok
1695 Phahonyothin Road
Tel: 541 1234
Fax: 541 1968
Midway between the airport and city, but a long way from anywhere except the popular weekend market at Catuchak Park.
Dusit Thani
946 Rama IV Road
Tel: 236 0450/9
Fax: 236 6400
Bangkok's first highrise hotel. Adjacent to major banks and business headquarters on Silom Road. Close to nightlife in Patpong.
Emerald
99/1 Ratchadapisek Road
Tel: 276 4567
Fax: 276 4555
A big, new establishment in a growing business, shopping and recreation quarter but a long journey from the center at peak traffic periods.
Evergreen Laurel
88 North Sathorn Road
(intersection with Soi Pipat)
Tel: 266 7223
Fax: 266 7222
Smallish but elegant, European atmosphere. On a busy thoroughfare but close to big business and foreign embassies.
Grand Hyatt Erawan
494 Ratchadamri Road
Tel: 254 1234
Fax: 253 5856
On a major intersection and home to the famous Erawan Shrine, one of the best known religious symbols in Bangkok. Adjacent to shopping malls, and horse-racing and golf courses.
Hilton International
2 Witthayu Road
Tel: 253 0123
Fax: 253 6509
Set in beautiful garden with pool. Close to embassies. Good access to and from the airport.
Holiday Inn Crown Plaza
981 Silom Road
Tel: 238 4300
Fax: 238 5289

Between business center and river. A choice location with small shops nearby.

Imperial Queen's Park
36 Soi 22
Sukhumvit Road
Tel: 261 9000
Fax: 261 9530
With 1,400 rooms it is Bangkok's biggest hotel. A cavernous place where guests must walk long distances between rooms and facilities. Interesting shops, bars and restaurants in the vicinity.

Imperial
6 Witthayu Road
Tel: 254 0023/100
Fax: 253 3190
Sprawling hotel with extensive sports facilities and choice of restaurants. Close to several foreign embassies.

The Landmark
138 Sukhumvit Road
Tel: 254 0404
Fax: 253 4259
Central location, and near airport road. Well-equipped for business travelers. Good shopping in and outside the hotel.

Le Merldien Hotels
135/26 Gaysorn Road
Tel: 656 0444
Fax: 253 7565 and 656 0555
Central location, walking distance to big shopping complexes. The hotel has a French flavor and the best hotel coffee shop in town.

Mansion Kempinski
75/23 Soi 11
Sukhumvit Road
Tel: 253 2655
Fax: 253 2329
In the big tourist district, this hotel offers discreet luxury and a hint of central Europe.

Marriot Royal Garden Riverside
257/1-3 Charoen Nakhon Road
Tel: 476 0022
Fax: 476 1120
A resort hotel with the conveniences of nearby downtown. On the western side of the river, a bit to the south, but there are fine views of the riverside life from the hotel terraces. Nearby streets offer tourists offbeat glimpses of Bangkok. Free river shuttle to Oriental Pier.

Monarch Lee Gardens
188 Silom Road
Tel: 238 1991
Fax: 238 1999
Situated in the heart of the banking and insurance district but conveniently placed for good shops and restaurants. The nightlife is also close.

Novotel Bangkok
Soi 6, Siam Square
Tel: 255 6888
Fax: 236 1937
French management. This is a busy quarter of small shops, movie theaters, eating places and traffic chaos.

Price Guide

Prices are for a double room in high season.
Expensive 4,000 baht plus
Moderate 2,500–4,000 baht
Inexpensive 1,000–3.000 baht
Budget less than 1,000

The Oriental
48 Oriental Avenue
Tel: 236 0400/20
Fax: 236 1937
A visit is a must, even if it is only to have a drink on the river terrace. The Oriental is part of the history of East meeting West. Repeatedly voted one of the world's best hotels, mainly because of its riverside location and its superb service.

The Peninsula Hotel
370 Charoen Nakorn Road
Tel: 861 1111
Fax: 861 1112
The latest hotel on the Chao Phraya riverside opened in 1988. Its is conveniently situated close to Sathorn Bridge with easy access to major business districts and Bangkok International Airport.

The Regent Bangkok
155 Ratchadamri Road
Tel: 251 6127
Fax: 253 9195
High luxury in the heart of the city. With music and tea in the lobby lounge, there are echoes of the old Orient. The best hotel swimming pool in Bangkok.

Royal Orchid Sheraton
2 Captain Bush Lane
Si Phraya Road
Tel: 234 5599
Fax: 236 8320
One of the big three riverside hotels with high levels of service and exceptional facilities. All have road access difficulties at peak traffic times but guests may travel by river and see little-known areas of Bangkok.

Shangri-La
89 Soi Wat Suan Plu
Charoen Krung Road
Tel: 236 7777
Fax: 236 8570
Every room has a river view. The evening buffet on the riverside terrace is famous. The biggest hotel on the river.

Siam City
477 Si Ayutthaya Road
Tel: 247 0120
Fax: 247 0178
A new hotel with good facilities near government offices and army headquarters. A good place to hobnob and people-watch.

Siam Intercontinental
967 Rama 1 Road
Tel: 253 0355
Fax: 253 2275
With 10 acres of gardens, tennis courts, jogging paths, swimming pools, golf greens and driving ranges, this is a cool retreat from the roar of the city. Big and small shops, movie houses and restaurants are just beyond the front gates.

Sukothai Bangkok
13/3 Sathorn Tai Road
Tel: 287 0222
Fax: 287 4980
Quiet, luxurious, a cool, green hotel favored by diplomats. Near the city's center on a busy thoroughfare but set well back amid tropical gardens.

Moderate
Asia
296 Phaya Thai Road
Tel: 215 0808
Fax: 215 4360
Many extra facilities available possibly to offset the noisy, non-stop traffic at its doors. The only

hotel that offers a cabaret show performed by transvestite dancers.

Ambassador
171 Soi 11–13
Sukhumvit Road
Tel: 254 0444
Fax: 253 4123
A long-established hotel with a big food mall in front. Situated in the middle of Sukhumvit night bazaar.

Best Western
Baiyoke Suite Hotel
130 Rajprarop Road
Tel: 253 0362
Fax: 255 0330
The city's tallest landmark provides a panoramic view. Also more than 200 export garment shops are located on the lower floors of Baiyoke Tower.

Chaophya Park Hotel
247 Ratchadapisek Road
Tel: 290 0125
Fax: 275 8585
Half-an-hour drive from the airport. Business and leisure facilities including disco and fitness are provided.

First
2 Petchaburi Roa
Tel: 255 0111
Fax: 255 0121
Situated on the main road just a 10-minute walk to the famous Pratunam and Baiyok markets. The building has been recently renovated.

Four Wings Hotel
40 Soi 26, Sukhumvit Road
Tel: 260 2100
Fax: 260 2300
Green surroundings in the heart of the city. International cuisine and live entertainment plus outdoor pool and health center.

Imperial Impala Hotel
9 Soi 24, Sukhumvit Road
Tel: 259 0053
Fax: 258 8747
A few minutes' walk to the central Benjasiri Park. Easy access to the Queen Sirikit National Convention Center and shopping areas.

Indra Regent
120/126 Ratchaprarop Road
Tel: 252 1111
Fax: 253 3849
Surrounded by old markets and eating places which are gradually making way for Thailand's largest wholesale center for garments.

Maruay Garden
1 Soi 40, Phahonyothin Road
Tel: 561 0510/29
Fax: 579 1182
A hotel in the outskirts of Bangkok about a 15-minute drive to the airport. Facilities including karaoke singing rooms.

New Peninsula
293/3 Suriwongse Road
Tel: 234 3910/7
Fax: 236 5526
An ideal choice for travelers who want a hotel in the central business district.

Novotel Bangna Bangkok
14/49 Moo 6 Srinakarin Road
Tel: 366 0505
Fax: 366 0506
Located in the eastern part of Bangkok, the hotel is a shorter distance from Pattaya. The fitness center with outdoor swimming pool is quite satisfactory though not on a grand-scale. Major international cuisines are on offer.

Royal Princess
269 Lan Luang Road
Tel: 281 3088
Fax: 280 1314
Owned and run by the long-established Dusit Thani hotel chain and famous for its Dim Sum, this low-rise hotel is friendly and hospitable.

Royal Princess Srinakarin
905 Moo 6 Srinakarin Road
Tel: 721 8400
Fax: 721 8432/3
Located just next to one of Thailand's largest shopping malls, Seacon Square. Restaurant offers all major international cuisines. The outdoor pool is big.

Tai-Pan
25 Soi 23, Sukhumvit Road
Tel: 260 9898
Fax: 259 7908
Enjoy a well-equipped fitness center with a pool-side bar and Thai massage. Guests can choose from a selection of sightseeing tours to all major sites in town. Internet service available to business travelers.

Windor
8-10 Soi 20, Sukhumvit Road

Tel: 258 0160/5, 258 1524/6
Fax: 258 1491
Located in the business Sukhumvit area the hotel provides a bookstore, shopping arcade and coffee house. Sightseeing tours are also available.

Hotel Reservations

Hotel reservations can be made in the airport arrival lounge once you have passed through customs. It is recommended that you book a room in advance during the Christmas, New Year and Chinese New Year holidays, and outside of Bangkok for Songkran in mid-April.

Inexpensive

In this category you get what you pay for. However, you can expect a better accommodation than at 2-star hotels in Europe. Every room comes with a private bathroom and toilet and in fairness there isn't much to choose from between the different hotels apart from location.

Bangkok Centre
328 Rama IV Road
Tel: 238 4848/57
Fax: 236 1862
Central location; convenient for railway station. Over 200 rooms.

Euro Inn
249 Soi 31, Sukhumvit Road
Tel: 259 9480/7
Fax: 259 9490/1
Convenient for shopping and entertainment areas.

Golden Dragon
20/21 Ngam Wong Wan Road
Tel: 589 0130/4
Fax: 589 8305
Close to airport; 20 minutes from the center of Bangkok. Swimming pool. Good service.

Grand Inn
2/7-8 Soi 3, Sukhumvit Road
Tel: 254 9021/7
Fax: 254 9020
24 rooms at the lower end of the Sukhumvit corridor.

Jim's Lodge
125/7 Soi Ruam Rudi,
Ploenchit Road

Tel: 255 3100, 255 0190/9
Fax: 253 8492
Near many embassies, pleasant restaurant, good service.
Malaysia Hotel
119 Rama IV Road
Tel: 679 7127/36
Fax: 287 1457
Service is not what it was, but the rooms are large and there is a swimming pool.
New Trocadero
343 Suriwongse Road
Tel: 234 8920/9
Fax: 236 5526
Good travel servcies and coffe shop, popular with Westerners.
Park
6 Soi 7, Sukhumvit Road
Tel: 255 4300/8
Fax: 255 4309
140 rooms, most bright and cheerful. Restaurant, coffce shop and bar. Small pool set in peaceful garden.
President Inn
155/14-16 Soi 11
Sukhumvit Road
Tel: 255 4230/4
Fax: 255 4235
Conveniently located in the heart of Sukhumvit, handy for shops and entertainment.
Rajah
18 Soi 4, Sukhumvit Road
Tel: 255 0040/83
Fax: 255 7160
Same handy location near good shopping and restaurants.
Silom Street Inn
284/11-13 Silom Road
Tel: 238 4680
Fax: 238 4689
Pleasant restaurants and shopping in the vicinity.
Thai
78 Prachathipatai Road
Tel: 282 2831/3
Fax: 280 1299
Pleasant surroundings, convienient for the TAT office, Banglamgpoo market and other attractions.
Tower Inn
533 Silom Road
Tel: 234 4051/4053
Fax: 234 4051
140 rooms. Midway between Patpong and the river. Good shopping in the area.

Viangtai
42 Tani Road, Banglampoo
Tel: 280 5392/9
Fax: 281 8153
In central Banglampoo on the edge of the Khao San Road area. Close to the National Museum and Sanam Luang.
White Orchid
409-421 Yaowarat Road
Tel: 226 0026
Fax: 255 6403
In the heart of Chinatown with good Dim Sum restaurant.
YWCA
13 Sathorn Tai Road
Tel: 286 1900
Fax: 287 1996
50 rooms, some cottages, sports facilities, European, Thai and Chinese restaurants. Quiet.

Price Guide

Prices are for a double room in high season.
Expensive 4,000 baht plus
Moderate 2,500–4,000 baht
Inexpensive 1,000–3,000 baht
Budget less than 1,000

Budget

If you are on a really tight budget but prefer a room with bathroom, head to these hotels. The hotels below have standard air-conditioned rooms with bathroom. Telephone lines are provided but don't expect other luxury facilities like a business or fitness center.

A One Inn
13-15 Soi Kasemsan 1
Tel: 216 4770
Fax: 216 4771
Located beside Siam Square and close to the World Trade Center and Chulalongkorn University. Spacious rooms, friendly service.
Burapa
160/14 Charoen Krung Road
Tel: 221 3545/9
Fax: 226 1723
On the edge of Chinatown and therefore a little noisy. Reasonable service.
Classic Inn
120/51-54 Ratchaprarop Road

Tel: 255 3988
Fax: 255 3886
Rooms are adequate and air-conditioned.
Comfort Inn
153/11 Soi 11
Sukhumvit Road
Tel: 251 9250, 254 3559/60
Fax: 254 3562
60 rooms. Convenient location close to shopping and restaurants.
Florida
43 Phayathai Road
Tel: 247 0990, 247 0103
Fax: 247 7419
This old, intresting building is near Victory Monument.
Siam
1777 New Petchaburi Road
Tel: 252 4967/8, 252 5081
Fax: 255 1370
Modest hotel with not much to shout about.

Guesthouses

Predominantly backpacker accommodation, most guesthouse rooms are clean and economical. Facilities vary: some have ceiling fans and shared bathroooms while others have air-conditioned rooms and a hot water bath. Some low budget guesthouses offer beds in dormitory type accommodation.

Although low on facilities, places to eat and telephones can be easily found in the locality as most guesthouses are situated in backpacker areas with easy access to shops, places to eat and night-time venues.

Guesthouse Prices

The price range for a night's stay in a guest house depends on the facilities offered but most places cost between 100–500 baht, with a bed in a dormitory costing from 80–150 baht depending on location. For more up-market guesthouses like the Bangkok Christian Guest House, which includes breakfast in the price, you can expect to pay around 650 baht a night.

Apple Guest House
10 Phra Athit Road
Tel: 281 6838
The guesthouse is part of a Thai family home and has a restaurant. Aimed at budget travelers, the rooms are quite small and basic but are cheap enough to fit into a limited budget.

Bangkok Christian Guest House
123 Soi Saladaeng 2
Silom Road
Tel: 233 2206
Fax: 237 1742
Good central location in missionary house with quiet rooms and bathrooms with good atmosphere. More expensive than most guesthouses, breakfast included in the price.

Chart Guest House
61 Khao San Road
Tel: 280 3785
Small rooms, some with air-con and a bathroom, in the central backpacker location of the Khao San Road. Rooms range in price depending on facilities and size.

Peachy Guest House
10 Phra Athit Road
Tel: 281 6471, 281 6659
Good value, sparse rooms with either air-conditioning or fans. Pleasant garden with bar which is popular with long-term residents. Not far from the Khao San Road.

Santi Lodge
37 Sri Ayutthaya Road
Tel: 281 2497
Quiet well-run guesthouse in the Dusit area with pleasant rooms and shared bathrooms. There is a vegetarian restaurant downstairs which is excellent.

Tavee Guest House
83 Sri Ayutthaya Road
Tel: 280 1447
In the area of Dusit with shared bathrooms but good sized rooms; some with air-con. Dormitory beds available.

Serviced Apartments
The slump in property prices has produced some good bargains for people looking for serviced apartments. Rental terms can be as short as a few days or be as long as a year. All serviced apartments are equipped with a kitchen, and facilities include maid service. Most apartment buildings have at least one good restaurant.

Rental Fees
Rental fees for serviced apartments vary from 10,000 baht to over 40,000 baht a month depending on facilities and location.

Bangkok Garden Apartments
289 New Sathorn Road
(Naradhiwat Ratnakarin Soi 24)
Tel: 672 0001
Fax: 672 0010
Claimed to be the serviced apartment complex with the biggest private garden after planting almost 1,500 trees. The place is brand-new and good for those looking for places to rent on Sathorn Road.

Chin House
75/1 Saladaeng Soi 1
Silom Road
Tel: 266 0505, 236 8265/9
Fax: 236 8206
These brand-new apartments have a squash court, pool, sauna and exercise room. Short and long-term rental are available.

Comfort Inn Serviced Apartments
153/11-14, Soi Chaiyot 11
Sukhumvit Road
Tel: 254 3559/61
Fax: 254 3562
Fully furnished apartments with facilities and kitchens. Located near to the main road and night bazaar.

Floraville
Soi Floraville 55/3
Pattanakarn Road
Tel: 320 2921/4
Fax: 320 2920, 320 2880
Famous for its resort club environment with a big swimming pool in the middle of the apartments. Buffet lunch and dinner are on offer and there is a play room for young residents.

Galleria Serviced Mansion
24 Soi 1, Pracharajbumphen Road
Tel: 276 4378/84
Reasonably-priced apartments with weekly and monthly rents available.

Grand President
14-16 Soi 11
Sukhumvit Road
Tel: 651 1200
Fax: 651 1260/1
Superior accommodation located in the heart of the city with full dining and leisure facilities.

Kanary House
2230 Soi 42,
Ramkamhaeng Road
Tel: 374 5544, 374 8941/3
Fax: 374 4490
This chain of serviced apartments offers a comfortable place and good business center for expats and executives.

Monterey Tower
398 Soi Rimklong Paisingto
Rama IV Road
Tel: 663 1037
Fax: 663 1050
Located in the central business district. Fully equipped with modern facilities to accommodate all business needs.

Oakwood City Residence
291 Naradhiwat Ratnakarin Road
Tel: 672 0200
Fax: 672 0199
Fully-equipped one, two, and three-bedrooms; the apartments have cable TV and VCR. Grocery store within the building, and lavish tropical garden and pool.

Palm Court Bangkok
27 Soi Saladaeng 1
Sathorn Road
Tel: 267 4050
Fax: 2674080
Managed by Ascott International, Palm Court's rooms are fully equipped and tenants can enjoy an extensive health club.

Riverfront Residence SV City
912 Rama III Road
Tel: 682 7888/9
Fax: 682 7888/9
Residents can enjoy a free breakfast, parking space, water and electricity all included in the price of the monthly rental. Run by the Accor group, these brand-new apartments offer great views of Chao Phraya River.

Riverine Place
9/280 Piboonsongkram Road
Tel: 966 6111
Fax: 966 6288

Situated by the Chao Phraya River, the building offers river scenery with natural surroundings. Sport club, fitness and restaurant are provided.

Royal President
43 Sukhumvit Soi 15
Tel: 253 9451
Fax: 253 8959, 651 1502
Up-market serviced apartments in a family atmosphere. Provides decent dining and leisure facilities.

Sathorn Saintview Serviced Apartments
201/1 Soi 15-17
Sathorn Road
Tel: 675 8921/30
Fax: 212 1231
Good location on the road with coffee shop, minimart, laundry and business center. Also satellite, cable TV with fitness and pool are provided.

Songvit Serviced Apartment
19 Soonvijai Soi
3 Petchaburi Road
Tel: 318 1633, 319 9288
Fax: 718 2461
A moderately-priced apartment located near the hip RCA nightclub and Bangkok General Hospital. It has all standard facilities including pool, TV, telephone, parking, and kitchen.

Sukhumvit
39 Sukhumvit Soi 10
Tel: 653 1783
Fax: 653 1824
This chain of serviced apartments have standard facilities for all locations including a daily cleaning service. The service is friendly and available around the clock.

V P Tower
21/45 Soi Chawakun
Rangnam Road
Tel: 246 8800/14
Fax: 246 8789
Situated in the bustling area near Victory Monument and Expressway. It has fully-decorated rooms for monthly and weekly rental at economic prices. Pool, garden, and cable TV in every room.

Where to Eat

What to Eat

The base for most Thai dishes is coconut milk. Ginger, garlic, lemon grass and fiery chilies give Thai dishes a piquancy that can set tender palates aflame. While many of the chilies are mild, their potency is in obverse proportion to their size; the smallest, the *prik kii noo* or "rat dropping chilies," are guaranteed to dissolve your sinuses and cloud your vision with tears. For those averse to spicy food, chefs can bland the curries or serve one of the dozens of non-spicy curries.

Restaurant Listings

In Europe, the very best restaurants are not usually to be found in hotels. In Thailand, the reverse is true. There are, of course, exceptions to both these generalities. The following restaurants are some of the best in town.

Thai Cuisine

All Gaengs
173/8-9 Suriwongse Road
Tel: 233 3301
Elegant, modern decor and delicious Thai cuisine. **$$**

Baan Khanitha
36/1 Sukhumvit 23
Tel: 258 8141
Relaxing and homey atmosphere in a remodeled Thai house decorated with antiques. Wide variety of Thai food presented in excellent ways. Private rooms for parties. **$$**

Benjarong
Dusit Thani Hotel
946 Rama IV Road
Tel: 236 0450/9
Superlative Royal Thai cuisine served on exquisite *benjarong* ware – a dining experience. **$$$**

Bon Vivant
Tawana Ramada Hotel
80 Suriwongse Road
Tel: 236 0361
Splendid cuisine with a host of traditional Thai dishes, all beautifully prepared and presented. **$$–$$$**

Bussaracum
35 Soi Pipat
2 Convent Road
Tel: 235 8915
Extremely popular with local connoisseurs of classical Thai cuisine; pleasant, informal atmosphere. **$$**

Cabbages and Condoms
8 Soi 12
Sukhumvit Road
Tel: 252 7349, 251 5552
Value for money and first-class cuisine. If you are not familiar with Thai food, this should be among one of your first choices. The profits support various family planning and HIV awareness programs and other charitable projects. **$$**

Price Guide

Prices are for a meal for two, excluding alcoholic beverages:
$ under 600 baht
$$ 600–1,000 baht
$$$ 1,000 baht plus

Celadon
Sukhothai Bangkok
13/3 South Sathorn Road
Tel: 287 0222
Exceptional cuisine in the setting of an exotic water garden. **$$$**

Chilli House
(near the Rome Club)
Patpong 4
Silom Road
Tel: 237 2777
You can enter either via Silom Road or through the Patpong Car Park Building on Patpong 2. Everything expertly prepared and presented by a top Thai chef, especially the seafood dishes; reasonable prices. **$$**

D'Jit Pochana
62 Soi 20 Sukhumvit
Tel: 258 1597; with branches at
1082 Phahonyothin Road

Tel: 279 5000/2; and
New Phahonyothin Road
Tel: 531 1644.
A long-established Thai restaurant with moderate prices. **$$**

Hualumphong Station Restaurant
88/167 Soi Onnuj
(Sukhumvit 77)
Tel: 332 3161
Authentic Thai cusine from all parts of the country. Country-style atmosphere with traditional Thai music from 8 pm to 10pm. **$$–$$$**

Laicram
120/1-2 Soi 23
Sukhumvit Road
Tel: 259 9604
Variety of tasty Thai dishes at moderate prices. **$$**

Price Guide

Prices are for a meal for two, excluding alcoholic beverages:
$ under 600 baht
$$ 600–1,000 baht
$$$ 1,000 baht plus

Lemongrass
5/1 Soi 24
Sukhumvit Road
Tel: 258 8637
Well known for its excellent cuisine at moderate prices. **$$**

Nipa Thai
Landmark Hotel
138 Sukhumvit Road
Tel: 254 0404
As with all the many restaurants in this hotel, its Thai restaurant is of the highest standard. **$$–$$$**

Pan Kitchen
Tai-Pan Hotel
25 Soi 23
Sukhumvit Road
Tel: 260 9888
Tasty Thai cuisine at reasonable prices. Worth going out of your way to try the inexpensive buffet set lunch which also includes some European dishes. **$–$$**

Salathip
Shangri-la Hotel
89 Soi Wat Suan Phlu
Tel: 236 7777
Superb Thai dining in pleasant surroundings on the river's edge. **$$$**

Sara Jane's Larb Lang Suan
36/2 Soi Lang Suan
Tel: 252 6572
Large variety of traditional, spicy Northeastern dishes to try. **$$**

Sidewalk
855/2 Silom Road
Tel: 236 4496
The owner is French born Pierre Chaslin, the author of the best selling *Discover Thai Cooking*. Superb cuisine, ordinary decor at very reasonable prices. **$–$$**

Sorn Dang
(at Democracy Monument)
78/2 Ratchadamnern Road
Tel: 224 3088
One of the oldest restaurants in town, known for good Thai food and relaxed atmosphere. Set menu. **$**

Spice Market
The Regent Hotel
155 Rachadamri Road
Tel: 251 6127
Beautifully decorated restaurant, with dishes that the chef can adapt to suit Western palates if necessary. **$$$**

Thai Pavilion
Holiday Inn Crown Plaza
Tel: 238 4300
Traditional Thai cuisine served in a traditional setting with pleasant atmosphere. **$$–$$$**

Thai Room
37/20-5 Patpong 2 Road
Tel: 233 7920
Serving Thai, Mexican, Chinese and European food. One of the oldest restaurants in the city. **$$$**

Thanying
10 Pramuan Road, Silom
Tel: 236 4361
Serves excellent Thai food. Set in very pleasant surroundings. **$$**

The Glass
22/3-5 Soi 11
Sukhumvit Road
Tel: 254 3566
As well known for its food as its live music in the evenings. **$$**

Whole Earth Cafe
93/3 Soi Lang Suan
Tel: 258 4900; and
71 Soi 26, Sukhumvit Road
Tel: 258 4900
Bangkok's best known Thai vegetarian restaurant, comfortable and friendly. There is also a tasty

menu of non-vegetarian fare with excellent Indian dishes. **$$**

Thai Dinner and Cultural Shows
A relaxing and enjoyable way to see traditional Thai dance-theater is to book an evening at a restaurant which features a cultural show.

Baan Thai
7 Sukhumvit Soi 32
Tel: 258 5403
Pleasant atmosphere in a group of old Thai houses in a tropical garden. Open daily 7.30pm with Thai dancing starting at 9pm. **$$$**

Maneeya Lotus Room
518/4 Ploenchit Road
Tel: 251 0382.
Open daily. Lunch 10am–2pm. Nightly 7pm with Thai classical dance performance at 8.15pm. **$$**

Sala Rim Nam
Oriental Hotel
Tel: 437 6211
Located in a beautiful, temple-like building across the river from the Oriental – particularly good Thai dancing. Free boat service from Oriental Hotel landing. **$$$**

Sala Thai
Indra Hotel
120-126 Ratchaprarop Road
Tel: 208 0022
Attractive reproduction of a classic building on an upper floor of the hotel. **$$**

Silom Village Trade Center
286 Silom Road
Tel: 235 8760/1, 234 4448
Open-air and indoor restaurants, traditional food stalls, Thai cultural show presented every Saturday and

Hotel Buffets

Many hotels in Bangkok vie with each other to prove that their lunch and dinner buffets surpass that of their competitors both in quality and value for money. The result is an overwhelming choice of prices.

You will not be disappointed wherever you choose to go, and even the least-expensive buffets offer a bewildering variety of dishes. All are come highly recommended.

Sunday from 12.45am and Thai classical dance shows daily at 8pm. Informal atmosphere. **$$**

Seafood
Dusit Rimtarn Seafood Restaurant
Supakarn Shopping Center
Sathorn Bridge
Tel: 437 9671
A view of the river. Seafood and other Thai and Chinese cuisine superbly prepared under the supervision of the Dusit Thani Hotel. **$$–$$$**
Lord Jim's
Oriental Hotel
48 Oriental Avenue
Tel: 236 0400
Top quality restaurant noted for its good atmosphere, excellent food and service; expensive prices. **$$$**
Sammuk Seafood
2140-4 Lardprao, Soi 90
Tel: 539 2466/9
One of many inexpensive Thai seafood restaurants in Bangkok. This particular one has won many accolades for the quality of its food and is very popular. **$**
Sea Food Market
388 Sukhumvit Road
(opposite Soi Asoke)
Tel: 258 0218
Pick out the seafood of your choice from a vast variety on ice and have it cooked to suit your taste. Informal and can be expensive if you succumb to the temptation of ordering too much. **$$–$$$**
Sea Food Restaurant
1980 New Petchaburi Road
Tel: 314 4312
Under the same management as Sea Food Market. **$$–$$$**
Somboon Seafood
895/6-21 Chula 8,
Bantadthong Road, Patumwan
Tel: 216 4203; also at
169/7-11 Suriwong Road, Bangrak
Tel: 233 3104, 234 4499; and
167/9-12 Ratchada Road,
Ratchada-Huaykwang Intersection
Tel: 692 6850/3.
Fresh seafood with a friendly picture menu. **$$–$$$**
Talay Thong
Siam Inter-Continental Hotel
967 Rama I Road
Tel: 253 0355

High quality dining, decor and service. **$$–$$$**
Wit's Oyster Bar
20/10-11 Soi Ruam Rudi
Ploenchit Road.
Tel: 252 1820.
A plush English style oyster bar. **$$**

Outdoor Thai Restaurants
When giving instructions to the taxi driver, tell him "Suan Aahaan" (garden restaurant) before giving him the name of one of the restaurants below.
Baanbung
32/10 Soi Intramara 45
Ratchadapisek Road
Tel: 275 7806 Road
Serves wide variety of local favorites with Chinese and seafood specialities. Grilled river prawns with garlic and chili sauce is highly recommended. **$–$$**
Bua Garden
Bangkhen
Tel: 579 6596
Al fresco dinning with large variety of Thai, Chinese, Japanese, and seafood dishes at reasonable prices. Relaxing garden atmosphere. **$–$$**
Goong Luang
1756 Boromrat Chonnani Road
Tel: 423 0748
Long-established garden restaurant on Thonburi side of Chao Phraya River. Delicious Thai, Chinese, and seafood at reasonable prices. **$–$$**

Riverside Restaurants
Baan Khun Luang
131/4 Khaw Road
Tel: 241 0928
Thai, Chinese and Japanese cuisine in a riverside setting. **$–$$**
Savoey Seafood Restaurant
River City Complex
23 Yotha Road
Tel: 237 7557/8
Excellent Thai and Chinese seafood dishes. **$$**

Chinese
Canton Palace
Evergreen Laurel Hotel
88 North Sathorn Road
Tel: 234 9829
A new restaurant in an elegant new hotel that has already received

many accolades for the high standard of its Cantonese cuisine. **$$–$$$**
Chinatown
Dusit Thani Hotel
946 Rama IV Road
Tel: 236 0450
Less expensive than the Mayflower also within the hotel, but just as delicious. **$$**
Chiu Chau
Ambassador Hotel
171 Soi 11-13
Sukhumvit Road
Tel: 254 0444
Delicacies from the Southern Chinese province of Chiu Chau (Guangchao). **$$**
Coca Noodles
8 Soi Tantawan
Suriwong Road
Tel: 236 9323
Has branches in Siam Square, Ramkamhaeng and Sukhumvit roadss. Cantonese hot pot, *sukiyaki* and noodle dishes. **$$**
Dynasty
Central Plaza Hotel
1695 Phaholyothin Road
Tel: 541 1234
Traditional cuisine with Peking duck, shark's fin and *abalone* all featured in the extensive menu. **$$**
Great Wall
Asia Hotel
296 Phaya Thai Road
Tel: 215 0808
The heart of any good hotel is in the kitchen and at the Asia Hotel, there are several different kinds of restaurants of which this is one of the best. **$$$**
Hoi Tien Lao
762 Laadya Road
(Thonburi bank of river, opposite the

Tea Rooms

Afternoon tea is an English custom that is followed in several of the major hotels. The most famous is in the Authors' Lounge at the prestigious Oriental Hotel. The buffet style afternoon teas in some of the hotels are so lavish and the choice so varied that they may easily be mistaken for a full gourmet dinner.

Royal Orchid Sheraton Hotel)
Tel: 437 1121
Cantonese food; one of Bangkok's oldest and most popular Chinese restaurants. **$$**

Hong Teh
Ambassador Hotel, 171 Soi 11–13 Sukhumvit Road
Tel: 254 0444
A favorite with local gourmets for banquet entertaining. **$$–$$$**

Jade Garden
Montien Hotel
54 Suriwongse Road
Tel: 234 8060
Southern Chinese dishes prepared by Hong Kong chefs in an elegant setting. **$$**

Lin-Fa
Siam City Hotel
477 Sri Ayutthaya Road
Tel: 247 0130
An elegant Chinese restaurant in one of Bangkok's most stylish hotels. **$$$**

Lok Wah Hin
Novotel, Siam Square
Tel: 255 6888
Cantonese and Szechuan cuisine at its best. **$$**

Mayflower
Dusit Thani Hotel
946 Rama IV Road
Tel: 236 0450
Without doubt, one of Thailand's best hotel Chinese restaurants. **$$$**

Ming Palace
Indra Regent Hotel,
120/126 Ratchaprarop Road
Tel: 208 0022
Southern Chinese dishes in pleasant atmosphere. **$$**

Nguan Lee
101/25-26 Soi Lang Suan
Ploenchit Road
Tel: 251 8366, 252 3614
Covered market; real atmosphere. One of the few restaurants where you can eat the famous Mekong giant catfish. **$$**

Rice Mill
Marriott Royal Garden Riverside
257/1–3 Charoen Nakhon Road
Tel: 476 0022
Built on the site of an old rice mill, this new, luxury riverside hotel has a splendid Chinese restaurant. **$$$**

Royal Kitchen
46/1 North Sathorn Road

Tel: 234 3063/5
More elegant and expensive than others but serving good food. **$$–$$$**

Scala Restaurant
218-218/1 Soi 1,
Siam Square
(near Scala Theater)
Tel: 254 2891
One of the house specialities is Peking Duck. The adjoining restaurant specializes in shark's fin. **$$**

Shang Palace
Shangri-La Hotel
89 Soi Wat Suan Phlu
Tel: 236 7777, ext. 1350 & 1358
Superb Cantonese and Szechuan specialties. The lunchtime dim sum is a real treat. **$$–$$$**

Silom Restaurant
793 Silom Road
Tel: 236 4442
One of the oldest Chinese restaurants in town. Northern Chinese dishes. **$$**

Silver Palace Restaurant
5 Soi Pipat
Silom Road
Tel: 235 5118/9
Well known for the variety of its delicious dim sum menu. Cantonese cuisine in opulent surroundings. **$$–$$$**

Sui Sian
Landmark Hotel
138 Sukhumvit Road
Tel: 254 0404
Cantonese and other regional delicacies of the highest standards. **$$$**

Tai-Pan
Imperial Hotel
6 Wireless Road
Tel: 254 0111, ext. 1473
Cantonese fare in elegant surroundings. **$$–$$$**

The Chinese Restaurant
Grand Hyatt Erawan
494 Rachadamri Road
Tel: 254 1234.
Sophisticated Cantonese specialties prepared by Hong Kong chefs. **$$–$$$**

The Empress
Royal Princess Hotel
269 Lan Luang Road
Tel: 281 3088
Delicious lunchtime dim sum. **$$**

Ti Jing
Monarch Lee Gardens Hotel
188 Silom Road
Tel: 238 1999
A dazzling array of dim sum and other Cantonese delicacies. **$$**

Tien Tien Restaurant
105 Patpong I Road, Bangrak
Tel: 234 8717, 234 6006
Located in the middle of busy, bustling Patpong. Moderate prices. The decor takes second place to the food. **$–$$**

Price Guides

Prices are for a meal for two, excluding alcoholic beverages:
$ under 600 baht
$$ 600–1,000 baht
$$$ 1,000 baht plus

Indian/Arabic/Muslim

Akbar Restaurant
1/4 Soi 3, Sukhumvit Road
Tel: 253 3479
Northern Indian food at very reasonable prices. Try the prawn korma. **$–$$**

Bangkok Brindawan
44/1 Soi 19, Silom Road
Tel: 233 4791
Simple decor and some excellent vegetarian dishes. Great value daily buffet lunch. **$**

Bukhara
Royal Orchid Sheraton Hotel
2 Captain Bush Lane
Tel: 234 5599
Superb Indian cuisine with impeccable service. **$$$**

Café India
460/8 Suriwongse Road
Tel: 233 0419
Northern Indian cooking in handsomely decorated surroundings. **$$–$$$**

Himali Cha Cha
1229/11 New Road
Tel: 235 1569
Northern Indian cuisine by a master chef named Cha Cha; ask him what he recommends from the daily menu. **$$**

Himali Cha Cha & Son Restaurant
2 Soi 35, Sukhumvit Road
Tel: 258 8843 and 258 8846
Another branch of Himali Cha Cha.

A place to enjoy delicious Northern cuisine such as tandoori and curry dishes. **$$**

Maharajah's
19/1 Soi 8, Sukhumvit Road
Tel: 254 8876
Some tasty tandoor dishes, good value for money. **$**

Moghul Room
1/16 Sukhumvit Road, Soi 11
Tel: 253 4465
Popular, but more expensive than some. **$$**

Mrs. Balbir's
155/18 Soi 11
Sukhumvit Road
Tel: 253 2281
Excellent cuisine with reasonable prices. **$$**

Rang Mahal
Rembrandt Hotel
19 Soi 18
Sukhumvit Road
Tel: 261 7100
First-class cuisine and impeccable service. **$$–$$$**

Shalimar
1/17 Soi Chaiyot Sukhumvit Soi 11
Tel: 255 7950
A little restaurant run by Sharma and his wife serving one of the best mutton curry dishes in Bangkok. Birayani is a must order dish. Reasonable prices. **$**

Tandoor
Holiday Inn Crowne Plaza
981 Silom Road

Tel: 238 4300
Northern Indian cuisine of exceptional quality. **$$**

Indonesian
Bali
15/3 Soi Ruam Rudee
Ploenchit Road
Tel: 254 3581
Customers can savor the best of Javanese cuisine at very reasonable prices. **$**

American
Bourbon Street
Washington Square, Soi 22
Sukhumvit Road
Tel: 259-0328-9
This friendly restaurant with its pub-like atmosphere is the place for good Cajun foods in Bangkok. Draft beer is available. **$**

Planet Hollywood
Gaysorn Plaza, 1st Floor
Ploenchit Road
Tel: 656 1358
Like any outlet under this brand name, it offers nachos, burger, ribs and much more American foods and snacks. Try spicy papapa salad (somtam) or tom yam goong. Live music every night from 10pm onwards. **$$**

British
The Bull's head
595/11 Sukhumvit Soi 33

Sukhumvit Road
Tel: 259 4444
English menu from fish and chips to cottage pie in a pub atmosphere. Reservation is needed for a group. The place gets crowded at night so it is recommended to get there early for dinner. **$$**

Bobby's Arms
Car Park Building, 2nd Floor
Patpong 2
Tel: 233 6828
Well-established haunt of mostly British and Australian regulars. Wide-ranging menu with the reasonably-priced roast dinners as highlights. Sunday night features a not-to-be-missed jazz band. **$$**

Jools Bar & Restaurant
21/3 Soi 4 Nana Tai
Sukhumvit Road
Tel: 252 6413
Excellent value for money for both food and drinks. Menu and decor come pretty close to an authentic English public house. The truly big English breakfast is served from 9 am to well past noon (costs 99–159 baht per person). **$$**

Witch's Tavern
306/1 Sukhumvit Soi 55
Tel: 391 9791
A pub cum restaurant founded by a Thai who studied in England. Live jazz makes the place lively every night. The upstairs restaurant serves English food from pies to

Internet Cafés

Bangkok has a number of places to surf the Net. Some offer only Internet services while others serve food and drinks. Prices are fairly reasonable.

Byte in a Cup
Siam Discovery Center, 4th Floor,
989 Rama I Road
Tel: 658 0433/5
A variety of coffees brewed in some fancy machines and delicious gourmet sandwiches are on offer apart from the reasonable online service.

Cyberia
654/8 Sukhumvit Road near Soi Sukhumvit 24 and Emporium

shopping mall
Tel: 259 3356/7
Enjoy a full bar and some food while surfing the Net. Open until midnight Thursday, Friday and Saturday.

Siam Square Imagine
Siam Square Imagine, 3rd Floor,
Siam Square Soi 7
Pathumwan
Tel: 658 3941/5
All the usual Internet and email facilities in a relaxed atmosphere.

Hello Internet Cafe
Second Floor of Hello Restaurant
63-65 Khao San Road (opposite D & D Inn)
Tel: 629 1280

A place to find very competitive fee for surfing the Net. Run by former staff of a big telecom firm, so the service is reliable. Food is also reasonably priced.

Explorer Internet Cafe
Patpong Soi 1
Silom Road
Tel: 634 0944
Internet services in the heart of Patpong.

Inter@ccess
43 Tanao Road
Banglamphoo
Tel: 629 4091
Reliable services. Good for backpackers if Hello Internet Cafe is too crowded.

fish and chips. Weekends can be crowded with night owls. **$$**

Japanese

Benihana
Marriott Royal Garden Riverside
257/1-3 Charoen Nakhon Road
Tel: 476 0022
The preparation of the dishes is a combination of knife-wielding and juggling. The end result is always a superb meal. **$$$**

Benkay
Royal Orchid Sheraton Hotel
2 Captain Bush Lane
Tel: 234 5599
The restaurant is noted for its exquisite Japanese cuisine served in an ambience of quiet elegance; a place for refined tastes. **$$$**

Endogin
Shangri-La Hotel
89 Soi Wat Suan Phlu
Tel: 236 7777
All you would expect from one of Bangkok's top hotels. **$$–$$$**

Genji
Hilton International Hotel
Wireless Road
Tel: 253 0123, ext. 8141
Excellent food in a refined atmosphere. **$$$**

Hagi
Central Plaza Hotel
1695 Phaholyothin Road
Tel: 541 1234
Very popular and with reasonable prices and good food. **$$**

Hanaya
683 Siphya Road
Tel: 234 8095

Clean and unpretentious with good service. **$**

Kagetsu
Asia Hotel
296 Phaya Thai Road
Tel: 215 0808
Popular restaurant offering traditional cuisine and setting at reasonable prices. **$$**

Kiku-No-Hana
The Landmark Hotel
138 Sukhumvit Road
Tel: 254 0404
First-class Japanese cuisine in a first-class hotel. **$$–$$$**

Miraku
Imperial Hotel
6 Wireless Road
Tel: 254 0023
Traditional Japanese dishes in a traditional Japanese setting. Good value for money. **$–$$**

Mizu's
32 Patpong Road
Tel: 233 6447
One of the oldest Japanese restaurants in the city. The house specialty is sizzling steak. Reasonable prices. **$–$$**

Shogun
Dusit Thani Hotel
946 Rama IV Road
Tel: 236 0450
Sashimi and other Japanese delicacies served; elegant decor. **$$$**

Teio
Monarch Lee Gardens Hotel
188 Silom Road
Tel: 238 1999
Sophisticated Japanese dining.

Special family buffet lunches on Saturday and Sunday. **$$**

Tokugawa
Ambassador Hotel
171 Soi 11–13
Sukhumvit Road
Tel: 254 0444, ext. 1569
The *teppanyaki* is delicious and fun to watch the chef displaying his skill. **$$**

Price Guides

Prices are for a meal for two, excluding alcoholic beverages:
$ under 600 baht
$$ 600–1,000 baht
$$$ 1,000 baht plus

Pacific

Trader Vic's
Marriott Royal Garden Riverside
257/1-3 Charoen Nakhon Road
Tel: 476 0022
The unique style of oven gives a different flavour to the dishes. A delightfully different dining experience. **$$$**

Vietnamese/Burmese

Le Dalat
47/1 Soi 23
Sukhumvit Road
Tel: 258 4192; and on
Patpong Building
2nd Floor
Suriwong Road
Tel: 234 0290
Two of the best in town in the medium price range. **$$**

Drinking Notes

Non-alcoholic drinks:
Shakes: Many restaurants catering to Western tastes whip up a delicious shake made of puréed fruit, crushed ice and a light syrup.
Coconuts: Chilled young coconuts are delicious; drink the juice, then eat the tender young flesh.
Soft drinks are found everywhere. Try Vitamilk, a health drink made from soya bean milk.
Coffee: Sip the very strong Thai coffee, flavored with chicory.
Tea: The odd orange Thai tea is

sticky sweet but delicious. On a hot day, the Chinese prefer to drink a hot, very thin tea, believing that ice is bad for the stomach. Try all over ice anyway.
Alcoholic drinks:
Beers: Local beers are Amarit, Singha, Singha Gold, Leo, Super Leo, and Chang. In addition to these, the most easily available international brands are Heineken, Kloster and Carlsberg. Carlsberg and Heineken are now brewed in Thailand. The end of the

rainy season sees beer gardens springing up in front of shopping malls and other vacant spaces. Most of them offer draft beers and serve local snacks.
Whiskeys: Of the many Thai cane whiskeys, Mekong and Saengthip are the most popular. They are drunk on the rocks, with soda, Cola, or water. Unfortunately, they are not available in most of the upmarket restaurants and leading hotels, but it is always good to ask if they are on offer.

Le Dalat Indochine
14 Sukhumvit Soi 23
Prasarnmitr
Tel: 661 7967-8.
Run by Le Dalat's owner, this
restaurant taps the high-end
bracket of Vietnamese cuisine. Nice
atmosphere and great for special
occasions. Reservation is
recommended. **$$**

Le Danang
Central Plaza Hotel
1695 Phaholyothin Road
Tel: 541 1234
A long-established Vietnamese
restaurant renowned for its
authentic cuisine. **$$**

Le-Ong
1091/50 Soi Chlarat
New Petchaburi Road
Tel: 251 4078
Vietnamese food served in a
tropical green setting. A private
meeting room is available. **$$–$$$**

Pho
25 Soi Chidlom
Ploenchit
Tel: 251 8900
Serving reasonaly priced authentic
dishes including a number of Pho
(Vietnamese noodles). Attentive
service. A pianist plays music from
7–9pm, Tuesday to Saturday. **$$**

Salgon
Asia Hotel
296 Phaya Thai Road
Tel: 215 0808
Luxury dining in an elegant setting
under the supervision of a
Vietnamese chef. **$$$**

Saigon Bakery
313 Silom Road
Tel: 231 0434
A Vietnamese restaurant and
bakery; inexpensive. **$**

Saigon-Rimsai
413/9 Soi 55
Sukhumvit Road
Tel: 381 1797
Small, beautifully decorated and the
Vietnamese chef produces a variety
of inexpensive dishes. **$–$$**

Vietnam
82-4 Silom Road
(opposite Convent Road)
Tel: 234 6174
Inexpensive tasty southern-style
Vietnamese cuisine. **$**

Culture

Sources of Information

Modern pop culture seems to have
gained ascendancy over traditional
Thai arts, despite government
support for Thai arts and
performers. The best sources of
information about what's going on
are *The Bangkok Post* and *The
Nation*, both of which have daily
listing sections and weekend
entertainment supplements. Other
sources of information include free
tourist leaflets from hotel and
guesthouse lobbies.

Art Galleries

Exhibitions of paintings, sculpture,
ceramics, photographs and weaving
are varied and numerous. Check
The Bangkok Post and *The Nation*
for details.

The National Gallery, to the north
of the National Museum in Bangkok
across the approach to the Phra
Pinklao Bridge at 4 Chao Fa Road,
tel: 281 2224, displays works by
Thai artists and offers frequent film
shows. Open daily from 9am–noon,
1–4pm except on Monday and
Friday.

Silpakorn University, opposite the
Grand Palace on Na Phralan Road,
is the country's premier fine arts
college. It frequently stages
exhibitions of students' work. Open
Monday to Friday, 9am–6pm and on
Saturday 9am–4.30pm. For more
details call: 221 0820.

Faculty of Decorative Arts,
Silpakorn University, holds
exhibitions with an emphasis on
interior design, visual
communications and applied arts.
Open daily, 10am–6pm (except
Sundays and public holidays).

Tel: 221 5874 for detials.

**Art Center, Chulalongkorn
University**, Center of Academic
Resources (Library Building), 7th
floor. This space of 260 sq. meters
(310 sq. yards) holds exhibitions of
international and established local
artists and photographers. Open
Monday to Friday, 9am–7pm,
Saturday 9am–4pm; tel: 218 2962.

About Studio/About Cafe,
Maitreejit Road. The young and
trendy come here to drink, eat and
catch the dance, music and
performance art shows held here.
Major exhibitions of visual art are
held on the second floor and the
café often has talks and
workshops. Open Monday to
Thursday noon–midnight; Friday and
Saturday noon–2pm; closed
Sunday; tel: 6723 1742/3.

Tadu Contemporary Art, Royal City
Avenue. This is a commercial
contemporary art gallery showing
well-known local artists. Open
Tuesday to Saturday
10.30am–7.30pm. For more details
call: 203 0926 ext. 15.

Co-Op Housing Building,
Thoetdamri Road. The Numthong
Gallery on the first floor displays
contemporary paintings by
established local artists. Open
Wednesday to Sunday 10am–8pm;
tel: 234 4326. On the third floor is
an art space called Project 304, a
venue for installations and
experimental film; tel: 688 5151 for
details of shows.

Visual Dhamma, Soi Asoke, in a
lane opposite the Singha Beer
House. Takes an active role in
ensuring that talented artists
exhibit their works. As its name
implies, it is interested primarily in
a new school of Thai art which
attempts to re-interpret Buddhist
themes.

Other promoters of Thai art and
photography are the:
British Council (Soi 9 Siam Square,
Rama I Road, tel: 652 5480/9); the
Goethe Institute (18/1 Soi
Ngamduplee, Rama IV Road,
tel: 287 0942–4); and the
Alliance Francaise (29 Sathorn Tai
Road, tel: 286 3841), all of which
sponsor exhibitions.

Concerts

Concerts of European music and dance are now regular events. The Bangkok Symphony Orchestra gives frequent concerts, as do groups from Western countries at various venues around the city (check the press for details).

Thai Dance-drama

The **Fine Arts Department** periodically offers concerts of Thai music and dance/drama at the **National Theater** (tel: 224 1342). On Saturday afternoons at 2pm, programs of Thai classical dance are presented at the auditorium of the Public Relations Building on Rachadamnern Klang Avenue opposite the Royal Hotel. Each Friday, **Bangkok Bank** offers traditional Thai music on the top floor of its Pan Fah branch (Rachadamnern Avenue at the intersection with Prasumane Road) at 5pm. *See also pages 115–117.*

Theaters

The **National Theater** (Ratchini Road, tel: 224 1342) presents Thai works and, occasionally, big name foreign ensembles like the New York Philharmonic. For more experimental works, Thai or foreign, look to the **Thailand Cultural Center** (tel: 245 7711). The center, which is a gift of the government of Japan, is located on Ratchadaphisek Road north of Bangkok. Its three stages present everything from pianists to puppets. See the newspapers for announcements of forthcoming performances.

It is also possible to find Chinese opera performed as part of funeral entertainment or during the Vegetarian Festival each September in Chinatown. These performances are normally not announced, but they are hard to miss; the clash of cymbals and drums and the screech of violins identify them.

Likay, the village version of the great *lakhon* and *khon* dance/dramas of the palace, was once staple fare at temple fairs. Alas, most of the fairs have faded away in the city and are found only in rural areas. About the only place one can see truncated *likay* performances is at Lak Muang, where supplicants pay a troupe to perform for the gods of the heavens and the angels of the city.

Foreign Cultural Organizations

Foreign culture is promoted by the respective country cultural organizations.
Alliance Française
29 S. Sathorn Road
Tel: 213 2122/3
Open Monday to Friday, 8am–7.30pm; Saturday, 9–7pm.
American University Alumni (AUA)
179 Ratchadamri Road
Tel: 252 8170/3; and in Chiang Mai: 24 Ratchadamnern Avenue. Tel: 211 377.
Lions Chaophaya (Bangkok) Association
1/3-4 Ekachai 2, Sukhumvit 3, Klongton
Tel: 391 4357. Meetings on the last Thursday of the month.
Rotary Club
Bangkok Rotary, Grand Hyatt Erawan Hotel
Tel: 254 1234, (Office) 258 9037. English is the medium.

Bangkok Cinemas

Hollywood 1-2, 420 Phayathai Road, Ratchathevee. Tel: 208 9194-5.
Lido 1-3, Siam Square, Rama I Road. Tel: 252 6498.
MGM 1-2, 1998 Ramkamhaeng Road. Tel: (MGM 1) 319 7269, (MGM 2) 319 5904.
Panthip 1-2, Panthip Plaza, New Phetchburi Road. Tel: 251 2390.
Pinklao 1-10, Central Plaza, 5th Floor, Pinklao. Booking tel: 884 8570. Information tel: 884 8578.
Rangsit 1-14, Future Park, 3rd Floor, Rangsit, Pahonyothin Road. Booking tel: 958 0600. Information tel: 958 0608.

Scala, Siam Square Soi 1. Tel: 251 2861.
Siam Square Multiplex 1-4, Siam Square. Tel: 252 7416.
United Artists Emporium, Sukhumvit 24. Tel: 664 8711.
Warner 1-3, 119 Mahesak Road, off Silom Road. Tel: 234 3700-9.
Wongsawang Center 1-2, Central Department Store, Rama VII. Tel: 587 2055 ext. 4321.
World Trade 1-3, World Trade Center, 6th Floor, Ratchadamri Road. Tel: 255 9555-6.
United Artists Yanawa, Central Department Store, Rama III. Tel: 673 6060.

Cinema

Bangkok movie theaters present Thai, Chinese and subtitled Western films. The Western films are either mega-hits or are filled with violence – gore being substituted for dialogue. Thai films are usually based on a set theme (good versus evil, with pathos, rowdy humor, ugly villains and plenty of fisticuffs), or are comedies on the theme of young love. Only rarely does a film of social significance appear.

Libraries

For reading or reference, stop in at one of these libraries. All carry books in English on Thailand.
AUA, 179 Ratchadamri Road. Tel: 252 8953. Open 8.30am–6pm, Monday to Friday; and 8am–1pm on Saturday. The library is sponsored by the US Information Agency.
British Council
428 Siam Square, Soi 2. Tel: 252 6136. Open 10am–7pm, Tuesday to Friday; and 10am–5pm, Saturday.
Neilson Hayes
195 Suriwong Road. Tel: 233 1731. Open 9.30am–4pm, Monday to Saturday; and from 9.30am–12.30pm on Sunday.
Siam Society
131 Soi 21, Sukhumvit Road. Tel: 258 3491. Open 9am–5pm, Tuesday to Saturday.

Festivals

Festivals and Fairs

Temple fairs upcountry are great fun to attend. They are usually held in the evenings during the cool season to raise money for repairs to temple buildings. There are carnival rides, freak shows, halls of horror, *rumwong* dances, food vendors and deafening noise – the one element without which a fair would not be a fair. If you see one in progress, stop, park and enjoy yourself.

Diary of Events

The dates for these festivals and fairs change from year to year. Check the exact dates by calling the TAT in Bangkok.

January
New Year's Day is a day of relaxation after the festivities of the night before. It is a public holiday.

February
Chinese New Year is not celebrated with the boisterousness of other Asian countries. The temples are a bit busier with people making

wishes made for good fortune in the coming year, but otherwise there is nothing to mark the period. Shops close and behind the steel grills, private family celebrations go on for three or four days.

Magha Puja, a public holiday in Bangkok and a Buddhist holiday on the full moon night of February, marks the spontaneous gathering of 1,200 disciples to hear the Lord Buddha preach.

In the evening, Thais gather at temples to hear a sermon by the chief monk of the *wat*. Then, when the moon is rising, they pray and, clasping candles, incense and flowers, follow the chanting monks around the *bot* of the *wat* three times before placing their candles and incense in trays at the front of the *bot*.

March
Barred Ground Dove Festival. Dove lovers from all over Asia come to Yala for this event. The highlight is a dove-cooing contest involving over 1,400 competitors.

April
Chakri Day on April 6 celebrates the founding in 1782 of the dynasty that presently rules Thailand. It is celebrated in the palace but there are no public ceremonies. An official holiday, most Thais celebrate it as a day off from work.
The Phra Chedi Klang Nam Fair in April is one of the larger temple fairs. It is celebrated at the *wat* on the river's edge at Prapadaeng, 15 km (9 miles) south of Bangkok, on the Thonburi side of the river.

May
Labor Day (May 1) is a public holiday.
Coronation Day (May 5) is a private royal affair and a public holiday.
The Plowing Ceremony is a colorful ancient tradition celebrated only in Bangkok. Held at Sanam Luang, it is presided over by King Bhumibol and marks the official start of the rice planting season. Crimson-clad attendants lead bullocks, drawing an old-fashioned plow, around a specially prepared ground. The lord of ceremonies, usually the minister of agriculture, follows behind, scooping rice seed out of baskets and sowing it in the furrows left by the plow, all to the accompaniment of blaring conch shells and drums.
Visakha Puja is a public holiday on the full moon night of May that commemorates the birth, enlightenment and death of Buddha. The three things are all said to have happened on the same day. Visakha Puja is celebrated like Magha Puja, with a triple circumambulation around the temple as the moon is rising.

June
Sunthorn Phu Day. This annual celebration in late June commemorates the birth of the Thai poet Sunthorn Phu. The festivities include dramatic performances and puppet shows depicting his literary works and poetry recitals.

July
Asalaha Puja on the full moon night of July is the third most important Buddhist holiday and marks the

Songkran

Songkran (usually April 13–15) is a public holiday which, in the past, was the traditional Thai New Year – until royal decree shifted the date to January 1. It most closely resembles the Indian festival of Holi which occurs at the same time. Songkran is a time of wild revelry. The central event is the sprinkling of water on one's friends to bless them, but this usually

turns into a boisterous throwing of buckets of water on passersby.

The celebration of Songkran in Bangkok is a little more subdued than in the north, and while it may be safe for a visitor to ride in an open-windowed bus down the street, you are advised to be prepared when walking in the street, riding a tuk-tuk or visiting nightlife areas.

To see Songkran at its most riotous, travel down the western bank of the Chao Phraya River to the town of Prapadaeng. There, no one is safe, but in the April heat, who cares?

Songkran in the north of Thailand, particularly in Chiang Mai, is fervently celebrated over several days and attracts many visitors from Bangkok.

occasion when Buddha preached to his first five disciples. It is celebrated on the full moon night in similar manner to Magha Puja and Visakha Puja. It also marks the beginning of the three-month Lenten season. According to tradition Buddha was asked by farmers to bar monks from going on their morning alms rounds for a period of three months, because they were trampling on the rice shoots they had just planted. They offered instead to take food to the monks at the temple during this period, a practice which has been followed ever since.

Khao Phansa is celebrated immediately after Asalaha Puja and marks the commencement of the annual three-month Rains Retreat.

August
Queen Sirikit's birthday (August 12) is marked by religious ceremonies and private celebrations. It is a public holiday.

September
On the first day of the eighth lunar month, the Chinese celebrate the **Moon Festival**. They place small shrines laden with fruit, incense and candles in front of their houses to honor the moon goddess. The highlight of the festival are the utterly scrumptious cakes shaped like a full moon. They are specially prepared, often by chefs flown in from Hong Kong, and found no other time of the year.

October
The Chinese Vegetarian Festival, held in mid-October, is a subdued affair in Bangkok by comparison with the "firewalkers" of Phuket version. Enormous amounts of vegetarian food, Chinese operatic performances and elaborate offerings are made at various Chinese temples around the city. Only those wearing all-white attire are allowed in the area of the altar, so dress appropriately.

Ok Pansa marks the end of the three-month Lenten season, and the beginning of the Kathin season when Buddhists visit *wats* to present monks with new robes and other necessities. Groups will rent boats or buses and travel long distances to spend a day giving gifts to monks of a particular *wat*.

Chulalongkorn Day (October 23) honors King Rama V (1868–1910), who led Thailand into the 20th century. On this public holiday, students lay wreaths before his statue in the Plaza at the old National Assembly building during an afternoon ceremony.

November
Golden Mount Fair held the first week of November in Bangkok is one of the noisiest of temple fairs. Carnival rides, food concessions, variety performances and product stalls are the main attractions. Buddhist temple fairs all over Thailand are held throughout the cool season to raise money for reparations.

Loy Krathong is on the full moon night of November. It is said to have started in Sukhothai in the 13th century when a young queen, Nang Nopamat, floated a small boat laden with candles and incense downstream past the pavilion where her husband was talking with his friends. Whatever its origins, on this night Thais everywhere launch small candle-laden boats into the water and ask for blessings.

December
Trooping of the Colors (December 3). The royal regiments dressed in brilliantly colored costumes pass in review before the king. Held on the Plaza before the old National Assembly building, the Trooping of the Colors is the most impressive of martial ceremonies.

King Bhumibol celebrates his birthday (December 5) with a ceremony at Wat Phra Kaeo only for invited officials and guests and with a private party. It is a public holiday.

Constitution Day (December 10) is a public holiday in Thailand.

Christmas may soon be a Thai public holiday if shopkeepers have any say in the matter.

New Year's Eve on December 31 is a public holiday.

Nightlife

For years, Bangkok has enjoyed a lusty reputation as a center for sex of every paersuasion and interest. While the reputation was not altogether undeserved, times and clienteles have changed. The American GIs of the 1960s and the German and Arab sex tourists of the 1970s have been replaced by upmarket tourists, usually traveling as couples. Also common are Japanese men on packaged sex tours. Western paedophiles are a continuing, and unwelcome, problem.

While there has been no diminution in the number of massage parlors and bars, there has been an increase in other activities to meet the needs of the new breed of travelers, most of them in the 20–50 age range. Jazz clubs, videotheques, discos and open-air restaurants are the most popular form of entertainment in towns. A sign of the drastic changes is that the queen of night-time activities in Bangkok is shopping. Night markets have sprung up along Sukhumvit and Silom roads. Even that wrinkled old harlot of a street, Patpong, has not been immune to the breezes of change. Vendors' tables choke the street, drawing more patrons than the bars with a wealth of counterfeit Rolex watches, Benetton shirts and cassette tapes. The change has rubbed off on the bars as well. Many of Patpong's bars have metamorphosed into discos, which begin to get going after 11pm.

Go-go Bars

There are three key areas in Bangkok where the types of entertainment for which the city has become famous can be found.

Patpong Road describes three streets: Patpong itself and Patpong 2, which is a welter of bars and bright lights, and Patpong 3, which is almost exclusively gay. Soi Cowboy is a somewhat downmarket version of Patpong. Here, the entertainment is more basic.

Midway between the two in geographic and entertainment terms, is the Nana Entertainment Plaza off Soi 4, Sukhumvit Road.

Discos

Patpong also offers discos, many of which continue long after the bars have closed down. As with all nightlife establishments, vogue and fashion play a part. Clubs, bars and discos come and go quite frequently, but the venues listed below have been around for a number of years. If you're looking for something hip and very happening, check the local press for club reviews. At upmarket or very trendy venues dress policy play its part, so make sure you dress according to where you are going.

Ratchadaphisek Road has been a magnet for Bangkok young nightowls for years. The discos appeal more to Thais than to foreigners, but there is room for both.

The biggest and most frequented is **Hollywood** and the **Phuture Pub**. However, the newest entertainment venue, **Studio Music Style**, is located in Sukhumvit Soi 24. The place is a one-stop entertainment venue which features discos, karaoke rooms and pubs. Open from noon over the weekend; tel: 661 0900 29 ext. 198.

Music Clubs

The jazz played in Thailand is not the kind of jazz you will find in New York, London or Tokyo but it is still very listenable and some of it is very innovative. Jazz clubs proliferate along Soi Sarasin, Lang Suan, and a new venue is **Pathumwan Princess Hotel** on Phayathai Road. They are usually glass-fronted with sidewalk tables – the emphasis being on good live music and good conversation.

These clubs appeal as much to middle class Thais as they do to visitors. Among the most popular with mixed nationality crowds is **Brown Sugar** (Soi Sarasin) and **Round Midnight** (Soi Lang Suan). Musicians at **Saxophone** at the Victory Monument (3/8 Phya Thai Road) play jazz standards. Open until 3am.

If you like Dixieland jazz and a lively atmosphere, **Bobby's Arms** at 8.30 Sunday evenings is where you should head. The band comprises local residents who play for the fun of it. Bobby's offers good British cuisine and lots of beer in a convivial setting. Located on the first floor of the car park behind Foodland on Patpong 2 Road.

Most of the more sophisticated nightclubs are found in first-class hotels. Classy and classic, the Oriental Hotel's famed **Bamboo Bar** nightclub is for dressier occasions. The scene is chic, normally with jazz singers from the United States playing long-term engagements. You can also find imported acts at the Dusit Thani Hotel's **Tiara Lounge**. Most hotels have lounge bars with good musical acts.

For other night-time activities, check the daily newspapers for announcements of concerts, art shows, lectures and other events around the city.

Sport

Participant Sports

Thailand has developed its outdoor sports facilities and air-conditioned indoor facilities to a considerable degree. Nearly every major hotel has a swimming pool and a fitness center; some have squash courts and jogging paths.

Fitness Centers

In Bangkok, the Asia-wide **Clark Hatch** has a branch in the Thaniya Plaza, off Silom Road, tel: 231 2250. **Fitness International** is located in the Dusit Thani Hotel, tel: 236 0450/9. Part-time membership is available. All the top hotels in Bangkok have well-equipped fitness centers. There is also a fitness park in Lumpini Park.

Golf

Thais are great golfing buffs, going so far as to employ some of the golfing worlds stellar architects to design international-class courses. The best courses are in Bangkok, Phuket and Pattaya, with other courses in Chiang Mai, Khao Yai and Hua Hin. Green fees range from 500–1,000 baht per round on weekends and it is generally not difficult to reserve a time.

Among Bangkok's courses is;

Navathanee Golf Course
22 M.1, Sukhapibal 2 Road
Tel: 376 1020
Designed by Robert Trent Jones Jr.
It is open from 6am–6pm

Army Golf Course
459 Ram Intra Road
Tel: 521 1530
Open from 5am–9.30pm

Railway Training Center Golf Course
Phahonyothin Road
Tel: 271 0130

West of the Hyatt Central Plaza Hotel opens at 6am, closes at 8pm
Krungthep Sports Golf Course
522 Huamark Road
Tel: 379 3732
Opens at 5am, closes at 5pm.

Jogging

Two jogging sites for those wise enough not to challenge Bangkok's traffic for right of way are in **Lumpini Park** and **Chatuchak Park**. The Siam Intercontinental Hotel, Rama Gardens, and the Hilton hotels have jogging paths.

Spectator Sports

Despite the hot climate, Thai men and women are avid sports enthusiasts, actively playing both their own sports and those adopted from the West.

The king of foreign sports is soccer and is played by both sexes. Following a close second is badminton, with basketball, rugby, track and field, swimming, marksmanship, boxing, tennis and golf trailing only a short way behind. Check the English-language newspapers for schedules.

The principal sports venues in Bangkok are the **National Stadium**, on Rama I Road just west of Mahboonkrong Shopping Center, tel: 318 0940/4; the **Hua Mark Stadium**, east of the city next to Ramkamhaeng University and the **Thai-Japanese Sports Center**, at Din Daeng near the northern entrance to the expressway, tel: 465 5325.

Thai Sports

Thailand has a number of unique sports well worth watching as much for the grace and agility displayed as for the element of fun that pervades every competition (see page 119).

Takraw

Tournaments are held at the **Thai-Japanese Sports Center** (tel: 465 5325 for dates and times) four times a year; admission is free. Competitions are also held in the

northwest corner of Bangkok's Sanam Luang during the March–April kite flying contests. Free admission. During the non-monsoon months wander into a park or temple courtyard anywhere in the country in the late afternoon.

Thai Boxing

In Bangkok, **Ratchadamnern Stadium** on Ratchadamnoen Nok Avenue offers bouts on Monday, Wednesday, and Thursday at 6pm and on Sunday at 4.30 and 8.30pm. The Sunday matinee at 4.30pm is recommended, as it has the cheapest seats. Ticket prices are between 500 and 1,000 baht for ringside seats (depending on the quality of the card), running downwards to 100 baht.

Lumpini Boxing Stadium, on Rama IV Road, stages bouts on Tuesday and Friday at 6.30pm and on Saturday at 1 and 6.30pm. Ticket prices are the same as at Ratchadamnern. As above, weekend afternoon matinees are the cheapest.

There are also televised bouts on Saturday and Sunday, and at 10.30pm on some week nights.

Snooker

In recent years, Thailand has produced some excellent snooker players who are currently nipping at the heels of world champions in international competitions. As a result, parlors have sprung up everywhere in Thailand as budding players focus their eyes on complex shots and potential riches. There are numerous snooker parlors in Bangkok. The **Rooks** chain is the most popular and dozens of its snooker parlors can be found around the city.

Shopping

Where to Shop

Whatever part of your budget you have allocated for shopping, double it or regret it. Keep a tight grip on your wallet or you will find yourself being seduced by the low prices and walking off with more than you can possibly carry home. If you cannot resist, see the "Export" section for an inexpensive way to get souvenirs home.

Over the years, there have been two major changes in the shopping picture. First, there have been subtle design alterations to make the items more appealing to foreign buyers. The purists may carp, but the changes and the wider range of products are welcomed by shoppers. At the same time, new products have been introduced which have found popular reception among visitors.

The other change is that while regional products were once found only in the places that produced them, there has been a homogenization of distribution, so that it is now possible, for example, to buy Chiang Mai umbrellas in Bangkok. The widest range of items are found in Chiang Mai and Bangkok, but if you never have a chance to leave Bangkok, do not despair; nearly everything you might want to buy in upcountry towns can be found in the capital.

Shipping

Most shops will handle documentation and shipping for you. Alternatively, the General Post Office on New Road, near the Oriental Hotel, offers boxes and a packing service for goods sent by sea mail. Packages can be shipped from most post offices. Post offices in most towns sell cardboard boxes specially created for shipping packages.

Thai International in Bangkok also offers a special service called "Thaipac" that will air freight your purchases (regardless of the mode of transportation or the airline you are using) to the airline's destination closest to your home for 25 percent of the normal rate. Just take your goods to the airline office at 485 Silom Road (tel: 233 3810). They must fit into a special box and weigh no more than 33 kg (73 lbs) per box. Thaipac will also handle the documentation and customs clearance for a small charge.

Export Permits

The Fine Arts Department prohibits the export of all Thai Buddha images, images of other deities and fragments (hands or heads) of images dating from before the 18th century.

All antiques and art objects, regardless of type or age, must be registered with the Fine Arts Department. The shop will usually do this for you. If you decide to handle it yourself, take the piece to the Fine Arts Department on Na Prathat Road, across from Sanam Luang, together with two postcard-sized photos of it. The export fee ranges between 50 and 200 baht depending on the antiquity of the piece.

Fake antiques do not require export permits, but airport customs officials are not art experts and may mistake it for a genuine piece. If it looks authentic, clear it at the Fine Arts Department to avoid problems later.

Complaints

The customer is (nearly) always wrong might be the most candid way of putting it. Apart from when large shops are involved, expect that once you have paid for an item and left the store, that's it in terms of possible refunds –

Shopping Areas

If you cannot find it in Bangkok, you will not be able to find it anywhere else in the country. Aside from the traffic problems, Bangkok is the most comfortable place to shop. Shopping venues range from huge air-conditioned malls to tiny hole-in-the-wall shops, to crafts sections of large department stores (see page 91).

Huge air-conditioned malls like Amarin Plaza, Oriental Place (New Rd), World Trade Center, Siam Center, Mahboonkrong, Gaysorn Plaza and Central Plaza are filled with shops selling a variety of items. Some malls specialize in particular types of items; River City, for example, has dozens of shops selling superb antiques.

Queen Sirikit's Chitralada stores sell the rare crafts she and her organization have worked so diligently to preserve by teaching the arts to village women. There are branches in the airport, Grand Palace, Oriental Plaza, Hilton Hotel and Pattaya. The Thai government's handicraft center, **Narayana Phand**, at 127 Ratchadamri Road, displays the full array of Thai handicrafts.

Most major department stores have special handicrafts departments carrying a wide selection of items. New Road between Silom and Suriwong, Silom Road in the vicinity of the Narai Hotel, upper sections of Suriwongse Road, and Sukhumvit Road are lined with crafts shops. Traditional shopping areas like Sampeng Lane, the Thieves' Market, the Buddha amulet markets at Tha Prajan and Wat Ratchanadda have lost some of their allure over the years as new businesses have moved in, but one

unless, that is, the defect is very glaring and there is no possible way you could have caused it.

You can report the shop to the Tourist Police, but they are not usually interested. Shop carefully. *Caveat emptor.*

can still find the occasional bargain. By far the most challenging (and often most rewarding) is the huge weekend market at Chatuchak (see page 98), which has special sections for porcelain, brassware and a number of old oddities that don't fit into any particular category.

Shopping hours

Large department stores in Bangkok are open from 10am to 9pm. Most ordinary shops open from 9am to 6pm.

What to Buy

Real/Fake Antiques

Wood, bronze, terracotta and stone statues from all regions of Thailand and Burma can be found in Bangkok. There are religious figures and characters from classical literature, carved wooden angels, mythical animals, temple bargeboards and eave brackets.

Although the Thai government has banned the export of Buddha images, there are numerous deities and disciples which can be sent abroad. Bronze deer, angels and characters from the Ramakien cast in bronze do not fall under the export ban.

Chiang Mai produces beautiful wooden replicas modeled on antique sculptures. Sold as reproductions, they make lovely home decor items.

Chiang Mai also produces a wide range of beautifully-crafted wooden furniture. Cabinets, tables, dining room sets, elephant howdah, bedroom sets or simple items like wooden trays are crafted from teak or other woods and carved with intricate designs.

Baskets

Thailand's abundant bamboo, wicker and grasses are transformed into lamps, storage boxes, tables, colorful mats, handbags, letter holders, tissue boxes and slippers. Wicker and bamboo are turned into storage lockers with brass fittings

Bookstores

English-language books are sold at the many outlets of Asia Books, Bookazine, DK Books and Kinokuniya.

Below are listed their flagship stores. DK also operates small French and German shops at the Alliance Française and the Goethe Institute. On Khao San Road, a half-dozen shops and stalls sell and buy used foreign-language books. Besides English, French, German and Japanese titles are common. The bookstores sell foreign-language magazines (at daunting prices), as do branches of **Central** and **Robinson**

department stores.

Asia Books
221 Sukhumvit Road
(between Sois 15 & 17)
Tel: 252 7277.
Bookazine
Siam Square
(opp. Siam Centre), Rama I Road
Tel: 255 3778.
DK Book House
2F Seacon Square, Srinakarin
Road (off Bangna-Trad Highway)
Tel: 393 8040
This is the largest bookstore in
Southeast Asia, but reaching it
may take an entire day.

Elite Used Books
593/5 Sukhumvit Road
(near Soi 33/1)
Tel: 258 0221; also at
1/12 Sukhumvit Soi 3
Tel: 258 0221
More than English titles.
Kinokuniya
The Emporium, 3rd Floor,
Sukhumvit Road
Tel: 664 8554/6; also at
Isetan, 6th Floor
Ratchadamri Road
Tel: 255 9834/6
The latest in Bangkok, this chain
probably stocks the largest
number of titles in all categories.

and furniture to fill the entire house. Shops can provide the cushions as well. *Yan lipao*, a thin, sturdy grass, is woven into delicate patterns to create purses and bags for formal occasions. Although expensive, the bags are durable, retaining their beauty for years.

Ceramics

Best known among the distinctive Thai ceramics (*see page 91*) is the jade green celadon, which is distinguished by its finely crazed surface. Statues, lamps, ashtrays and other items are also produced in dark green, brown and cobalt blue hues.

Modeled on its Chinese cousin, blue-and-white porcelain includes

Street Shopping

You will not find high-ticket items nor will the quality equal that found in finer stores, but for gift items, there are few better places to look. In Bangkok look in Pratunam market – now being redeveloped – and along both sides of Rachaprarop Road. Try both sides of Sukhumvit Road, between Soi 3 and 11, where you will find Burmese puppets, handicrafts and, perhaps most important, suitcases and bags to put it all in.

pots, lamp bases, household items and figurines. Quality varies according to the skill of the artist, and of the firing and glazing.

Bencharong (five colors) describes a style of porcelain derived from 16th-century Chinese art. Normally reserved for bowls, containers and fine chinaware, its classic pattern features a small religious figure surrounded by intricate floral designs. The whole is rendered in five colors – usually green, blue, yellow, rose and black.

Earthenware includes a wide assortment of pots, planters and dinner sets in a rainbow of colors and designs. Also popular are the big, brown glazed Shanghai jars bearing yellow dragons, which the Thais use to hold bath water and which visitors use as planters. Antique stoneware includes the double-fish design plates and bowls originally produced at Sawankhaloke, the kilns established near Sukhothai in the 13th century.

Some of the best ceramics come from Ratchaburi, southwest of Bangkok. The wide variety makes a special trip there worthwhile.

Decorative Arts

Lacquerware comes in two styles: the gleaming gold-and-black variety normally seen on temple shutters, and the matte red type with black and/or green details, which

originated in northern Thailand and Burma. The lacquerware repertoire includes ornate containers and trays, wooden figurines, woven bamboo baskets and Burmese-inspired Buddhist manuscripts. The pieces may also be bejeweled with tiny glass mosaics and gilded ornaments.

Black lacquer is also the base into which shaped bits of mother-of-pearl are pressed. Scenes from religious or classical literature are rendered on presentation trays, containers and plaques. Beware of craftsmen who take shortcuts by using black paint rather than the traditional seven layers of lacquer. On these items, the surface cracks, often while the item is still on the shelf.

Fabrics and Clothes

Thai silk is perhaps Thailand's best-known craft. Sold in a wide variety of colors, its hallmark is the tiny nubs which, like embossings, rise from its surface. Unlike sheer Indian silks and shiny Chinese-patterned silks, Thai silk is a thick cloth that lends itself to clothes, curtains and upholstery.

Burmese in origin and style, *kalaga* wall hangings depicting gods, kings and mythical animals are stuffed to make them stand out from the surface in bas-relief.

Gems and Jewelry

Thailand is one of the world's exporters of cut rubies and sapphires. The rough stones are mostly imported from Cambodia and Burma, as local mines are not able to meet the demand. Customers should patronize only those shops that display the trade's official emblem: a gold ring mounted with a ruby, which guarantees the dealer's integrity.

Thailand is now regarded as the world's leading cutter of gemstones, the "Bangkok cut" rapidly becoming one of the most popular. Thai artisans set the stones in gold and silver to create jewelry and bejeweled containers. Artisans also craft jewelry to satisfy the tastes of an international clientele. Light-green Burmese jade (jadeite) is carved into jewelry and art objects. The island of Phuket produces international-standard natural, cultured, "mob" (teardrop), and artificial pearls (made from pearl dust glued to form a globule). They are sold as individual items or are set into gold jewelry.

Costume jewelry is a major Thai business with numerous items available. A related craft which has grown rapidly in the past decade is that of gilding Thai orchids for use as brooches.

Metal Art Objects

Although Thai craftsmen have produced some of Asia's most beautiful Buddha images, modern bronze sculpture tends to be of less exalted subjects and execution. Minor deities, characters from classical literature, deer and abstract figures are cast up to 2 meters (7 ft) tall and are normally clad with a brass skin to make them gleam. Bronze is also cast into handsome cutlery and coated in shiny brass.

Silver and gold are pounded into jewelry items, boxes and other decorative pieces; many are set with gems. To create nielloware boxes and receptacles, a design is incised in silver or gold. The background is cut away and filled with an amalgam of dark metals, leaving the figures to stand in high relief against the black background.

Tin, mined near Phuket, is the prime ingredient in pewterware, of which Thailand is a major producer. Items range from clocks and steins to egg cups and figurines.

Paintings

Modern Thai artists paint everything from realistic to abstract art, the latter often a weak imitation of Western art. Two areas at which they excel are depictions of everyday village life and of new interpretations of classical Buddhist themes. Artists can also work from live sittings or photographs to create superb charcoal or oil portraits. A family photograph from home can be transformed into a painting. The price depends on size: a 40cm x 60cm (16" x 24") charcoal portrait costs around 1,000 baht. There are several street-side studios in Bangkok that specialize in this art. Works of local artists are regularly exhibited at various art galleries and cafés (see page 283). Check the press for details of art sales.

Theatrical Paraphernalia

Papier-mache khon masks, like those used in palace dance/drama, are painted and accented with lacquer decorations and gilded to create superb works of art.

Shadow puppets cut from the hides of water buffaloes and displayed against backlit screens in open air theaters tell the Ramakien story. Check to be sure the figure is actually cut from hide and not anything else. Brightly-colored shadow puppets cut from buffalo hide make excellent wall decorations.

Inspired by the Ramakien, craftsmen have fashioned miniature models of chariots and warriors in gilded wood or glass sculpture. These two materials are also employed to create reproductions of the famous Royal Barges.

Umbrellas

Chiang Mai produces lovely umbrellas and fans made from silk or "sa" paper, a fine parchment often confused with rice paper but made from pounded tree bark.

Hilltribe Crafts

Northern hilltribes produce brightly-colored needlepoint work in a wide variety of geometric and floral patterns. These embroideries are sold either as produced, or else incorporated into shirts, coats, bags, pillowcases and other items.

Hilltribe silver work is valued less for its silver content (which is low) than for the intricate work and imagination that goes into making it. The genre includes necklaces, headdresses, bracelets and rings the women wear on ceremonial occasions. Enhancing their value are the old British-Indian rupee coins that decorate the women's elaborate headdresses.

Other hilltribe handicraft items on sale include knives, baskets, pipes and gourd flutes (that look and sound like bagpipes.)

Children

Activities for Children

Children enjoy the unusual animals of **Dusit Zoo**, or paddling boats in its lake or in **Lumpini** or **Chatuchak Park**. **Magic Land** at 72 Phahonyothin Road, near the Hyatt Hotel, is an amusement park with a ghost house, bumper cars and carnival rides. On weekdays, the ticket covers an unlimited number of rides; on weekends the number of rides is limited. Open 10am–5pm Monday to Friday; 10am–7pm Saturday and Sunday.

East of town at 101 Sukhapiban 2 Road, **Siam Park City** is a theme park with water-slides and flumes. It is open 10am–6pm, Monday to Friday; and 9am–7pm, Saturday and Sunday. A word of warning: The park prohibits the wearing of T-shirts in the swimming areas so take plenty of suntan oil for tender young skins.

Dream World, the latest theme park, is on Rangsit-Nakornnayok Road and it features what is called an "amazing snow land". It is open 10am–5pm on weekdays, and 10am–7pm on weekends.

Safari World is an amusement park with animal shows every weekend about 10 km (6 miles) from the center of town. The place has special facilities for the disabled, elderly and children. It is open 9am–5pm on weekdays, and 9am–5.30pm on weekends. Children can also make merry in the mini-amusement parks in some of the mega shopping malls such as Central Bangna, Seacon Square, and The Mall Thonburi.

Language

Origins and Intonation

For centuries, the Thai language, rather than tripping from foreigners tongues, has been tripping them up. Its roots go back to the place Thais originated from in the hills of southern Asia, but are overlaid by Indian influences. From the original settlers come the five tones which seem designed to frustrate visitors; one sound can have five different tones to mean five different things.

When you mispronounce, you don't simply say a word incorrectly, you say another word entirely. It is not unusual to see a semi-fluent foreigner standing before a Thai running through the scale of tones until suddenly a light of recognition dawns on his companion's face. There are misinformed visitors who will tell you that tones are not important. These people do not communicate with Thais, they communicate at them in a one-sided exchange that frustrates both parties.

Thai Names

From the languages of India have come polysyllabic names and words, the lexicon of literature. Thai names are among the longest in the world. Every Thai person's first and surname has a meaning. Thus, by learning the meaning of the name of everyone you meet, you would acquire a formal, but quite extensive vocabulary.

There is no universal transliteration system from Thai into English, which is why names and street names can be spelled three different ways. For example, the surname Chumsai is written Chumsai, Jumsai and Xoomsai depending on the family. This confuses even the Thais. If you ask a Thai how you spell something, he may well reply "how do you want to spell it?" Likewise, Bangkok's thoroughfare of Ratchadamnern is also spelled Rajdamnern. Ko Samui can be spelled Koh Samui. The spellings will differ from map to map, and book to book.

Phonology

The way Thai consonants are written in English often confuses foreigners. An "*h*" following a letter like "*p*," and "*t*" gives the letter a soft sound; without the "*h*" the sound is more explosive. Thus, "*ph*" is not pronounced "*f*" but as a soft "*p*." Without the "*h*," the "*p*" has the sound of a very hard "*b*." The word *Thanon* (street) is pronounced "*tanon*" in the same way as "Thailand" is not meant to sound like "*Thighland*." Similarly, final letters are often not pronounced as they look. A "*j*" on the end of a word is pronounced "*t*;" "*l*" is pronounced as an "*n*." To complicate matters further, many words end with "*se*" or "*r*" which are not pronounced.

Vowels are pronounced like this: **i** as in *sip*, **ii** as in *seep*, **e** as in *bet*, **a** as in *pun*, **aa** as in *pal*, **u** as in *pool*, **o** as in *so*, **ai** as in *pie*, **ow** as in *cow*, **aw** as in *paw*, **iw** as in *you*, **oy** as in *toy*.

In Thai, the pronouns "*I*" and "*me*" are the same word, but it is different for males and females. Men use the word *phom* when referring to themselves; women say *chan* or *diichan*. Men use *khrap* at the end of a sentence when addressing either a male or a female i.e. *pai* (f) *nai*, *khrap* (h) (where are you going? sir). Women add the word *kha* to their statements as in *pai* (f) *nai*, *kha* (h).

To ask a question, add a high tone *mai* to the end of the phrase i.e. *rao pai* (we go) or *rao pai mai* (h) (shall we go?). To negate a statement, insert a falling tone *mai* between the subject and the verb i.e. *rao pai* (we go), *rao mai pai* (we don't go). "Very" or "much" are indicated by adding *maak* to the end of a phrase i.e. *ron* (hot), *ron maak* (very hot).

Listed below is a small vocabulary intended to get you on your way. The five tones have been indicated by appending letters after them viz. high (h), low (l), middle (m), rising (like asking a question) (r), and falling (like suddenly understanding something as in "ohh, I see") (f).

Useful Words & Phrases

Days of the Week
Monday *Wan Jan*
Tuesday *Wan Angkan*
Wednesday *Wan Phoot*
Thursday *Wan Pharuhat*
Friday *Wan Sook*
Saturday *Wan Sao*
Sunday *Wan Athit*
Today *Wan nii* (h)
Yesterday *Mua wan nii* (h)
Tomorrow *Prung nii* (h)
When *Mua* (f) *rai*

Greetings and Short Phrases
Hello, goodbye
Sawasdee (a man then says *khrup*; a woman says *kha*; thus *sawasdee khrup*)
How are you?
Khun sabai dii, mai (h)
Well, thank you
Sabai dii, khapkhun
Thank you very much
Khapkhun maak
May I take a photo?
Thai roop (f) *noi, dai* (f) *mai* (h)
Never mind *Mai* (f) *pen rai*
I cannot speak Thai
Phuut Thai mai (f) *dai* (f)
I can speak a little Thai
Phuut Thai dai (f) *nit* (h) *diew*
Where do you live?
Khun yoo thii (f) *nai* (r)
What is this called in Thai?
An nii (h), *kaw riak aray phasa Thai*
How much? *Thao* (f) *rai*

Directions and Travel
Go *Pai*
Come *Maa*
Where *Thii* (f) *nai* (r)

Right *Khwaa* (r)
Left *Sai* (h)
Turn *Leo*
Straight ahead *Trong pai*
Please slow down *Cha cha noi*
Stop here *Yood thii* (f) *nii* (f)
Fast *Raew*
Hotel *Rong raam*
Street *Thanon*
Lane *Soi*
Bridge *Saphan*
Police Station *Sathanii Dtam Ruat*

Other Handy Phrases
Yes *Chai* (f)
No *Mai* (f) *chai* (f)
Do you have...? *Mii...mai* (h)
Expensive *Phaeng*
Do you have something cheaper?
Mii arai thii thook (l) *kwa, mai* (h)
Can you lower the price a bit?
Kaw lot noi dai (f) *mai* (h)
Do you have another color?
Mii sii uhn mai (h)
Too big *Yai kern pai*
Too small *Lek kern pai*
Do you have bigger?
Mii arai thii yai kwa mai (h)
Do you have smaller?
Mii arai thii lek kwa mai (h)
Hot (heat hot) *Ron* (h)
Hot (spicy) *Phet*
Cold *Yen*
Sweet *Waan* (r)
Sour *Prio* (f)
Delicious *Aroy*
I do not feel well *Mai* (f) *sabai*

Numbers

1 nung (m)
2 song (r)
3 sam (r)
4 sii (m)
5 haa (f)
6 hok (m)
7 jet (m)
8 pat (m)
9 kow (f)
10 sip (m)
11 sip et (m, m)
12 sip song (m, r)
13 sip sam (m, r) and so on
20 yii sip (m, m)
30 sam sip (f, m) and so on
100 nung roi (m, m)
1,000 nung phan (m, m)

Further Reading

General

Culture Shock: Thailand, by Cooper, Robert and Nanthapa, Singapore: Times Books, 1990. Very useful look at Thai customs and how to avoid faux pas. Written and illustrated in a highly amusing manner.
Mai Pen Rai Means Never Mind, by Hollinger, Carol, Tokyo, 1977. A very personal book that describes hilarious experiences in Thailand half a century ago. Both amusing and informative.
Siam Society, Culture and Environment in Thailand by Siam Society: Bangkok, 1989.
Thailand: The Environment of Modernisation, by Sternstein, Larry, Sydney: McGraw-Hill, 1976. Excellent geography text.
Thai Boxing, by Stockmann, Hardy. Bangkok: D.K. Books, 1979. Excellent, well-illustrated book on the basics of Thai boxing.
The Legendary American, by Warren, William, Boston: Houghton Mifflin. The intriguing story of American Thai silk king Jim Thompson.

History

Lords of Life, by Chakrabongse, Prince Chula. London: Alvin Redman, 1960. A history of the Chakri kings.
The Rise of Ayudhya by Kasetsiri, Charnvit. London: East Asian Historical Monographs, 1976. A narration of the history of early Ayutthaya.
The Indianized States of Southeast Asia by Coedes, George, Trans. Susan Brown Cousing. Ed. Walter F. Vella. Honolulu: East-West Center Press, 1968. Well written scholarly work.
A History of Southeast Asia, by Hall, D.G.E, 3rd ed. London: Macmillan, 1968. The classic text.

Revolution in Siam by Hutchinson, E.W, 1688: Hong Kong University Press. The events leading to the expulsion of the foreigners from Ayutthaya.

Mongkut, the King of Siam by Moffat, Abbot Low, Ithaca, New York: Cornell University Press, 1961. Superb history of one of Asia's most interesting 19th-century men.

A King Of Siam Speaks by Pramoj, M.R. Seni and M.R. Kukrit Pramoj. Bangkok, The Bangkok Siam Society, 1987.

Bangkok Only Yesterday by Van Beek, Steve, Hong Kong: Hong Kong Publishing, 1982. Anecdotal history of Bangkok illustrated with old photos.

Chaiyo! by Vella, Walter F, Honolulu University of Hawaii Press, 1979. The life and times of King Vajiravudh (1910-1925).

Jim Thompson: The Legendary American by Warren, William, Boston, 1970.

The Balancing Act: A History of Modern Thailand by Wright, Joseph, Oakland: Pacific Rim Press, 1991. Accessible and detailed history of modern Thailand.

Thailand: A Short History by Wyatt, David K, Bangkok/London: Thai Wattana Panich/Yale University Press, 1984. Concise and well-written.

People

The Falcon of Siam by Aylwen, Axel, London: Methuen, 1988. A fictionalized story of Constantine Phaulkon, Greek adventurer in Siam in the late 1600s.

Teak-Wallah by Campbell, Reginald, Singapore: Oxford, 1986. Adventurers of a teak logger in northern Thailand in the 1920s.

Siamese White by Collis, Maurice, London: Faber, 1965. Fictionalized account of a contemporary of Constant Phaulkon in 1600s Siam.

Behind the Smile, Voices of Thailand by Ekachai, Sanitsuda, Thailand. Thai Development Support Committee, 1990. Well-written and informative portraits of Thai life by a local journalist.

Chinese Society in Thailand by Skinner, G. William, Ithaca, New York: Cornell University Press, 1957. Gives an insight into an important segment of Bangkok's history.

Religion

Buddhist Monk, Buddhist Layman by Bunnag, Jane, Cambridge: Cambridge University Press, 1973. Gives an insight into the monastic experience.

A History of Buddhism in Siam by Nivat, Prince Dhani, Bangkok: Siam Society, 1965. By one of Thailand's most respected scholars.

What the Buddha Taught by Rahula, Walpola, New York, Grove Press, 1974. Comprehensive account of Buddhist doctrine; other editions available.

Art and Culture

Reflections on Thai Culture by Klausner, William J, The Siam Society: Bangkok, 1987. Observations of a longtime resident anthropologist.

Essays on Thai Folklore by Rajadhon, Phya Anuman, Bangkok: D.K. Books. A description of Thai ceremonies, festivals and rites of passage.

The Arts of Thailand by Van Beek, Steve & Tettoni L.I, London, Thames & Hudson, 1991. Lavishly illustrated, includes the minor arts.

The House on the Khlong by Warren, William, Tokyo: Weatherhill. The story of the Jim Thompson House.

Ten Lives of the Buddha; Siamese Temple Paintings and Jataka Tales by Wray, Joe, Elizabeth Wray, Clare Rosenfeld and Dorothy Bailey, Tokyo: Weatherhill, 1974. Well illustrated, valuable for understanding Thai painting and the Tosachat (Jataka Tales).

Gardening in Bangkok by Amranand, Pimsai, Bangkok: Siam Society. Good work on plants although it could do with more pictures.

Thai Writers

Letters from Thailand by Botan. Bangkok: DK, 1977. A novel in letters, reflects a Chinese immigrant's views of his new compatriots.

The Path of the Tiger by Khoamchai, Sila, Bangkok: Thai Modern Classics, 1994. Originally published in 1989. Jungle lore and philosophy by a former guerrilla. This is among the first in a series of English translations of the best 20 novels of Thailand.

The Judgment by Korpjitti, Chart, Bangkok: Thai Modern Classics, 1995. Originally published in 1981. Chart is the most popular living writer of quality fiction.

Si Phaendin by Pramoj, Kukrit, Bangkok: DK, 1981. The nostalgia is sometimes cloying, but this is the work of a consummate Renaissance man.

Behind the Painting (and Other Stories) by Saipradit, Kularp (Seebeorapha), Singapore: Oxford, 1990. Kularp was a crusading journalist and fiction writer who died in Chinese exile.

The Prostitute by Surangkhanang, K. London: Oxford, 1994. Originally published in 1937. Attitudes towards prostitutes haven't changed much.

Other Insight Guides

In the acclaimed original **Insight Guide** series titles covering Southeast Asia include: Southeast Asia, Burma, Indonesia, Bali, Java, Malaysia, Singapore, Thailand, Vietnam and Southeast Asia Wildlife.

Pocket Guides have planned one-day itineraries written by a local resident and easy-to-use full-size pull-out map. There are numerous Pocket Guides to cities in Southeast Asia. In addition, more than 80 **Compact Guides** offer the traveler a highly portable encyclopedic travel guide packed with carefully cross-referenced text, photographs and maps. Southeast Asian titles are: Bali, Singapore, Thailand and Bangkok.

ART & PHOTO CREDITS

INSIGHT GUIDE
BanGKOK

Cartographic Editor **Zoë Goodwin**
Production **Stuart A Everitt**
Design Consultants
Carlotta Junger, Graham Mitchener
Picture Research **Hilary Genin, Georgina Vacy-Ash**

Index

Numbers in italics refer to photographs

The World of Insight Guides

400 books in three complementary series cover every major destination in every continent.

Insight Guides

Alaska
Alsace
Amazon Wildlife
American Southwest
Amsterdam
Argentina
Atlanta
Athens
Australia
Austria
Bahamas
Bali
Baltic States
Bangkok
Barbados
Barcelona
Bay of Naples
Beijing
Belgium
Belize
Berlin
Bermuda
Boston
Brazil
Brittany
Brussels
Budapest
Buenos Aires
Burgundy
Burma (Myanmar)
Cairo
Calcutta
California
Canada
Caribbean
Catalonia
Channel Islands
Chicago
Chile
China
Cologne
Continental Europe
Corsica
Costa Rica
Crete
Crossing America
Cuba
Cyprus
Czech & Slovak Republics
Delhi, Jaipur, Agra
Denmark
Dresden
Dublin
Düsseldorf
East African Wildlife
East Asia
Eastern Europe
Ecuador
Edinburgh
Egypt
Finland
Florence
Florida
France
Frankfurt
French Riviera
Gambia & Senegal
Germany
Glasgow

Gran Canaria
Great Barrier Reef
Great Britain
Greece
Greek Islands
Hamburg
Hawaii
Hong Kong
Hungary
Iceland
India
India's Western Himalaya
Indian Wildlife
Indonesia
Ireland
Israel
Istanbul
Italy
Jamaica
Japan
Java
Jerusalem
Jordan
Kathmandu
Kenya
Korea
Lisbon
Loire Valley
London
Los Angeles
Madeira
Madrid
Malaysia
Mallorca & Ibiza
Malta
Marine Life in the South China Sea
Melbourne
Mexico
Mexico City
Miami
Montreal
Morocco
Moscow
Munich
Namibia
Native America
Nepal
Netherlands
New England
New Orleans
New York City
New York State
New Zealand
Nile
Normandy
Northern California
Northern Spain
Norway
Oman & the UAE
Oxford
Old South
Pacific Northwest
Pakistan
Paris
Peru
Philadelphia
Philippines
Poland
Portugal
Prague

Provence
Puerto Rico
Rajasthan
Rhine
Rio de Janeiro
Rockies
Rome
Russia
St Petersburg
San Francisco
Sardinia
Scotland
Seattle
Sicily
Singapore
South Africa
South America
South Asia
South India
South Tyrol
Southeast Asia
Southeast Asia Wildlife
Southern California
Southern Spain
Spain
Sri Lanka
Sweden
Switzerland
Sydney
Taiwan
Tenerife
Texas
Thailand
Tokyo
Trinidad & Tobago
Tunisia
Turkey
Turkish Coast
Tuscany
Umbria
US National Parks East
US National Parks West
Vancouver
Venezuela
Venice
Vienna
Vietnam
Wales
Washington DC
Waterways of Europe
Wild West
Yemen

Insight Pocket Guides

Aegean Islands★
Algarve★
Alsace
Amsterdam★
Athens★
Atlanta★
Bahamas★
Baja Peninsula★
Bali★
Bali Bird Walks
Bangkok★
Barbados★
Barcelona★
Bavaria★
Beijing★
Berlin★

Bermuda★
Bhutan★
Boston★
British Columbia★
Brittany★
Brussels★
Budapest & Surroundings★
Canton★
Chiang Mai★
Chicago★
Corsica★
Costa Blanca★
Costa Brava★
Costa del Sol/Marbella★
Costa Rica★
Crete★
Denmark★
Fiji★
Florence★
Florida★
Florida Keys★
French Riviera★
Gran Canaria★
Hawaii★
Hong Kong★
Hungary
Ibiza★
Ireland★
Ireland's Southwest★
Israel★
Istanbul★
Jakarta★
Jamaica★
Kathmandu Bikes & Hikes★
Kenya★
Kuala Lumpur★
Lisbon★
Loire Valley★
London★
Macau★
Madrid★
Malacca★
Maldives★
Mallorca★
Malta★
Mexico City★
Miami★
Milan★
Montreal★
Morocco★
Moscow
Munich★
Nepal★
New Delhi
New Orleans★
New York City★
New Zealand★
Northern California★
Oslo/Bergen★
Paris★
Penang★
Phuket★
Prague★
Provence★
Puerto Rico★
Quebec★
Rhodes★
Rome★
Sabah★

St Petersburg★
San Francisco★
Sardinia
Scotland★
Seville★
Seychelles★
Sicily★
Sikkim
Singapore★
Southeast England
Southern California★
Southern Spain★
Sri Lanka★
Sydney★
Tenerife★
Thailand★
Tibet★
Toronto★
Tunisia★
Turkish Coast★
Tuscany★
Venice★
Vienna★
Vietnam★
Yogyakarta
Yucatan Peninsula★

★ = Insight Pocket Guides with Pull out Maps

Insight Compact Guides

Algarve
Amsterdam
Bahamas
Bali
Bangkok
Barbados
Barcelona
Beijing
Belgium
Berlin
Brittany
Brussels
Budapest
Burgundy
Copenhagen
Costa Brava
Costa Rica
Crete
Cyprus
Czech Republic
Denmark
Dominican Republic
Dublin
Egypt
Finland
Florence
Gran Canaria
Greece
Holland
Hong Kong
Ireland
Israel
Italian Lakes
Italian Riviera
Jamaica
Jerusalem
Lisbon
Madeira
Mallorca
Malta

Milan
Moscow
Munich
Normandy
Norway
Paris
Poland
Portugal
Prague
Provence
Rhodes
Rome
St Petersburg
Salzburg
Singapore
Switzerland
Sydney
Tenerife
Thailand
Turkey
Turkish Coast
Tuscany
UK regional titles:
  Bath & Surroundings
  Cambridge & East Anglia
  Cornwall
  Cotswolds
  Devon & Exmoor
  Edinburgh
  Lake District
  London
  New Forest
  North York Moors
  Northumbria
  Oxford
  Peak District
  Scotland
  Scottish Highlands
  Shakespeare Country
  Snowdonia
  South Downs
  York
  Yorkshire Dales
USA regional titles:
  Boston
  Cape Cod
  Chicago
  Florida
  Florida Keys
  Hawaii: Maui
  Hawaii: Oahu
  Las Vegas
  Los Angeles
  Martha's Vineyard & Nantucket
  New York
  San Francisco
  Washington D.C.
Venice
Vienna
West of Ireland